VISUAL CULTURE IN FREUD'S VIENNA

PSYCHOANALYTIC HORIZONS

Psychoanalysis is unique in being at once a theory and a therapy, a method of critical thinking and a form of clinical practice. Now in its second century, this fusion of science and humanism derived from Freud has outlived all predictions of its demise. **Psychoanalytic Horizons** evokes the idea of a convergence between realms as well as the outer limits of a vision. Books in the series test disciplinary boundaries and will appeal to scholars and therapists who are passionate not only about the theory of literature, culture, media, and philosophy but also, above all, about the real life of ideas in the world.

Volumes in the Series:

Mourning Freud
by Madelon Sprengnether

Does the Internet Have an Unconscious?: Slavoj Žižek and Digital Culture
by Clint Burnham

In the Event of Laughter: Psychoanalysis, Literature and Comedy
by Alfie Bown

On Dangerous Ground: Freud's Visual Cultures of the Unconscious
by Diane O'Donoghue

For Want of Ambiguity: Order and Chaos in Art, Psychoanalysis, and Neuroscience
by Ludovica Lumer and Lois Oppenheim

Life Itself Is an Art: The Life and Work of Erich Fromm
by Rainer Funk

Born After: Reckoning with the German Past
by Angelika Bammer

Critical Theory Between Klein and Lacan: A Dialogue
by Amy Allen and Mari Ruti

Transferences: The Aesthetics and Poetics of the Therapeutic Relationship
by Maren Scheurer

At the Risk of Thinking: An Intellectual Biography of Julia Kristeva
by Alice Jardine, edited by Mari Ruti

The Writing Cure
by Emma Lieber

The Analyst's Desire: The Ethical Foundation of Clinical Practice
by Mitchell Wilson

Our Two-Track Minds: Rehabilitating Freud on Culture
by Robert A. Paul

Norman N. Holland: The Dean of American Psychoanalytic Literary Critics
by Jeffrey Berman

Psychological Roots of the Climate Crisis: Neoliberal Exceptionalism and the Culture of Uncare
by Sally Weintrobe

Circumcision on the Couch: The Cultural, Psychological and Gendered Dimensions of the World's Oldest Surgery
by Jordan Osserman

The Racist Fantasy: Unconscious Roots of Hatred
by Todd McGowan

Antisemitism and Racism: Ethical Challenges for Psychoanalysis
by Stephen Frosh

The Ethics of Immediacy: Dangerous Experience in Freud, Woolf, and Merleau-Ponty
by Jeffrey McCurry

Analyzed by Lacan: A Personal Account
by Betty Milan

Visual Culture in Freud's Vienna: Science, Eros, and the Psychoanalytic Imagination
by Mary Bergstein

VISUAL CULTURE IN FREUD'S VIENNA

Science, Eros, and the Psychoanalytic Imagination

Mary Bergstein

BLOOMSBURY ACADEMIC
NEW YORK • LONDON • OXFORD • NEW DELHI • SYDNEY

BLOOMSBURY ACADEMIC
Bloomsbury Publishing Inc
1385 Broadway, New York, NY 10018, USA
50 Bedford Square, London, WC1B 3DP, UK
29 Earlsfort Terrace, Dublin 2, Ireland

BLOOMSBURY, BLOOMSBURY ACADEMIC and the Diana logo are trademarks of Bloomsbury Publishing Plc

First published in the United States of America, 2024

Cover design by Daniel Benneworth-Gray
Cover images supplied by the author

Library of Congress Cataloging-in-Publication Data
Names: Bergstein, Mary, author.
Title: Visual culture in Freud's Vienna : science, eros, and the psychoanalytic imagination / Mary Bergstein.
Description: New York : Bloomsbury Academic, 2024. | Series: Psychoanalytic horizons | Includes bibliographical references and index. | Summary: "Shows how visual culture in turn-of-the-century Vienna (the birthplace of psychoanalysis) not only reflected modernist ideas already gaining in force, but helped to bring into being our modern "psychoanalytic imagination." "– Provided by publisher.
Identifiers: LCCN 2023030943 (print) | LCCN 2023030944 (ebook) | ISBN 9798765111963 (hardback) | ISBN 9798765111956 (paperback) | ISBN 9798765111970 (epub) | ISBN 9798765111987 (pdf) | ISBN 9798765111994
Subjects: LCSH: Photography–Social aspects–Austria–Vienna. | Psychology and art–Austria–Vienna–20th century. | Art and society–Austria–Vienna–20th century. | Vienna (Austria)–Moral conditions–19th century. | Vienna (Austria)–Moral conditions–20th century.
Classification: LCC TR65.2.V54 B47 2024 (print) | LCC TR65.2.V54 (ebook) | DDC 770.9436/13–dc23/eng/20230824
LC record available at https://lccn.loc.gov/2023030943
LC ebook record available at https://lccn.loc.gov/2023030944

ISBN: HB: 979-8-7651-1196-3
PB: 979-8-7651-1195-6
ePDF: 979-8-7651-1198-7
eBook: 979-8-7651-1197-0

Series: Psychoanalytic Horizons

Typeset by Integra Software Services Pvt. Ltd.

To find out more about our authors and books visit www.bloomsbury.com and sign up for our newsletters.

CONTENTS

NOTES ON THE ILLUSTRATIONS

The illustrations in this book, which is itself largely about the history of photography and graphic design, constitute a mixed bag of images gathered over a long period of time. Every attempt to secure permissions to publish these pictures has been made. If in any case photo credits or copyrights are not accurate, the error should be brought directly to the attention of the author.

The unconscionable exploitation of children for erotic or pornographic images in printed matter (including photography) is illegal in 2024. This includes any visual depiction of sexually explicit content involving a child, no matter where or when the image was made. A number of my original illustrations came under this category and therefore were kept back from publication. I should add that such illustrations proved my arguments (Chapter 3) all too well. But these pictures, in addition to being deemed unfit for publication, called forth to me and to the editors at Bloomsbury Press the sorrows of the disenfranchised young girls (children) who had been obliged to pose for them over a century ago. These misfortunes, sorrows, and deprivations belong to us, too.

LIST OF ILLUSTRATIONS

ACKNOWLEDGMENTS

The topics presented in this book have been of interest to me for a long time. Several friends and colleagues have supported my research and writing. The descendants of Else Kotanyi de Widakovich (Else Jerusalem) supplied me with the use of a copy of R. I. Marchant's (1932) English translation of Jerusalem's novel, *The Red House*, from which I quote throughout this study. *The Red House* is no less than a "magic lantern" of material about the underside of Viennese society around 1900. Matt Seccombe kindly edited my original manuscript with an astute critique. I am grateful for Matt's expertise and his interest in my work.

Many thanks to Peter Rudnytsky for having included this study in the series *Psychoanalytic Horizons*. Peter has long advised and inspired me, dating back to his time as editor of *Imago*. Diane O'Donoghue deserves gratitude for her learned understanding and advice in the evolution of this project. I look back with a certain nostalgia to the days of my fortunate meeting with Diane by way of the brilliant Austrian historian of psychoanalysis, Lydia Marinelli (1965–2008), who should also be remembered. I would like to thank Murray Schwartz, with whom I worked on *Imago*, for his encouragement and erudition. Jeffrey Slater kindly encouraged me throughout the process of thinking and writing this book. The late Marcin Gizycki (1951–2022) supplied me with out-takes from pertinent films. He made the stunning photograph of a gilded reticule in the illustrations—an image that gives fuel to Freud's arguments about the female sexuality of such luxurious objects. I owe an immense gratitude to the people at Bloomsbury Press, especially Editorial Director Haaris Naqvi and his brilliant assistant Hali Han, whose intelligence and tact have guided me through the publication of this book.

I still remember my parents, Evelyn M. Berg (1917–86) and Harry Benjamin Bergstein (1916–2003), for having long ago introduced me to the satisfactions of dedicated study and hard work.

Above all, this book is dedicated to David M. Slater, and to our amazing grandchildren Anna and Ellis, with much love.

INTRODUCTION

VISUAL CULTURE IN FREUD'S VIENNA: SCIENCE, EROS, AND THE PSYCHOANALYTIC IMAGINATION

Visual Culture

Sigmund Freud's great modernist invention, the theory and practice of psychoanalysis, occurred in a visual atmosphere where representations of erotic and scientific knowledge were frequently similar, contiguous, or superimposed. This study illuminates the social history of visual culture around 1900 in Vienna, with particular attention to representations that hovered around the uneasy junctures of erotic love and scientific discourse. I shall argue that photography and film not only reflected ideas already in force in Vienna around 1900, but established networks of cultural meaning, bringing into being what might be referred to as a "psychoanalytic imagination."

Psychoanalysis here refers not only to Freud's writings directly, but should be taken in the spirit of the "whole climate of opinion" that W. H. Auden (1907–73) spoke of in his poem "In Memory of Sigmund Freud" of 1939.[1] Each of the following chapters is meant to demonstrate that visual images not only illustrated but actually invented ways of seeing social, psychological, and scientific discourse at a particular time and place.

At its most analytical, the present book argues that visual culture, involved as it so frequently is with the act of reading, initiated pertinent aspects of psychoanalytic thought. I should clarify from the outset that in this book eros signifies sexual love or desire, or even the exigencies of romantic love, as opposed to the more essential "life instinct," or the fundamental creative impulse, as sometimes thought of by philosophers and psychologists.

1. Auden 1991, 273–76.

What do we mean by visual culture in this context? The three chapters look at systems of images within what contemporary scholars like Alexis Boylan would consider a totalizing "visual atmosphere."[2] Each of the chapters is devoted to technologies of visual production in Vienna around 1900. Constellations of images to be sited in the visual atmosphere include published photography (in books and journals), images viewed through epidiascopic projection, and the fascinating, sometimes disorienting, immediacy of moving images in cinema. These mediums all gave rise to new ways of imagining reality and fantasy.

I intend to locate the uneasy junctures of science and eros in visual culture; and ponder these sites according to what I call "the psychoanalytic imagination." In order to understand the production and function of visual culture in turn-of-the-century Vienna, one might sample deeply from the fields of literature, medicine, biology, psychoanalysis, graphic design, industrial design, and the historiography of art. Photography is perhaps the most elusive medium for exploration of these issues, but also, I would venture to claim, the most interesting.

Among art historians it is now tacitly agreed that rather than abiding by a chronological parade of culturally accepted artistic "masterpieces," the historian or theorist ought to look, instead, at "everything." This "everything" includes even the most vulgar and decrepit evidence. It includes traces of discarded materials and tools, vernacular depictions of sentimental topics ("low" art), and conscious and unconscious designs located in the everyday world.

Objects "hiding in plain sight" ought to be considered just as apposite for consideration as the most aesthetically and historically charged antiquities conserved in museums and illustrated in comprehensive art history textbooks. Such relatively neglected, or even repudiated, objects (whether hiding in plain sight or lingering in historical shadow) should be as compelling to the cultural historian as is the most famous or fully resonant work of art.

All of this material, high and low, together with recognized monumental productions described in the most celebrated *ekphrases* from antiquity, is categorized, together with fine and commercial art and design, under the rubric of what we call visual culture. Within this distinction, photography, and the photographic reproduction of art, like the rhetorical structure of ekphrasis, is always in some way about its own embedded referent.

2. Boylan 2020, 190.

Psychoanalysis

Social historians can imagine that a psychoanalytic situation prevailed not only in the individual case histories analyzed by Freud, but also for society at large around 1900. As such, some of the rhetoric of psychoanalytic thinking can be discovered in the study of photography and film in modern life.

The present book asks how the craft of making, publishing, and apprehending photographs came into play in this psychological environment. The three chapters will demonstrate that as well as "reflecting" certain norms and fashions like a hypothetical mirror of memory, photography and film created the operative visual environment of Vienna 1900.

In exploring visual representation in Freud's Vienna, a few important precepts from the social history of visual culture need to be reiterated. First, that the past is always already genuinely different from the present. Additionally, that everyday life in the present is forever informed, troubled, and haunted by the past. Furthermore, visual culture is everywhere in the historical past *and* the present, in our unconscious reminiscences and unconscious expectations, like the air we breathe, or, as David Foster Wallace might have put it, the water we (fish) swim in.[3]

We should also agree that social habits (including the education of children, attention to material objects, and sexual mores) vary from one society to another, historically and culturally. With a nod to cultural anthropology, it ought to be the rule rather than the exception that the sum total of visual production, from the most profound object or image to the most trivial, be interrogated with the special attention we art historians typically reserve for that which was long ago, far away, legendary, obscure, arcane, spiritually esoteric, or intellectually abstruse. Visual culture, including the photographic reproduction of works of art, deserves as much attention as any authored work of fine art.

Two Case Studies: Eros and Science

As the Viennese were particularly oriented to technical issues in photography and book design, I propose to introduce this book with two pertinent case studies in visual culture. First, I shall explore the

3. Wallace 2009.

system of photographic illustration for Paul Schultze-Naumburg's *Culture of the Female Body as a Foundation for Women's Clothing Design* (*Kultur des Weiblichen Körpers als Grundlage der Frauenkleidung*). My second case study will focus on a scientific illustration, Adolf Strümpell's *Radiogram of a Right-sided Pneumothorax*, which was published in his *Lehrbuch der speziellen Pathologie und Therapie der inneren Krankenheiten*.

Schultze-Naumburg's *Kultur des Weiblichen Körpers als Grundlage der Frauenkleidung* was presumed to introduce the educated, or cultivated, reader ("der gebilditer Mann") to the supposedly hygienic advantage of women's loosely fitting reform dresses (*Reformkleider*) (1901). The text was ostensibly meant to serve as an anti-corseting treatise. But there is a more complex presentation of meaning here by way of the illustrative material. Regarding the book's design, I shall analyze the German graphic designer Johann Vincenz Cissarz's brilliant arrangements for Schultze-Naumburg's book. The German Art-Nouveau designer Cissarz (1873–1942) used photos presumably provided, or at least selected, by the author. Cissarz was an interesting protagonist: his works were infused with German nationalism throughout his career, particularly during the Nazi regime of the 1930s. Here, his ensembles of photographic illustrations emphasized the erotic and fetishized capacities of the corseted or nude female body. Whether it be in spite of, or because of, its ostensible anti-corset position, Schultze-Naumburg's book circulated in Vienna as erotica (by way of the strategic layout of the text and illustrations) during the twentieth century. What the reader absorbs here is rapidly synthesized material from the optical (photographic) unconscious.

For the most part, Schultze-Naumburg (**fig. 21**), who eventually became a prominent Nazi architect and theorist, held to a traditionalist, nationalist aesthetic in the face of modernism, which he rejected on racial and social grounds. When Alfred Rosenberg testified at the International Military Tribunal of April 15, 1946, he stated that the works of Schultze-Naumburg represented a protest against industrial culture, and not a movement of retrospective sentimentality.[4]

4. This reference was provided to me by Matt Seccombe in April 2023, on the basis of *Trial of the Major War Criminals before the International Military Tribunal* (Nuremberg 1947), vol. 11, 448.

Schultze-Naumburg's earlier racialist book *Kunst und Rasse* (*Art and Race*) was published in 1928 to the tune that so-called Jewish art was degenerate, and modernist art distorted the human body the way diseases such as neurosyphilis, cretinism, and microcephaly did. *Art and Race* famously included what Neil Levi called a "fascist photomontage" of works of modernist art paralleled with images of human illness and deformity.[5] According to Schultze-Naumburg, the German racial community produced the best human bodies and the best figurative art. In order to conserve a racially pure German aesthetic, any contact with foreigners, Jews, modernists, chronically ill or disabled people, or other "degenerates" was to be avoided.[6]

The pointedly rhetorical arrangement of images in *Kultur des Weiblichen Körpers* has been overlooked by historians of photography as well as scholars of psychoanalysis. Throughout the photographic illustrations of *Kultur des Weiblichen Körpers* women's bodies are fragmented and objectified.[7] Photographs of nude girls and women, which appear to be excerpted (fragmented) from pornographic contexts, ancient sculpture of female torsos, and elaborate undergarments (the ostentatious corsets Schultze-Naumburg claimed to despise) alternate across the pages, constructing a systematic series of erotic and sado-masochistic formulae in graphic design (**see fig. 12**). In the same book Schultze-Naumburg brought to witness some familiar *exempla* from the Greco-Roman canon of sculpture, as classical comparanda for the nude studies and photographs of corsets he published amongst them.

The pictures in Paul Schultze-Naumburg's book, which circulated in Vienna as erotica during the twentieth century, don't merely illustrate written ideas, but actually construct meaning, consciously or unconsciously, in the reader's gaze. Schultze-Naumburg's *Kultur des Weiblichen Körpers* communicates to the reader on at least two levels, as would a subject in a psychoanalytic session, who consciously tells the analyst an autobiographical story, but acts out psychic conflict with his or her body by means of coughing, involuntary tics, trembling, or skin ailments. Schultze-Naumburg tells us one thing in the text, that corseting was unhealthy for the human body. But he shows us something else in the pictures, namely the erotic or sadomasochistic

5. Levi 2014, 85–87.

6. English 2021.

7. For feminist views on objectification see Papadaki 2021.

lure of the corseted woman. The photographic illustrations across the pages (body=sculpture=corset) are openly sexual in content, presenting flamboyant corsets together with fragmented images of women's naked bodies. The illustrations speak most eloquently to each other within the framework of a single book. The fragmented photographs of nude women in *Kultur des Weiblichen Körpers* are redolent of pornography, and the originals may have been obtained from the stacks of photographs that were collected in brothels throughout the Austrian Empire and elsewhere in Europe. These fragmented bodies are legitimated in publications like this one by their two-dimensional proximity to partial or fully composed views of ancient classical sculpture.[8] The visual allusion to Greco-Roman statuary creates a kind of "flicker effect" where the guise of classical art flirts with contemporary erotic content. Notwithstanding the classical pretext of this book, *Kultur des Weiblichen Körpers* contained undercurrents of darkly erotic, fetishistic material. Ensembles of fragmented images anticipate or correspond with discussions of fetishism by psychoanalytically informed individuals in Freud's circle such as Paul Federn (1871–1950), Friedrich Salomon Krauss (1859–1930), and Eduard Hitschmann (1871–1957).

On Wednesday evening, March 15, 1911, the Vienna Psychoanalytic Society discussed the fetishism of corsets.[9] Freud's group was led that evening by the ethnologist and sexologist Friedrich Salomon Krauss, who stated that some men could only have intercourse with women who were tightly laced into a corset, and that this tendency had a sadomasochistic root. The minutes were transcribed by ego-psychologist Paul Federn. Krauss offered the idea that corsets were required by men as "beauty aids." Federn, the scribe and translator of the Wednesday group's minutes, rounded out the discussion of March 15, 1911 by recalling that the music critic Max Graf (1873–1958) had presented a paper three years earlier on the psychology of clothing, "in which he tried to demonstrate that individual pieces of clothing, while veiling [the body as a whole], show precisely sexual characteristics."[10] Psychoanalytically informed, Graf was the father of Herbert Graf (1903–73), the "Little Hans" of Freud's *Analysis of a Phobia in a Five-year-old Boy* of 1909. Little Hans/Herbert seems to have survived all of

8. See below Chapter 3.

9. Nunberg and Federn vol. 3, 194–200.

10. Nunberg and Federn vol. 3, 200.

this analytic attention well enough, eventually becoming a successful opera producer in Vienna and New York.

Eduard Hitschmann pointed out that Schultze-Naumburg among others had written that the lacing up of women's bodies introduced "harmful consequences of the corset for an individual as well as for the [human] race."[11] (Compressing the gastric system could cause illness; and over time the woman's back muscles could weaken and atrophy.) Hitschmann maintained that "lacing-up in and of itself plays an important role in fetishism as can be inferred from shoe fetishism, in which, too, the lacing up of high shoes is significant."[12] Freud listened to all of this, calling Krauss's paper "comprehensive and interesting," adding, in general, noncommittal, terms, that, "It would be worthwhile to do some work on the psychoanalysis of attire and fashion."[13] That Wednesday (March 15, 1911) Freud summed things up in a rather anodyne statement: "It could easily be that there was an attraction to the other sex so strong that it caused the repression of the sexual ideal and its transformation into the aesthetic ideal."[14]

Friedrich Salomon Krauss was arrested for pornography in Berlin in 1913, given his open discussions of sex in his journal *Anthropophyteia* (1904–13), a yearbook that published erotic and sexual folklore, and featured some photographs of sexual oddities on its covers, and in his illustrated book of essays on female beauty *Streifzüge im Reiche der Frauenschönheit* (*Inroads into the Realm of Female Beauty*) of 1904. Krauss's *Streifzüge* presents about 300 photographs of women and girls, including photographs of a variety of well-nourished Viennese beauties *en déshabillé*. A child-like image of a naked fifteen-year-old Tyrolean girl by the eminent portrait photographer, Dominik Stahala (active 1875–1905) is typical of these offerings. Stahala's photograph, neither a portrait nor a classical nude, portrays a seductive child for the delectation of the reader. I shall revisit the phenomenon of the child-woman in erotic photography and in Viennese life in Chapter 3.

11. Nunberg and Federn vol. 3, 196.
12. Nunberg and Federn vol. 3, 197.
13. Nunberg and Federn vol. 3, 198–99.
14. Nunberg and Federn vol. 3, 199–200.

Racial Types of Women

Krauss's volume is a world unto itself, where Rudolf Krziwanek (1843–1905), Otto Schmidt, Dominik Stahala, and other photographers provided images of various "racial types" of women from the Austrian Empire such as Slavic types, North German types, Russian types, Jewish types, Magyar Types, and other ethnographic categories portrayed nude or semi-nude. These female "*Wiener Typen*" are highly sexualized in representation. Their images are also interspersed throughout the book with other "types," that is, photographs of naked or costumed women from around the world. Various ethnographic categories, such as Spaniards, Greeks, Serbians, Jewish women from Polish Galicia, Italians, Amerindians, "Hottentots" (a pejorative name for the Khoikhoi people of South Africa), Eskimos, and Asian women from a variety of locations, are exoticized and sexualized. Captions inform us that many of the girls are young teenagers. Some of the photographs are credited to the official Viennese Court Photographers (men like Angerer, Stahala, and Krziwanek) whereas others (the anthropological types) are taken from the photo-archive of the anthropological Museum für Wölkerkunde in Leipzig.

We twenty-first-century cultural historians already take it for granted that racialism, colonial expansion, and sexual fantasy were blended in European society around 1900. The fact that women were desirable according to racial types was illustrated photographically in C. H. Stratz's book project of the time, *Die Rassenschönheit des Weibes* (Stuttgart, 1911) about the particular physical charms to be seen in women from every continent and every "race" or ethnicity. Books like those of Stratz and Paul Schultze-Naumberg, which were widely read in Vienna, set the tone for this kind of photographic "evidence" in the connoisseurship of women's bodies. Cissarz, in his role as graphic designer, worked with photos from the German and Austrian archives, wove them into the text as subtle propagandistic "evidence" for the reader. This tactic constructed complex meaning with image and text operating together, indeed at a single glance. Such an illustration strategy was absorbed rapidly by the preconscious and even unconscious mind of the reader. Whether it be in theory or practice, women's bodies were manipulated in the clothing and lingerie of turn-of-the-century Vienna and such fetishistic phenomena were made manifest in numerous illustrative photographs.

A pair of photographs by Emil Brugsch (1842–1930) in Krauss's book precipitates a particularly uncanny mood (**fig. 33**). An

Egyptian mummy of a princess-priestess Nessi-ta-neb-asher (born ca. 1008 BCE) discovered at Deir-el-Bahri, now in the Cairo Museum, is represented in photographs by Brugsch before (R) and after (L) the unwinding of her bandages. The thrill of unwrapping an inanimate mummy was inevitably suggestive of the undressing of a living woman. Here in Brugsch's representations the un-bandaged mummy looks like a naked women shown with the companion photograph of the same mummy still half-unwrapped, who is seen in a large headscarf with her torso covered. An essay about this mummy appeared on New Year's Day 1910 in *The Sphinx*, an illustrated English-language weekly published from 1892 to 1947 in Cairo by the American Anglophile David Garrick Longworth.[15] In *The Sphinx*, the princess' mummy was characterized as a "portrait" of a beautiful woman in her prime, aged around 35 to 40. Friedrich Krauss, in the guise of an archaeologically informed ethnologist, served up a veritable encyclopedic catalogue of sexual consumption in a lavish Jugendstil volume produced in Leipzig.

Scientific Authority in Strümpell's Pneumothorax

At the threshold of the twentieth century, photography and psychoanalysis were new sciences, incorporating cognitive systems from the established fields of chemistry and medical learning (biology), as well as literature, ethnology, and the history of art. As in psychoanalysis itself, the reception of popular photographs and cinema involved memory-networks that were tied up with the unconscious content of fear, conflict, and desire. Freud's own practice of early psychoanalysis concerned itself primarily with the vicissitudes of European urban life in an extended family and social network, and the erotic imaginings, conscious or unconscious, in the life-history of an individual female or male personality.

Moving on from the picturesque photographs of women collected by Friedrich Krauss, let us now take up the case of a biological illustration, namely Adolf Strümpell's *Radiogram of a Right-sided Pneumothorax* which was published in his *Lehrbuch der speziellen Pathologie und Therapie der inneren Krankenheiten* (Leipzig: F. C. W. Vogel, 1886). This small but powerful picture (**fig. 24**) speaks as though it were

15. Anonymous 1910, 2.

an objective photographic X-ray of a human chest. The ribcage is heightened by the light of chiaroscuro and a shadowy indication of the lungs, as appropriate to a textbook explanation of tuberculosis. The heart is not visible, but rather indicated in a caption and connected by a thin diagrammatic line. Strümpell states that the heart is displaced in this picture, and in the left portion of the picture the shadow of the right lung indicates that it is entirely compressed against the vertebral column. But this photographic image is rich in ambiguity, and as such there is a great demand on the participation of a viewer's photographic imagination. Without its surrounding text and caption, the printed photograph could have easily served as a projective psychological test in the time it was composed. Scientific (biological, chemical, medical), erotic, and even religious images collided with and superimposed one another, creating a new vocabulary of content and forms. These images, where one thing means another, and interpretation is required, captivated various audiences from the Viennese bourgeoisie, including Freud and his contemporaries.

What exactly are we seeing in Strümpell's *Radiogram*? I have already stated that this photographic illustration invites and even requires interpretation. Although photographic illustrations such as the *Radiography of a Right-Sided Pneumothorax* rendered here may not be scientifically accurate according to twenty-first-century standards, publishers such as F. C. W. Vogel in Leipzig published such views as definitive in medical textbooks, such as Adolf Strümpell's (1853–1925) own textbook (1884) on internal medicine that was based upon his practical experiences as an internist and neurologist. This publication, *Lehrbuch der speziellen Pathologie und Therapie der inneren Krankheiten*, was then considered to be the definitive German-language textbook with regard to internal medicine. It was published in more than thirty editions and was translated into numerous languages (including English in 1887).

Strümpell's *Radiogram of a Right-sided Pneumothorax* is an illustrative photographic plate showing the radiogram of a right-sided pneumothorax wherein the lighter area corresponds to the large air space; and the left portion is the shadow of the lung, which is entirely infiltrated with tuberculosis, and compressed against the vertebral column. The *Pneumothorax* corresponds with the scientific authority of the text that surrounds it. But if received differently, the picture loses its biological pretense and becomes rather a weighted symbolic emblem—an uncanny *memento mori.* Freud himself must have encountered this illustration before 1899, because he quoted from Strümpell's *Lehrbuch* in *The Interpretation of Dreams* of 1899.[16] He cited Strümpell's detailed writings on the overdetermined forgetting of dreams, adding that all of those factors that produce forgetfulness in the waking state are also determinant for the forgetting of dreams. Strümpell stated that even the most vivid pictorial material in dreams can be rapidly forgotten, whereas some of the most enduring dream images are shadowy, hazy, and indistinct. On a speculative level we might propose that Strümpell's X-ray of the pneumothorax belongs to the shadowy, hazy, and frightening category of images that could be transported directly into the dream language of his contemporaries. I want to add here that Viennese posterity liked Strümpell, who was by all accounts a generous individual, and also an accomplished violinist.

Various sorts of visual materials and pertinent texts are considered in the chapters of my book. Many of these images belong to the realm of popular culture, including the erotic "Saturn Films" created by Johann Schwarzer (1880–1914), which I consider in Chapter 2 in terms of what popular movies communicated *in anteprima* (as it were a "sneak preview") of early psychoanalysis. We shall see that the "Saturn Films" loomed large in Vienna from circa 1906 to 1910. These comedic cinematic vignettes about love and sex are not subtle, but rather they display a clanking obviousness that is generally inherent in the earliest European movies. Throughout this book Schwarzer's films are viewed in terms of social history and early Freudian psychoanalysis. I have also given attention to women's dresses and shoes in a social context and as they are represented in photography. The shoe-and-ankle fetish is present in humorous examples such as the ubiquitous photographic postcards in circulation at the time (**fig. 62**). Design is at issue here, too, and the fashionable reticule (**figs. 64** and **65**), so feminine and vaginal to sight and touch, with its netted or soft mesh facture, is considered in terms of Freudian psychoanalytic concepts (see Chapters 1, 2, and 3, below).

Various domestic objects from Biedermeier Vienna, such as the standard nineteenth-century "Psyche Mirror," come to bear on everyday life and play a role in the psychic life of the bourgeoisie (**fig. 49**). We recognize this in one of the family-oriented histories, namely that of Breuer's "Anna O.," where Bertha Pappenheim hallucinated images of death-heads in such a mirror while at her dying father's bedside. In another case of domestic furniture design, an examination couch and operating table designed by the French surgeon

16. Freud 1900, 36–37, citing Strümpell 1877, 119.

Eugène-Louis Doyen (1869–1916) are examples of the most modernized medical apparatuses to be photographed, filmed, and published in Vienna. Doyen's patient daybed, to be installed in a hospital room, is represented photographically in his widely circulated book *Surgical Therapeutics and Operative Technique* of 1897. The daybed (**fig. 55**) as a place for the patient to relax while she recuperates, is a precursor to Freud's psychoanalytic couch in its function as well as design.

At my most purposeful, I shall continue to argue that popular visual mediums such as photography and film not only furnished, but actually constructed the psychoanalytic visual environment. I attempt to be incisive about popular visual culture, involved as it was with the activity of reading. I argue that popular culture was constitutive of a particular visual environment, as if it were a pictorial humus from which the psychoanalytic imagination coalesced. Each of the three chapters here propose that visual images, including "documentary" photographs, not only recorded, but actually initiated, cultural meaning and hierarchical structures.

The New Art: Youth Style

The beginning of modernist art and design in Austria began with the Vienna Secession in 1897, thus ending the pervasiveness of the painterly Romanticism of the ubiquitous Hans Makart (1840–84), of Biedermeier ornamental decoration, and of other classical or historicist styles that had prevailed since the early nineteenth century, so abjured by Adolf Loos (1870–1933) in *Ornament and Crime* of 1908. The Secession, led by Gustav Klimt (1862–1918), Koloman Moser (1868–1918), Josef Hoffman (1870–1956), Mileva Roller (1886–1949), and Joseph Maria Olbrich (1867–1908), brought the ideals of Romanticist, academic, and neoclassical thinking to a close, initiating dramatically new ventures in painting and design and the exposition of these ideas in their splendid illustrated journal, *Ver Sacrum* (published 1898–1903), which also advocated an "artistic way of life," including a new way of looking at life via photographic representation.[17] The Jugendstil (or Youth Style) and the Secession (separation from the Academy) in art and design was more or less contemporary with Art Nouveau in France, and shared many of Art Nouveau's stylistic nuances.

17. See Faber 2006.

In Vienna the new art (Jugendstil) commenced, not necessarily in painting or sculpture, but rather, first in the field of photography and graphic design. Such design projects followed closely upon the founding in 1888 of the important K. K. (Kaiserlich Königlich) Graphische Lehr- und Versuchsanstalt für Photographie und Reproductionsverfahren in Wien (Imperial Viennese Graphic Institute for the Teaching and Research of Photography and Reproductive Printing) (hereafter GLV) initiated by the renowned photochemist Josef Maria Eder (1855–1944).[18]

Josef Maria Eder and the Imperial Institute

Why is the early history of photography so essential to the study of visual culture? Let me focus my interests by pointing to the life of a single individual, namely the Austrian photochemist Josef Maria Eder (1855–1944) who was portrayed by Nadar in 1887 (**fig. 2**). Eder was perhaps the most prominent European innovator in the field of photography and its allied interests. Of all the photographers working in Europe and North America around the turn of the century, Eder not only did the most to gather and divulge new photographic technologies, but he was able to apply these technologies to the historical and cultural context of his own photographic research and representation.

By 1905 Eder had written a definitive history of photography, *Geschichte der Photographie* (*History of Photography*). This *History of Photography* in its English translation by Edward Epstean (1868–1945) was reviewed positively by the American photography historian Beaumont Newhall in the *Art Bulletin* of June 1946.[19] Newhall (1908–93) recognized the importance of the book, calling it an "almost indispensable" reference work. Eder's first book (*Die Momentenphotographie in ihrer Anwendung auf Kunst und Wissenschaft*) was about the application of photography to science and art.[20] In the year 1887 (the same year he was photographed by Nadar) Eder had several epiphanies. He visited important institutions such as the

18. Presently called the Austrian Federal Education and Research Institute for Graphics, the Institute's collection is now conserved in the Albertina Museum.

19. Hewhall 1946, 135–36.

20. See Eder 1886.

Photochemische Laboratorium in Berlin and the photographic studios at the Pitié-Salpêtrière University Hospital in Paris. The same year Eder attended the International Astronomical Congress for the Creation of Photographic Maps of the Heavens in Paris, and maintained a long correspondence with the experimental photographer Étienne-Jules Marey (1830–1904), and with Albert Londe (1858–1917), a formidable personality in the history of French scientific photography, the head of photographic technology and radiology at the Salpêtrière, where, as we know, Freud had spent a crucial residency with Jean-Martin Charcot in 1885–86. Londe, of course, is best remembered for his work with Charcot (1825–93) as a medical photographer at the Salpêtrière in Paris, where among his subjects were female patients suffering from a shape-shifting ailment (known as "hysterical epilepsy" in the terminology of the Salpêtrière). Some of these "hysterical" women were photographed while under hypnosis. Paul Regnard's (1850–1927) documentary photographs of "Hysterical Epilepsy" presented an evidentiary gaze at women who were medical subjects, including plate XXXIX, *Hysterical Epilepsy After the Attack*, where we see a young woman carrying a basket, walking with a clumsy gait with the help of her nurse (**fig. 3**).

It was also in 1887 that Eder founded the annual *Jahrbuch für Photographie und Reproductionstechnik*, a journal that published photographs and texts on photography and photographic printing. Additionally, Eder founded and edited the *Photographische Correspondenz*, an *omnium gatherum* of technical and aesthetic themes contributed from around the world. His five-volume *Ausführliches Handbuch der Photographie* (*Complete Handbook of Photography*) was published from 1892 to 1899, illustrated copiously not only with reproductions of photographs, but also with many wood engravings (made *from* photographs) detailing particular equipment and methods.

One of Eder's most important contributions was as founder in 1888 of the important, and previously mentioned, GLV, where he remained director until 1923. This research institute was of maximum importance in the scientific and artistic cultures of Vienna. Students at the institute had courses in drawing for re-touching techniques, and learned how to transfer photographic "sketches" to other media, such as the end-blocks of wood for engraving.[21] One pertinent example of the technical transfer of photography to wood engraving is an anonymous illustration titled

21. Eder 1886, 170.

Photographie im Hospital (**fig. 4**).[22] Here, a sick woman in her hospital bed is observed, not by a physician, but by a photographer who tends his heavy, almost architectural, equipment.

Women and men who were trained at the institute, or any other heirs to the Viennese tradition, were masters in the craft of photographic representation and transformation. One such photographer was Max Jaffé (1841–1911). An advertisement published by Jaffé's Graphische Kunstanstalt (Graphic Arts Institute) in 1918 listed among his skills: "Schwartz und Farben Lichtdruck" (black-and-white and color callotypes); "Autochromie" (autochromes); "Schwartz und Farben Klischees" (color and black-and-white negative plates); "Weitraumphotographie" (long-distance photography); "Photolith" (photolithography); and "Fettabzug" (printing with oil).

In considering the period of around 1850 to 1950, we may ask whether photographs are "naturally" more naturalistic than drawings and paintings. Is realism construed by the fact that photography always contains and displays its own referent? In Vienna at the Graphic Institute, the principles of photography were profoundly allied with experimentation in the physical sciences. In 1890, for example, the physiologist Sigmund Exner (1846–1926) set up complex experiments at the GLV to examine the visual capacities of the compound eyes of insects. Not only did biological and chemical research flourish at the institute, but physics was also investigated there. The physicist Ernst Mach (1838–1916) and his son Ludwig Mach (1868–1951) carried out their famous experiments with the hyperbolic shock waves of flying bullets at the institute in 1889. The photographs—"instantaneous photographs of projectiles meeting an obstacle and their shock waves"—show variously shaped bullets with their variations in shock waves and trajectories.[23] The velocities of Mach's bullets exceeded the speed of sound, and the photographic evidence showed that shock waves traveled *in advance* of the bullet, reversing commonly held beliefs about the physical event of a bullet moving in space, by showing what had previously not been visible.[24]

It is important to note that Mach also invented X-ray stereoscopy soon after Röntgen's initial discovery of 1895. This invention made possible, among other images, a stereoscopic view of two mice by the

22. Eder 2013, 53, 54, *passim*.
23. Frizot 1998, 252–53, 255.
24. Crary 2001, 142.

physiologist Johann Nepomuk Czermak (1828–73) at Graz, published in the *Bullettino della società fotografica italiana* (**fig. 5**).[25] Czermak, whose brother Jaroslav (1830–78) was an accomplished painter, put a premium on visual observation. He founded the Leipzig "Spectatorium" just prior to his death in 1873.

Two years after Josef Maria Eder had observed Londe in Paris, he and his technician, Johann "Hans" Lenhard (1853–1920), took serial photographs of psychiatric patients suffering from various conditions at the Lower Austrian Provincial Lunatic Asylum (founded 1885), Kierling-Gugging hospital, under the invitation of the primarius, Dr. Krajatsch.[26] These photographs by Eder and Lenhard (credited to Eder's GLV) are known via copies by the firm Stengel & Markert. They correspond to particular illnesses, such as one of a woman diagnosed as suffering from a psychosis of acute delusion (**fig. 6**).

In 1889, the Kierling-Gugging photos were published in an illustrated exhibition catalogue, meant to serve as a reference tool for doctors and researchers, and to be divulgated widely as a working textbook. Eder and Lenhard were therefore arguably as important as Freud in importing the French morphological examination through photography practiced by Charcot to Vienna in the 1880s.

Although used by physicians as documentary evidence, here the unknown woman's *Angst* and totalizing pathos are rendered in dramatic terms as though staged for the photographer's lens. This project constitutes an important cultural alliance between psychoanalytic and photographic techniques of observation around the turn of the century in the Austro-Hungarian capital.

Under Hitler's rule, between 1939 and 1941, tens of thousands of patients were murdered at psychiatric hospitals. Kierling-Gugging was taken over by the Nazi euthanasia physician Emil Gelny (1890–1961) in 1943. It then became the site of mass exterminations by way of pills, injections (morphine, hyoscine, barbiturates), remodeled stun-guns,

25. Eder 1945, 384–85; Eder and Valenta 1896, 10. An undated note accompanying the copy of Eder and Valenta 1896 at the Vienna Institute for the History of Medicine states: "Enthält die ersten in Oesterreich hergestellten Röntgensphotos nebst ausführlicher Erklärung der Röntgenographie" (Contains the first X-ray photographs produced in Austria together with a detailed explanation of radiography).

26. Eder 1889, 467.

and lethal electroshock, by Gelny.[27] It is striking that the German-speaking lands of Europe were so suddenly distorted by the Nazi regime that Gelny's killing techniques replaced Eder and Lenhart's functional design projects within the space of about fifty years under the roof of the same institution.

How do theoretical questions about photography and science play out in the world of Josef Maria Eder? We can look to the images employed by Freud's teachers and colleagues as *exempla*. There were several artists and scientists who concerned themselves with seeing what was traditionally hidden or forbidden from sight. In the multi-cultural Austrian milieu of the turn of the twentieth century, biology, naturalism, and art were pressed (laminated) close together in scientific images. I shall point to a few pertinent examples in the paragraphs that follow.

In design, Martin Gerlach (1846–1918), who was a publisher, engraver, photographer, and graphic designer, published macroscopic and histological photographs of natural objects and effects, which were adapted for use according to the Jugendstil principles. Gerlach published the album *Formenwelt aus dem Naturreiche* (*A World of Forms from Nature*) between 1902 and 1904 for the inspiration of Secessionist artists and designers.[28] Following this documentary album (*Formenwelt*) photographic representations of plants and animals were consistently included in Gerlach's vocabulary as a designer. In many ways, Gerlach made natural objects look "strange" and intriguing by way of defamiliarization, what the Russian formalists called "*ostranenie*." The use of magnification by way of photomicrography aggrandized or minimized these forms and rendered them desirable to the eye and appropriate for design projects of any scale. These images insisted upon their own aesthetic system, which was close to the Freudian uncanny, whereby familiar objects were defamiliarized or abstracted from nature by way of the beholder's point of view, or by the photographer's use of light. Gerlach's enlargements of specimens such as insect wings, jellyfish medusae, radiolaria, and various forms of plant life (**fig. 20**), endowed even the most common natural objects with an elegant sense of revelatory power, indicating that some of the most splendid forms in nature were occult until revealed in all their elegance by the camera

27. Wheeling 2017.
28. Lechner 2005.

as an instrument of investigation.[29] Gerlach's photographic images revealed the underlying structures (as well as the surfaces) of natural forms, preparing the public for the reception of works by artists like the German zoologist Ernst Haeckel. Martin Gerlach's work, through the artful juxtapositions of nature photography, microscopic photography, and enlargements, had an important impact upon the art of Wiener Werkstätte designers such as textile designers Thomas Weigner, who produced *Studies from Nature and Composition* (1905) and Wilhelm Foltin (1890–1970).

As so often happened in the history of photography, the style and intention of some images were influenced by contemporary or earlier drawing, painting, and printmaking. The photographic designs made by Gerlach and his contemporaries looked, for example, to the brilliant drawings and paintings by his German contemporary Ernst Haeckel (1834–1919) (**fig. 19**). Haeckel was a naturalist, whose views of animal evolution spanned the theories of Jean-Baptiste Lamarck to those of Charles Darwin (1809–82). Haeckel is known for stating the so-called recapitulation theory—that "ontogeny recapitulates phylogeny"—and he also embraced the idea of "social Darwinism." In the same vein, Haeckel's *General Morphology of Organisms* (1866) was based on theories put forth by Jean-Baptiste de Lamarck (1744–1829). His monograph on radiolaria (1862) earned him the Cothenius Medal in 1864; his *The Riddle of the Universe* of 1899 also brought him abundant fame. Haeckel's *Kunstformen der Natur* (*Art Forms in Nature*) of 1899 was an important contribution to modernism that demonstrated the way abstract art forms were derived from illustrations of biological forms, merging, as it were, the concerns of science with art and design, in a harbinger of the new (twentieth) century. Among Haeckel's greatest contributions to visual culture were his colorful and precise illustrations such as the lithographs *Actiniae* (**fig. 20**) and *Trochilidae* of 1904. Haeckel's drawings and paintings of flora and fauna (including the flower-like animals that we call sea anemones—actiniae) still exercise a strong attraction for postmodern viewers.[30]

The strategy of making the commonplace strange (*ostranenie*) was one of sudden aesthetic revelation: Astrid Lechner, for example, has observed that the foot of a common dung fly (*Scataphaga stercoraria*) is infused with an ethereal elegance and grace when it is removed from

29. Lechner 2005, 30, 31, 50, 51, 60–65, 74, 75.

30. Haeckel 1998, plate 49.

its natural setting and transformed by photography into a work of art.[31] Certain photographs of plant life by Gerlach have the translucent look of X-ray negatives printed in positive, making the substance of geraniums look as translucent as the most delicate of translucent seaweed.

Gerlach's aesthetic evolved, too, under the German photographer Karl Blossveldt (1865–1932) in his botanical photographs, which suggest strong modernist architectural forms. Walter Benjamin, in his *Little History of Photography* commented on Blossfeldt's "astonishing plant photographs" (**fig. 22**). Karl Blossfeldt's works were published in 1929 in *Urformen der Kunst* (translated as *Art Forms in Nature*). Benjamin remarked on the way Blossveldt's famous plant studies "revealed the forms of ancient columns in horse willow, a bishop's crosier in the ostrich fern, totem poles in tenfold enlargements of chestnut and maple shoots, and gothic tracery in the fuller's thistle." Walter Benjamin recognized the importance of such photographic work, which he foresaw would form our concept of the world.[32] All of this had originated in the Viennese modernism of Martin Gerlach a decade earlier.

Many of Gerlach's images, including those by his historically neglected followers, were riveting unto themselves, as well as having educational value for artists and designers. S. Schenk, for example, published a series of photographs of the results of the arbitrary (accidental) effects of acid on metal (**fig. 23**). This photograph, a neglected print of which I found in the library files of the Rhode Island School of Design, where it may have languished unstudied for about a century, provides a surprising visual "key" to Viennese modernism, uniting scientific observation with two-dimensional design in an unprecedented manner. Photography was at the heart of this endeavor and reproducible images such as Schenk's were disseminated internationally from the hub of the Austro-Hungarian capital city.

Photography Disappears

As Hagi Kenaan has stated recently in *Photography and Its Shadow* (2020), "The history of photography is not a chronology of a given, essentially self-same, pictorial medium [that progressed over time]; but rather it is an account of a dialectical process that allowed photography to negotiate

31. Lechner 2005, 74–75.

32. Benjamin [1931] 1999, 59–77.

and sustain an identity."[33] It is with the visual culture of photography as a dialectical process that my work is concerned. Photography, to use a concept established by the American anthropologist Clifford Geertz (1926–2006), is itself nothing more nor less than a far-reaching "cultural system."[34] The present book is a study of photography in Vienna around 1900 as a cultural system with psychoanalysis as its corresponding verbal language—even its *Mameloshn* (mother tongue).

Photography was an ally of the scientific (and anthropological) disciplines from the start in Freud's Vienna. To cite a specific and rather obvious example, photographic social documentation such as the famous "Wiener Typen" (Vienna types), cabinet cards by Vienna's most prolific commercial photographers, including the ever-prosperous Otto Schmidt, are in their own way "species-specimen portraits." Such pictures pretended a certain veracity; as well as serving as stereotypes, they were likenesses that could be checked against "reality" for evidentiary proof and consistency.

In the practice of (modernist) art history, we spend a lot of time pretending to ourselves that photography does not prevail as intermediary to the studied object. Thus, photography as a medium of transmission effectively continues to escape, keeps disappearing into the beholder's visual imagination. It is precisely the dialectic of this "fort/da" vanishing process that makes possible the art of "specimen photography" (a kind of object portraiture), as in the photography of art objects, a practice, incidentally, which was at the very core of art-historical studies.

In the *Wiener Typen*, then, these most overdetermined, staged, and exoticized pictures of social types, each person/type is isolated as a separate societal specimen, with an exacting nomenclature as used in scientific classification. We may look, for example, at Schmidt's series of *Graben-Nymphen* (urban prostitutes). These pictures isolate and eroticize Viennese street-walkers of a particular time and place, and a very specific social echelon (**fig. 7**). It is also the case, of course, in Schmidt's photographic representation of Galician-born, kaftan-wearing, Viennese Jews who were photographically observed in their isolated presence for the visual delectation of mainstream Austrians and others (**fig. 8**). Such pictures and their attendant words (whether or not they meant to deprecate specific social groups or merely define

33. Kenaan 2020, 11.

34. Geertz 1976, 1473–499.

them from an authoritative point of view) afford the viewer a position of privilege, from which he can inspect the specimen in a handheld photographic print as if it were a newspaper or a book.

In exploring visual representation in Freud's Vienna, a few important precepts from the social history of visual culture ought to be reiterated. First, that the past is always already genuinely different from the present. Additionally, that everyday life in the present is forever informed, haunted, and likewise troubled by the past. Further, that visual culture is everywhere in the historical past *and* the present, in our unconscious reminiscences and unconscious predictions, like the air we breathe, or, as David Foster Wallace might have put it, the water we swim in.[35] We should also agree that social habits (including the education of children, attention to material objects, and sexual mores) vary from one society to another, historically and culturally. With a nod to cultural anthropology, it ought to be the rule rather than the exception that the sum total of visual production, from the most profound object or image to the most trivial, be interrogated with the special attention we art historians typically reserve for that which was long ago, far away, legendary, obscure, arcane, spiritually esoteric, or intellectually abstruse.

Apropos "species photography" and the *Wiener Typen*, it is here in the study of social systems that the cultural proximity of erotic themes to medical practice, like those familiar to us from Freud's case of "Dora," for example, come into sight. The difficulties inherent in the idealization and subsequent expectations of family life (what we would now refer to as lived experience in an extended family) in the second half of the nineteenth century, are already familiar to us by way of thinkers such as the playwright and short story writer Anton Chekhov (1860–1904), who, like Freud, qualified as a medical doctor. In a statement made in 1888 that might have resonated with Freud, Chekhov claimed that "Medicine is my lawful wife and literature is my mistress."[36] For Freud, of course, literature was the very muscle of Western culture, as well as being the medium that correlated most closely with the new science of psychoanalysis. In Lionel Trilling's classic essay of the mid-twentieth century dedicated to "Freud and Literature," he stated that psychoanalysis was "one of the culminations of Romanticist literature

35. Wallace 2009.

36. Chekhov, letter to Alexei Suvorin, September 11, 1888; Chekhov 2004.

of the nineteenth century."[37] Freud's case histories were written in the manner of fictional literature of a Romanticist stamp, incorporating and exploring what Trilling called the "rich ambiguity" of (the German) language.[38] Freud's case studies are indeed microhistories (such as those later addressed by Italian thinkers of the 1970s such as Giovanni Levi and Carlo Ginzburg), dealing with the mystifications of patriarchy, marriage, romantic love, the idealization and reality of family life. Freud wrote about various kinds of problematic, or unrequited, love in everyday life and the difficulty of finding satisfaction in the spheres of the nuclear or extended family.

What was the intellectual and art-historical climate in which the *Wiener Typen* functioned? It was an age of experimentation in medical studies and medicine's visual paraphernalia. To say that Freud had interesting professors would be an understatement, and several of these men were innovators in visual, as well as scientific, culture. Let me expand upon this point in the following paragraphs.

Vienna Life: Photography and Dreams

We can see that the realm of unconscious psychological motivation at the beginning of the twentieth century springs forth from the rich humus of visual representation and material culture. How does the craft of making, publishing, and apprehending photographs come into this picture? Photography, particularly in its art-historical application, is a hidden actor, not quite visible to the human eye. It is just this phenomenon of "hiding in plain sight," of residing deep inside the gaze, that is one of the most perplexing qualities of photography.

This "hiding" and "revealing" ("fort-da") or "invisibility" of the photographic medium is also problematic in terms of the interpretation and criticism of photographs as research tools or as representations per se. The communicative nature of photography is such that its presumed transparency, "looking through" the surface (rather than examining the surface, as we do with European painting), so mystifies the viewer as to keep them from critical discourse. This has been the case since the beginning of the medium's application around 1839. Depending upon the eye of the beholder, photographs themselves can appear either

37. Trilling 1947, 182.
38. Trilling 1947, 195.

obscure or explicit, inadvertent or carefully composed, freshly minted or dulled by cultural overload.

Concomitant to the transparency of photography is the idea that photographs frequently appear in an oneiric guise, complete with its characteristic tenebrous atmosphere. The psychological lamination of photography onto the rest of visual culture allows for unconscious content, and opens photography (for some people the most literally reproductive of all the visual arts) to the investigation of unconscious preoccupations and desires. Photographs, like dreams, contain latent as well as manifest content, and, like a dream, the interpretation, or analysis, of even the most "straightforward" photograph is never really quite finished, and disappears into chronic forgetfulness.

Whether or not unconscious visual ideation is truly structured like a language, as Jacques Lacan (1901–81) and his followers would have it, the interpretation of a photograph, as in the interpretation of a dream, is somewhat hallucinatory and never fully exhausted. This is because the arena of meaning around a cultural object is determined by intertextuality as well as by the subjective identity of the interpreter, particularly in the visual engagement with photographic illustrations to texts.

Photography and Science

Photography was an ally of the scientific disciplines from the start, and was important as such in Freud's Vienna. In *Photography and Science*, Kelley Wilder, who is trained in history of science as well as history of art, emphasized that "the sheer transparency of photography as a physical object is what is crucial to creating photographic records."[39] In Wilder's view, transparency "could be called one of the iconographic traits of the art of photography."[40] This "photographic disappearing act," working together with neutral visual grounds among other factors, creates effective "specimen photographs," by isolating the object of the photograph for close looking. In modernism, specimen photographs are like "portraits" of objects or individuals that seem to communicate directly through the adjustable veil of photography. Such "specimen portraits" encourage the observer to assume (consciously or not) they

39. Wilder 2009, 88.
40. Eder 1889, 467.

are looking directly at the primary referent object, and interpreting it, rather than at a printed or projected photographic representation of the object.

This set of photographs, which corresponded to particular diagnoses, are known via copies by the firm of Stengel & Markert of original photographs by Josef Maria Eder and Hans Lenhard, such as one of a woman at Kierling-Gugging diagnosed as suffering from a psychosis of acute delusion (**fig. 6**).

Salomon Stricker and Epidiascopic Projection

The pathologist Salomon Stricker (1834–98), another of Freud's professors, also a former pupil of Brücke, was named director of the Institute for General and Experimental Pathology at the University of Vienna in 1868. Freud took courses with Stricker in experimental physiology at the University of Vienna, including one on the general pathology of the nervous system, which took place in spring 1878. The epidiascope manufactured by Carl Zeiss (1816–88) (like the episcope from which it derived) was a kind of opaque projector; it became the mid-twentieth century's "overhead projector," which projected opaque objects or images placed in its box onto a screen of any kind. Optician Carl Zeiss was a German manufacturer of optical aids and systems who founded his company, Carl Zeiss, AG, in Jena 1846.

According to the American developmental psychologist G. Stanley Hall (1844–1924), the use of epidiascopes transformed the physiological laboratory into a sort of cinematic theater.[41] An original drawing of its early use by Moritz Ledeli (1856–1920) was reproduced in a contemporary illustration. This exciting picture (**fig. 16**), titled *Presentation of the Brain with the Electric Episcope in the Auditorium of Professor Dr. Stricker in Vienna*, shows a crowd of intensely attentive men in a darkened lecture hall gazing at a large-scale luminous image of a human brain, the projector apparently managed by Stricker himself. The image arose as an illustration to the Reports of the Ninth Congress of Internal Medicine held in Vienna from April 15–18, 1890, published in the *Pharmaceutische Post* of April 20, 1890.

Here the brain, disclosing itself as a large complete specimen to crowds of doctors, is the center of the moment of visual comprehension,

41. Stricker 1879, 90, 106, 497.

or *Anschauung*— and is the ultimate protagonist. In the realm of the lecture-hall spectatorium, all gazes fix upon the projected image of the human brain. Although not indicated in the wood engraving, we may imagine that among the astonished viewers depicted at Stricker's lecture was the young Freud. At this point in his studies, Freud was examining the biology of nervous tissue, specifically comparing the brains of humans and other vertebrates to those of invertebrates. Ledeli's chiaroscuro wood engraving is far more profound, in form as well as content, than his typical illustrations, which consisted of the courting couples and fast-moving fiacres of Viennese life and leisure.

Salomon Stricker was an innovative thinker in Vienna. Freud wrote about him in the *Interpretation of Dreams*, where he discussed a passage in Stricker's *Studien über das Bewusstsein* of 1879 (*Studies of Consciousness*) regarding the expression of emotional affect in dreams, the dream's conceptual structure, and how these two elements compare to the ideational–emotional dynamic in a waking state. In the *Interpretation of Dreams*, Freud discussed a passage in Stricker's writing regarding the expression of emotions (such as fear or joy) in dreams as opposed to the dream's narrative content, and how these two elements compare to the affective dynamic in a waking state. Freud cited Stricker's book about consciousness, where Stricker used the following example: "If I am afraid of robbers in my dreams, the robbers, to be sure, are imaginary, but the fear of them is real."[42] It was at Stricker's institute that the ophthalmologist Karl Koller (1857–1944) began his experimentation with cocaine as a local anesthetic for eye surgery at the suggestion of Freud. Koller, who was nicknamed "Coca Koller," for his expertise with cocaine, relocated to New York in 1888 and carried on his practice there until his death in 1944.

Histology, Drawing, and Painting: From Masaccio to Kaposi

Coinciding with the study of the mind (on the verge of being called the science of the brain, and then back again to the psyche), scientists such as the Hungarian-born Moritz Kaposi (1837–1902) (for whom the dreaded "Kaposi's sarcoma" was named) went on from microscopic observation to look at histological drawings, which explored microscopic life on or beneath the surface of the skin. A drawing from Kaposi's collection,

42. Freud 1900.

by Karl Henning (dated 1886) (**fig. 9**), shows the crust of the skin's surface at the top (epidermis), with the depths of the dermis (below the epidermis) roiling in granular motion below, incorporating various discrete forms. In a microscopic view like this drawing, we see various kinds of cells: fibroblasts, macrophages, and mast cells, which were also called mastocytes or labrocytes.

Although histologically produced images of such samples are also widespread in the digital images of twenty-first-century medicine, they somehow lack the energetic registration of forms in the earlier drawings, which are arguably more aesthetically sustaining, particularly because the act of histological representation itself was pioneering. In the history of art, "firsts," or pioneering attempts at representation, as in this important drawing, stand out for their lively descriptive and active qualities. Let us turn from this small informational format to a macro-heroic scale in the depiction of the human body. This is visible in the art of Renaissance Italy, to cite a familiar example, in the fresco painting of the shadow of Saint Peter in *The Healing of the Cripple and the Resurrection of Tabitha* at the Brancacci Chapel of Santa Maria del Carmine. Masolino (1383–1447) and Masaccio (1401–28) painted the healing shadows as colored cast shadows—a first in Florentine painting of the fifteenth century. In this case, Masaccio and Masolino's shadows are not just a device of visual mimesis, but rather become essential to the meaning of the religious narrative. The theme of Saint Peter healing with his shadow originates in Acts 5:15–16 "they brought the sick out into the streets and laid them on beds and couches, that at least the shadow of Peter passing by might fall on some of them." The shadows cast in the Brancacci Chapel are evidentiary indicators in terms of sacred history, active agents of healing in the life of Saint Peter (**fig. 10**), and material evidence of the corporeal states of a heroic Adam and Eve. Much of the same energy and "firstness" that we know from fifteenth-century Florence obtains in the scientific images that were made or used by Freud's teachers and colleagues at the turn of the twentieth century in the multiethnic metropolis.

Ernst Wilhelm Brücke and His World: Science and the History of Art

To say that Freud had interesting teachers would be an understatement, and several of these men were innovators in visual as well as intellectual (scientific) culture. Freud studied under the eminent physician and physiologist Ernst Wilhelm Brücke (1819–92) from 1877 until 1883. Brücke had been appointed teacher of anatomy in the Academy of Fine Arts in Berlin already in 1846, and maintained a lifelong interest in the visual arts as both practitioner and theorist. In art-historical analysis we see that Brücke the physiologist was above all a classicist with a prodigious knowledge of ancient Greco-Roman sculpture. He was also given to the study of Italian Renaissance painting and, perhaps because of his medical training, had an excellent "eye" and visual memory for artists' individual styles as well as for anatomical principles in the human form.

Scientific and artistic representation are all but inseparable in Brücke's worldview and in the concerns of those around him, casting him and his followers as the most typical Viennese observers of scientific and erotic images. Brücke, who like Schultze-Naumburg, Krauss, and Stratz, objected to the premature corseting of girls, spent a lot of time looking at photographs.[43] He worked from photographs of nude models, and his book on *The Human Figure* was illustrated with wood engravings made after such photographs from life. Brücke must have enjoyed looking at orientalist photographs, too, and recollected "a photograph of a poor Fellah girl, in whom the great toe was conspicuously longer than the second," from never having worn Western shoes.[44] Such photographs of Egyptian peasant women, like the one I illustrate by Jean Pascal Sébah (see **fig. 14**), were widely collected in Europe and America.

Brücke also commented on Turkish [Egyptian] dancers, "The so-called Almeh," who could move their breasts while "keeping the body perfectly still by contracting in an appropriate manner the great pectoral muscle lying beneath them."[45] Here I believe we must imagine a certain visual slippage among various pictures of bodies, with photography already taken for granted as a kind of reliable record of truth, as digested from books like those of Stratz and Schultze-Naumburg.

Brücke was a connoisseur of classical bodies among the male and female models who worked for academic artists in the mid to later nineteenth century too. Judging from his text, Brücke worked with nude models in the art academy, photographs of living models (both female and male), photographs of ancient sculpture, actual sculpture that he encountered in his Grand Tour travels in Italy, and people he chanced

43. Brücke 1891, 99, 111.
44. Brücke 1891, 172.
45. Brücke 1891, 172, 182.

to see in passing or whose bodies he observed at "bathing resorts."[46] Brücke even commented upon the "well-rounded upper arms" of Leona Dare (1855–1922), a sensational trapeze acrobat, who had appeared at the Circus Renz in Vienna during the 1870s as well as the Folies Bergère in Paris, and had "displayed the beauty of her arms in all of the great cities of the world."[47] Dare's beautiful arms are to be admired, for instance, in a cabinet card by the New York daguerreotypist Jeremiah Gurney (1812–95) (**fig. 15**).

Brücke travelled widely in Europe, above all in Italy, where he seems to have left no female thorax unstudied, and even examined the mummified body of an ancient Egyptian woman that was conserved at Parma.[48] Brücke particularly admired the posture and gait of women from the Romagna.[49] The Romagna region of Italy was known to be a culture of great antiquity (supposedly settled by Paleolithic times), and the women, who still carried heavy loads on their heads even throughout the nineteenth century, were in Brücke's view the most graceful and dignified, famous for the beauty of the attachment of the neck to the shoulders.[50] He stated that women of the Romagna, "especially those belonging to certain districts of the Sabine mountains, owe the regal bearing" and "the superiority of their gait" to the habit of carrying things on their heads.[51] Ernst Wilhelm Brücke would have seen nineteenth-century illustrations (engravings, paintings, and photographs) of Italian women carrying goods on their heads, like the popular prints and paintings of women at the *vendemmia* (vintage) carrying large baskets of grapes on their heads. Brücke took the time to distinguish among the photographs of various photographers, discussing in particular, for instance, "Lombardi's photograph" of the ancient *Three Graces* from Siena Cathedral.[52]

46. See Brücke 1891, 93.

47. Brücke 1891, 49. Circus Renz was a German company with stationary buildings in Vienna. It was established in 1842 by Ernst Jakob Renz (1815–92) in Berlin and existed until 1897.

48. Brücke 1891, ch. 3. For the female Egyptian mummy at Parma, see Brücke 1891, 121.

49. Brücke 1891, 146.

50. Brücke 1891, 21.

51. Brücke 1891, 147.

52. Brücke 1891, 159.

The touristic/ethnographic photography of Sicily included photographs of women with heavy baskets of grapes or jugs or wine on their heads. In a postcard entitled "Costumi Siciliani: Gruppo di Popolani" two women are charged with taking large, deep baskets on their heads. In a photo from the series titled "Tipi Siciliani" a beautiful young girl stands in pose with a large terra-cotta jug balanced on her head. She is a living personification of the balance and dignity of the Sicilian past and continuing Italian traditions of this kind (**fig. 11**). A bit of white paint daubed in at the girl's right shoulder gracefully suggests the presence of Mount Etna in the background.

The girl is labelled as a particular ethnographic species, or "type," the "Sicilian type" representing the physical type of a Sicilian woman. Such racialized generalizations chimed with Brücke's preference for classicism in the human figure. This ethnographic preference for a particular "race" of Italian women (let us say from the Romagna or from Sicily), coincided with the young Freud's "scientific" interest in the women of Trieste and Muggia, whom he considered "more attractive, mostly blonde, oddly enough, which accords with neither Italian nor Jewish descent."[53] Brücke differentiates throughout his treatise on the human figure between Aryan and Latin types of women and men. The ethnographic analysis of women was alive and well for scientists like Brücke and Freud.

X-ray Photography: Under the Skin

Whereas photographic negatives represented "latent" ideation in Freud's terminology, the metaphor shifts with X-ray photography, staking out new territory in the visual imagination. X-ray images (positives and negatives) go deep under the skin to reveal what is not only unconscious, but due to that fact also disorienting, uncanny, forbidden, or taboo. This precept is at the heart of Chapter 1 of the present study. X-ray photography "saw through" surfaces such as human skin, looking below the boundaries of the epidermis to the inner workings of the body. The X-ray technique has an obvious analogy in Freudian thought with its conscious and unconscious realms. The invention of X-ray photography (1895) had a glorious reception in Vienna by medical doctors and photographers alike.

53. Bergstein 2010, 238.

Because X-rays have a similar effect to rays of daylight as they strike silver bromide and gelatin-dry plates, the photographic method was perfectly suited to the documentary record of X-ray research experiments. X-ray photography fixed the image as a negative photogram lit from behind or as a positive photographic print.[54] Photography instantly became the means of representing and reproducing X-ray technology.

X-ray observations were fixed on paper via photography, and became (no less than the Kierling-Gugging portrait series) diagnostic tools that explained outward perception of illness such as physical pain, and the haunting *Unheimlich* oscillation between life and death that Thomas Mann wrote about in *The Magic Mountain*, written from 1912 and published in 1924.

The Future of the Uncanny, Then and Now

Recently, cultural historians in the twenty-first century have been captivated yet again by concepts and aesthetics from the turn of the twentieth century, including from just that time and place that we casually locate as "Vienna 1900." Vectors of meaning that have plotted back to the point in time-space that we call "Vienna 1900" edge into the thinking about several new complex notions. One of these fashionable topics is the aesthetic that Freud called the uncanny (*Unheimlich*) in his essay of 1919.

Now in the third decade of the twenty-first century, the Freudian uncanny is applied not only to literature but to diverse fields such as architecture theory, film studies, and radical philosophy.[55] We need not go as far as Anneleen Masschelein, who calls the Uncanny a "late-twentieth-century theoretical concept."[56] Instead, the uncanny has now (twenty-first-century) become one of the most attractive ideas in Freudian psychoanalysis, and one of the most difficult ideas to come to terms with in aesthetic terms. In Freud's world the uncanny oscillation between life and the image of death was weirdly frightening to the sensory receiver. As a field of research, the uncanny, in the words of

54. Eder and Valenta 1896, 2.
55. Masschelein 2011, 4.
56. Masschelein 2011, 126.

the contemporary British novelist, Nicholas Royle, "is a province still before us, awaiting our examination."[57]

In the ripeness of the middle of the twentieth century, photographic advertising strategies pressed hard upon the bourgeois imagination. According to theorist Jennifer Reinhardt, writing for the Chicago School of Media Theory, we interpret a photographic representation of a woman gazing at a bottle of perfume as a representation of desire, *tout court* (see **fig. 17**). There were numerous variations on this theme in the advertising art of the period. In this view, the registration of gazes provides a visual code with which to interpret interior desires and social behavior. Psychoanalysis allowed individuals (theorists, analysts, patients, the interested public) to see what was formerly hidden or forbidden from their operative gazes. In the modernist psychoanalytic model, the prize is life behind or outside of the conscious mind, the proverbial dark side of the moon.

I and others who write about visual culture employ these terms ("uncanny" and "optical unconscious") with frequency and conviction, but these topics are still somewhat fragile, haunted, frightening, and uncertain, even in the third decade of the twenty-first century. The present book aims to clarify and interpret such themes and related material by way of close looking. We shall see that Sigmund Freud, Josef Maria Eder, and their contemporaries participated in an important cultural alliance between psychoanalytic and photographic techniques of observation around the turn of the century in the Austro-Hungarian capital.

57. Royle 2003, 26–27.

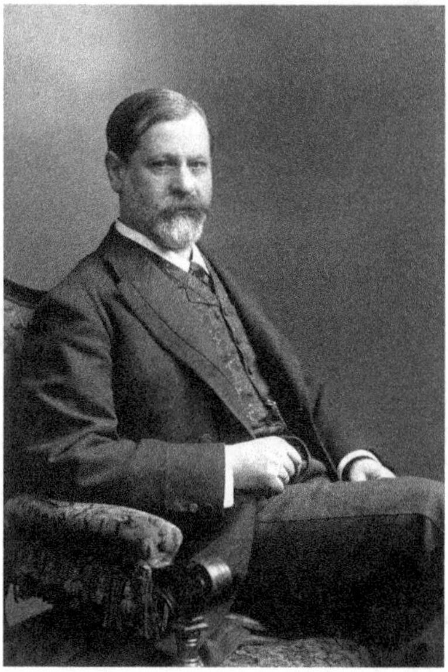

Fig. 1 Anonymous, *Photo-portrait of Sigmund Freud*, ca. 1906. Brandstaetter Images/Contributor, Hulton Archive. Courtesy of Getty Images.

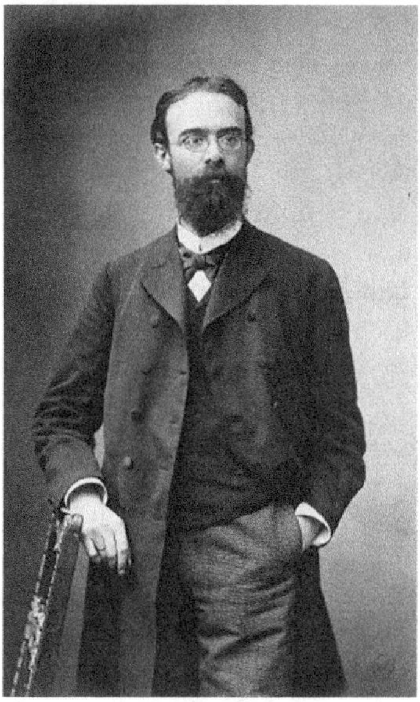

Fig. 2 Gaspard-Felix Tournachon, called Nadar, *Portrait of Josef Maria Eder*, age 32, 1887. Albertina, Vienna. Image in the public domain. Courtesy of Wikimedia Commons.

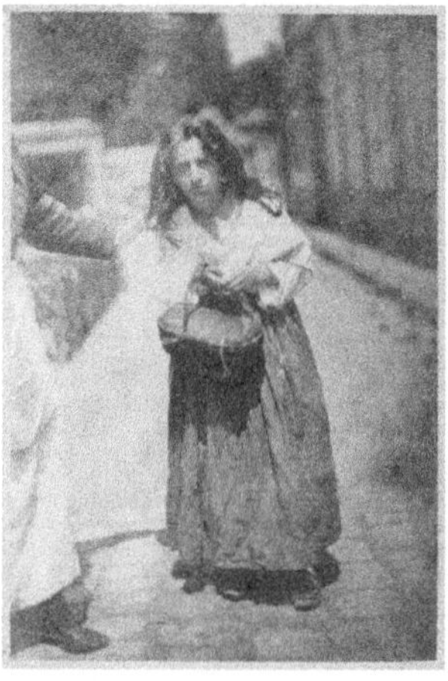

Fig. 3 Paul Regnard (1850–1927), *Hysterical epilepsy, after the attack*, plate XXXIX from Bourneville and P. Regnard, *Iconographie Photographique de La Salpêtrière* (Paris, 1876), albumen print. Private Collection. Image in the public domain.

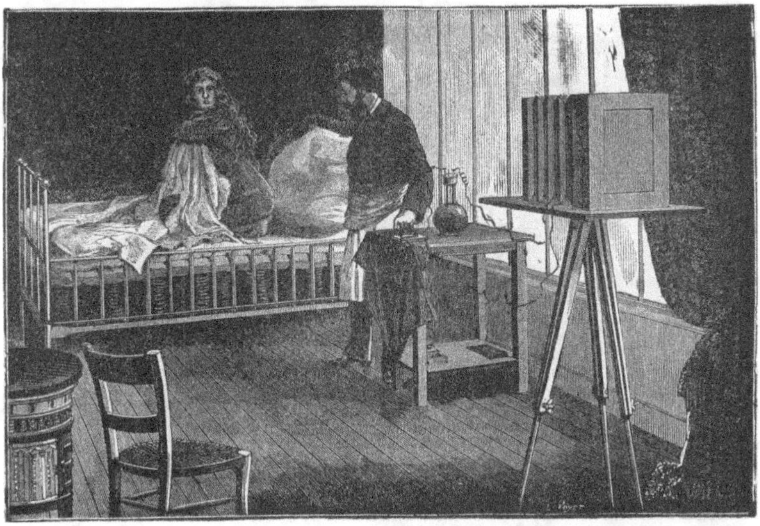

Fig. 4 Louis Poyet, *Charcot's Photographic Procedure*, wood engraving, in Josef Maria Eder, *Ausfürliches Handbuch der Photographie* (1891). Photo Kunsthistorisches Museum, Vienna. Image in the public domain. *"Disposition de l'appareil photo-électrique poire les études médicales,"* Albert Londe, *"La Photographie a la Salpêtriere", La Nature, 1883. CNAM.*

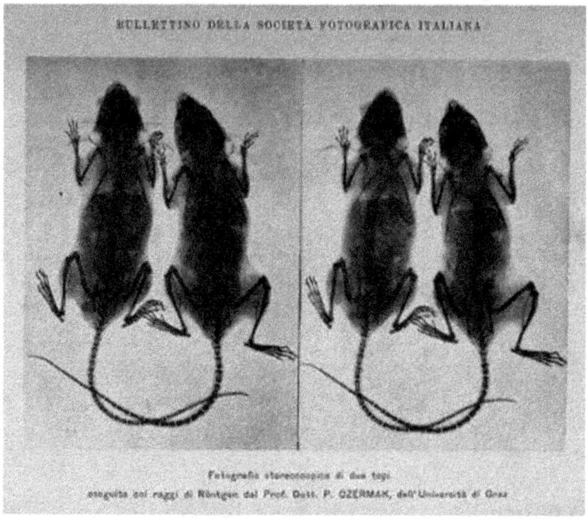

Fig. 5 Johann Nepomuk Czermak, *Stereoscopic View of Two Mice*, University of Graz, as published in *Bullettino della società fotografica italiana* (1896), A. 8, Plate, p. 347. Author's private collection. Image in the public domain.

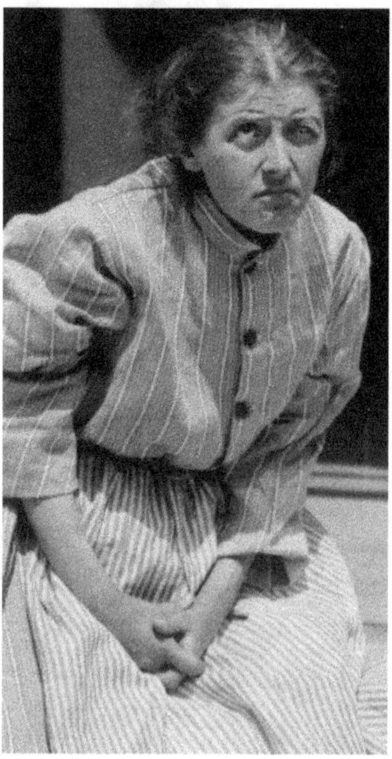

Fig. 6 *Geisteskranke, Psychose: Akuter Wahnsinn*, ca. 1885. Momentphotographie in der Irrenanstalt in Kierling-Gugging bei Wien. Original photograph by K. K. Lehr- und Versuchsanstalt für Photographie und Reproductionsverfahren in Wien. Rijksmuseum, Amsterdam. Reproduced by Eder and Lenhard, Kierling-Gugging, Stengel & Markert. Image in the public domain.

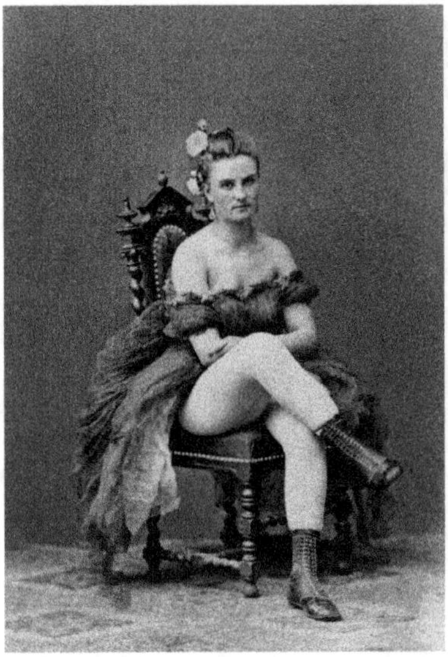

Fig. 7 Johann Baptist von Lakenbacher, *Graben-Nymphe* (Viennese prostitute in pose), cabinet card, 1865–80. Wien Museum. Brandstaetter Images/ Contributor. Courtesy of Getty Images.

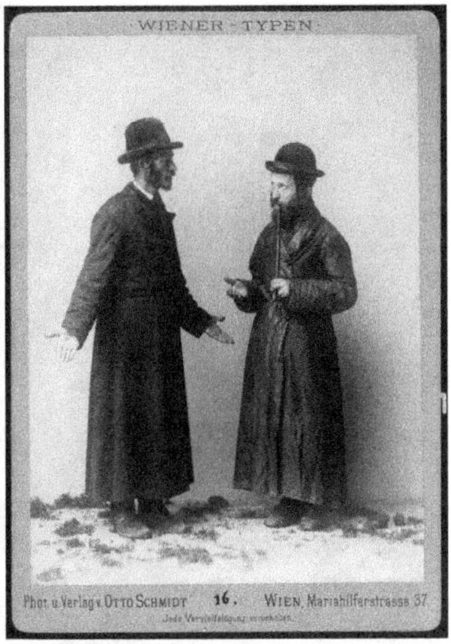

Fig. 8 Otto Schmidt, *Galician Jews,* from "Wiener Typen" series, 1887, albumin, cabinet card. Austrian National Library, Vienna. Image in the public domain.

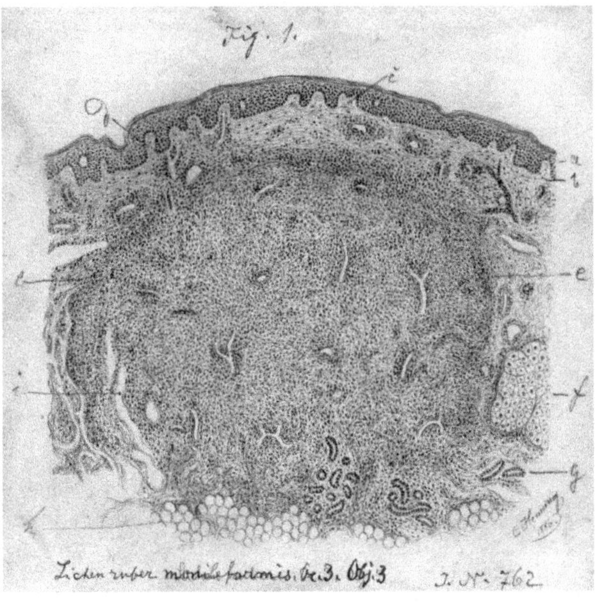

Fig. 9 Karl Henning, histological drawing marked "Lichen ruber multi formis." Vienna Medical University, 1886. Photo from author's collection. Image in the public domain.

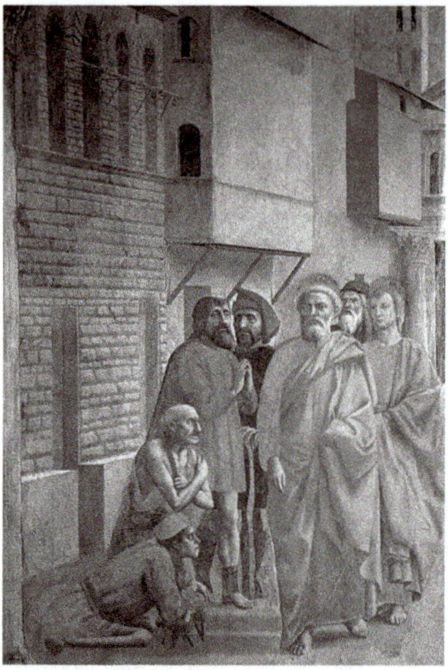

Fig. 10 Masaccio, *St. Peter Healing with His Shadow,* fresco painting, Brancacci Chapel, Santa Maria del Carmine, Florence. Image in the public domain.

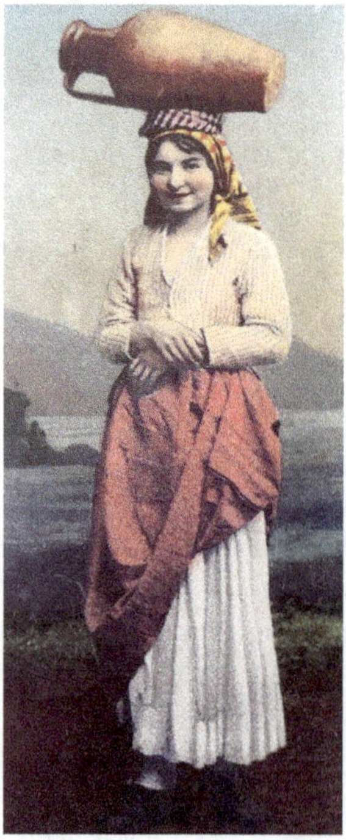

Fig. 11 Anonymous, *Girl Carrying an Amphora,* from "Tipi Siciliani" series. Hand-colored postcard. Author's private collection. Image in the public domain.

62

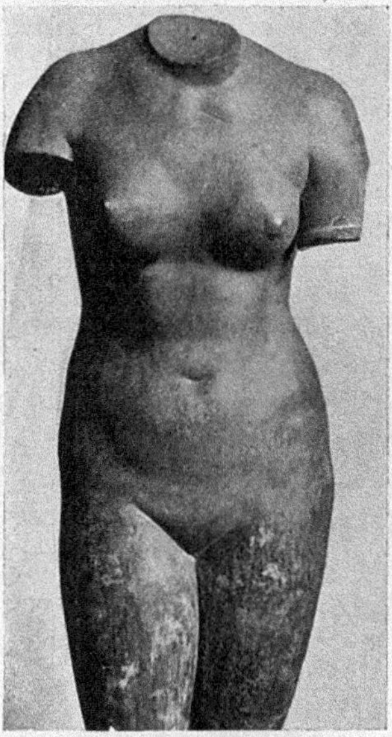

Abb. 59

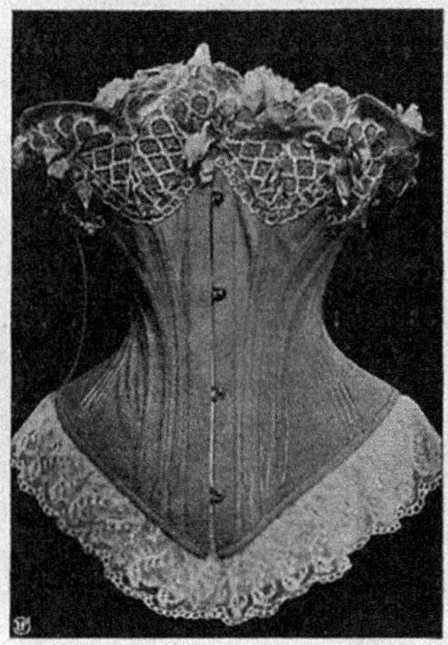

Abb. 60

ihren Kostümen zu Grunde legen. Ich weiss es, die Herausgeberinnen solcher Zeitungen schütteln sich selbst vor Abscheu davor, aber der Geschmack des Publikums diktiert diesen Typus. Wir können absolut sicher sein: dieses entsetzliche Zerrbild vom Menschenleib ist das Ideal des weitaus grössten Teiles der Menschheit.

Ich ziehe die Konturen des Körpers nach, wie er hierbei unter der Kleidung stecken müsste (Abb. 58).

Dies der entsprechende Körper. Man wird lachen und meinen, das gäbe es doch wohl kaum. Mag sein. Aber es ist das Ideal, dem mit allen Mittel näher zu kommen die Mehrzahl der Frauen bestrebt ist. Und leider, der Mann trägt vielleicht hieran die Haupt-

Fig. 12 Johann Vincenz Cissarz, facing pages 62–63, in Paul Schultze-Naumburg *Die Kultur des Weiblichen Körpers als Grundlage der Frauenkleidung* (Leipzig, 1901). Author's private collection. Image in the public domain.

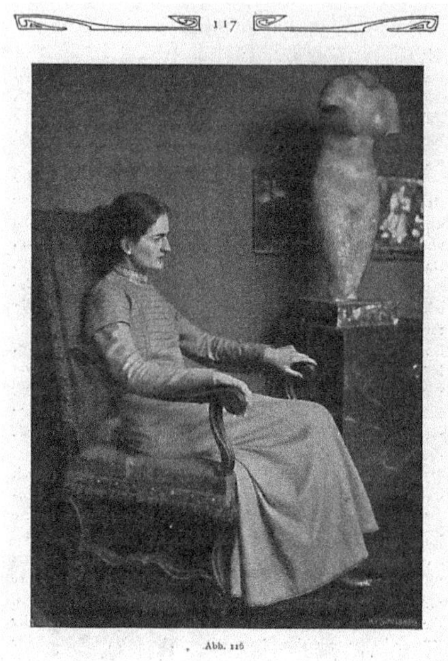

Fig. 13 Johann Vincenz Cissarz, *Reform dress*. Illustration 110, in Paul Schultze-Naumburg, *Die Kultur des Weiblichen Körpers als Grundlage der Frauenkleidung* (Leipzig, 1901). Author's private collection. Image in the public domain.

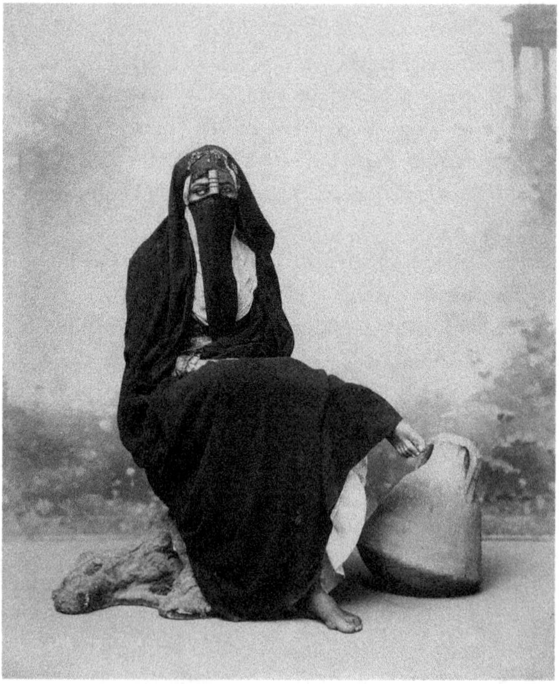

Fig. 14 Jean Pascal Sebah, *Femme Fallah*. Photograph © 2024 Museum of Fine Arts, Boston. Photograph, albumen print. Image/Sheet: 25.6 × 20.9 cm (10 1/16 × 8 1/4 in.). Stephen T. Rose. ACCESSION NUMBER 1974.432 Jean Pascal Sébah (Turkish, 1872–1947).

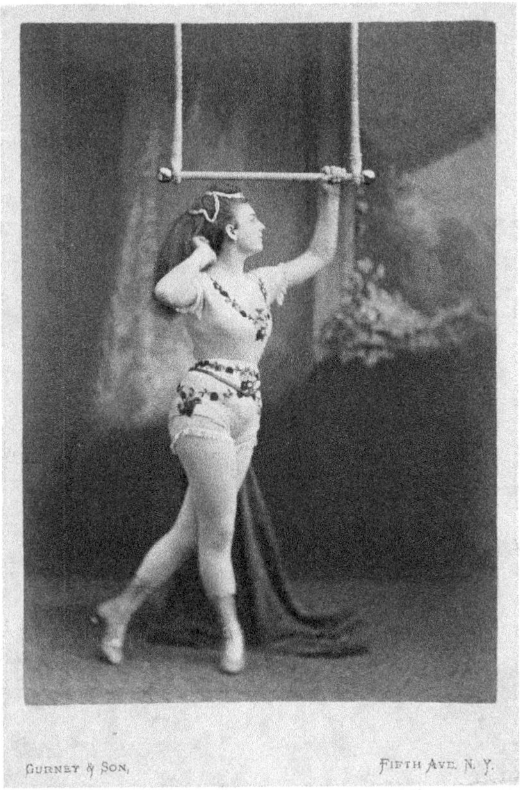

Fig. 15 Jeremiah Gurney and Son, New York, *Leona Dare,* photograph, cabinet card. Author's private collection. Image in the public domain.

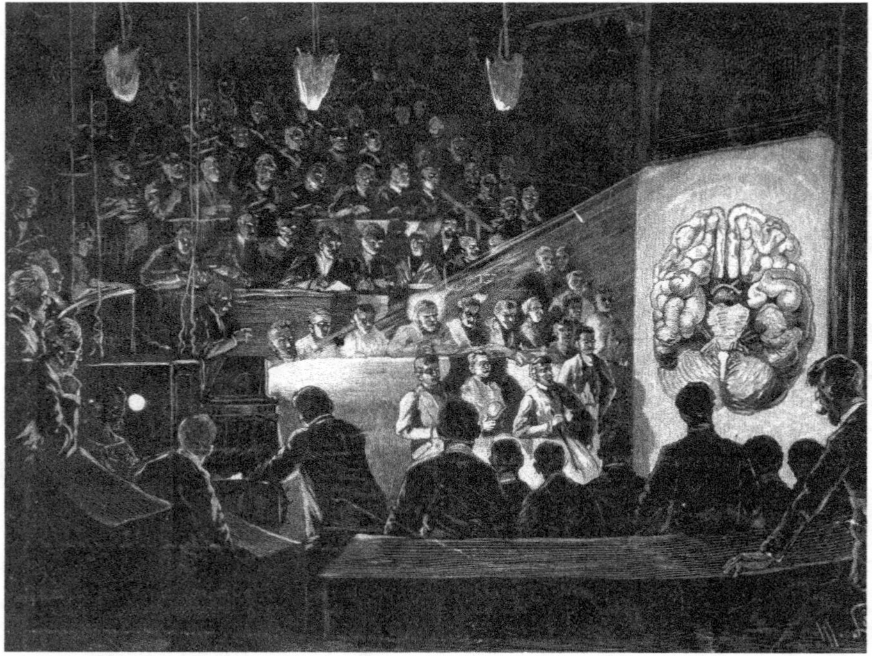

Fig. 16 Moritz Ledeli. *Demonstration of the pathologist Salomon Stricker on a brain with the help of an episcope*, original drawing by Moritz Ledeli. Courtesy of the Archive of University of Vienna. AT-UAW/135.828. Licensed under CC BY-NC-SA 4.0.

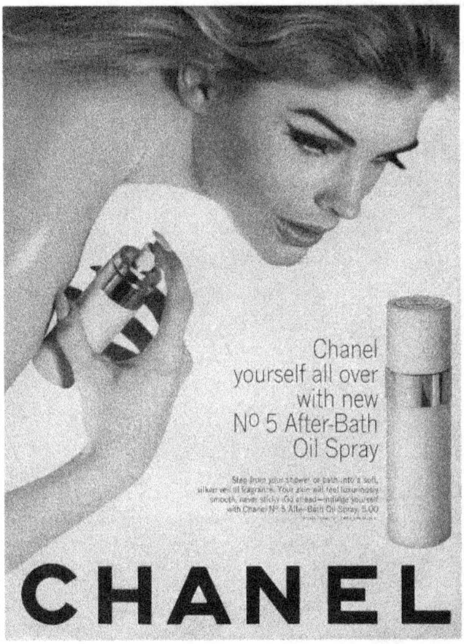

Fig. 17 Advertisement for Chanel No.5 After-Bath Spray, 1960s. Advertising Archive Everett Collection.

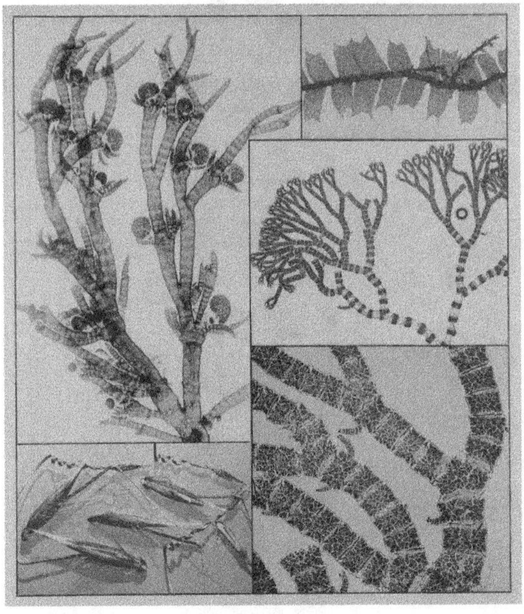

Fig. 18 Martin Gerlach, *Formenwelt aus der Naturreich: photographische Naturaufnahmen* (Vienna and Leipzig: Verlag von Martin Gerlach & Co. 1902–1904). Author's private archive.

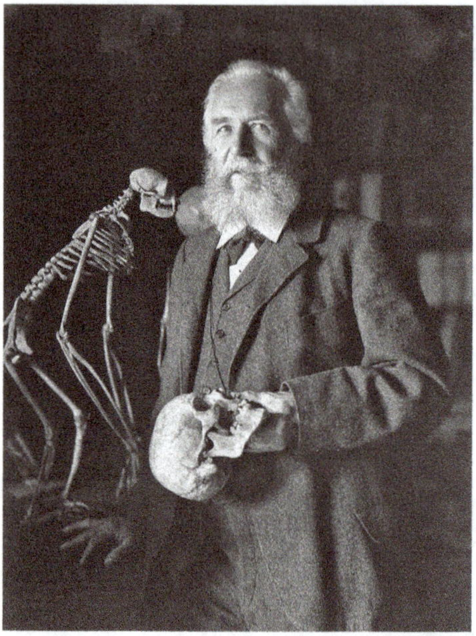

Fig. 19 Nicola Perscheid, *Portrait of Ernst Haeckel with the Skeleton and Skull of an Ape,* ca. 1904. Bridgeman Archive DGC3432991. Published in *Deutsche Kunst und Dekoration* 15 (October 1904–March 1905). Image in the public domain.

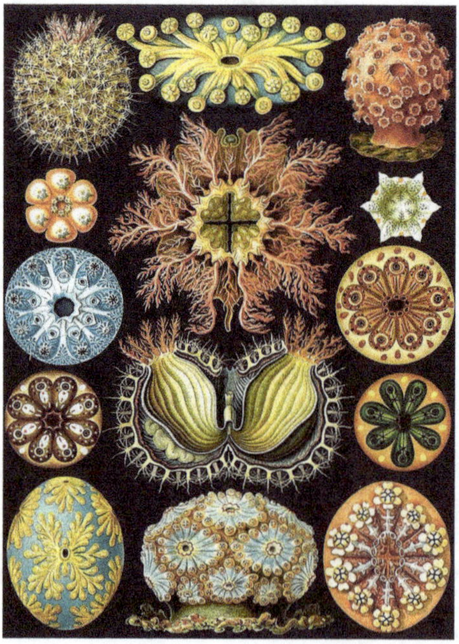

Fig. 20 Ernst Haeckel, *Ascidiacea (sea squirts),* color lithograph, 1904. From *Kunstformen der Natur,* plate 85. Image in the public domain.

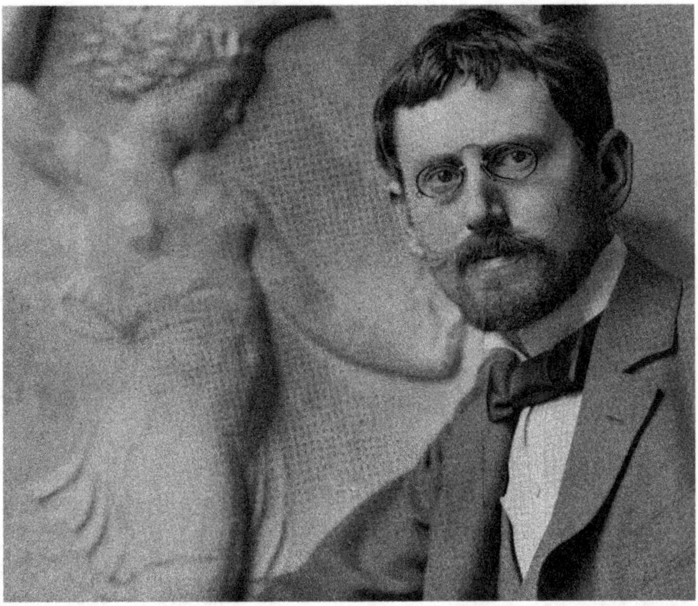

Fig. 21 Anonymous, *Portrait of Paul Schultze-Naumburg*, photograph, stamped: "Reclams Universum Leipzig." Author's private collection.

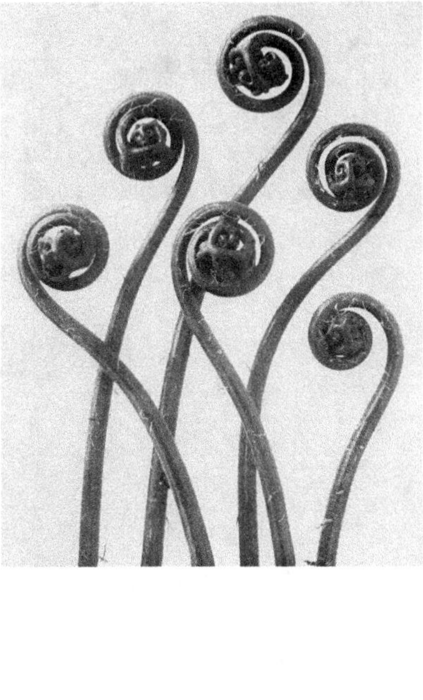

Fig. 22 Karl Blossfeldt, plant study from *Urformen der Kunst* (Bertlin: Ernst Wasmuth, 1928). Image in the public domain.

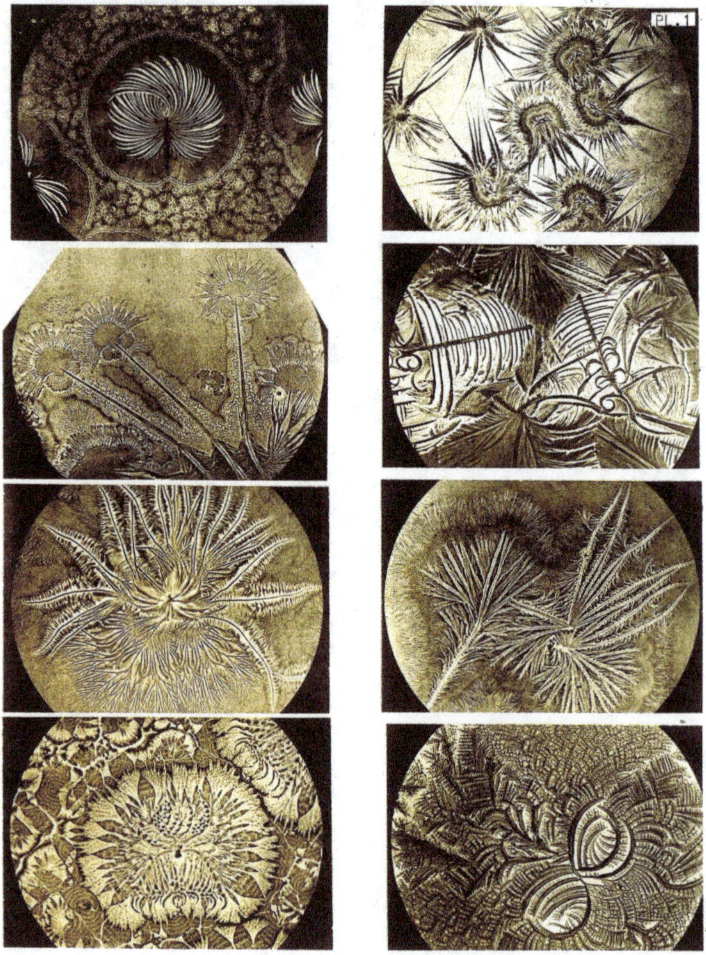

Fig. 23 S. Schenk, *Various Effects of Acid on Metal,* Vienna, ca. 1900. Credit: Rhode Island School of Design. Photo in the author's private collection. Image in the public domain.

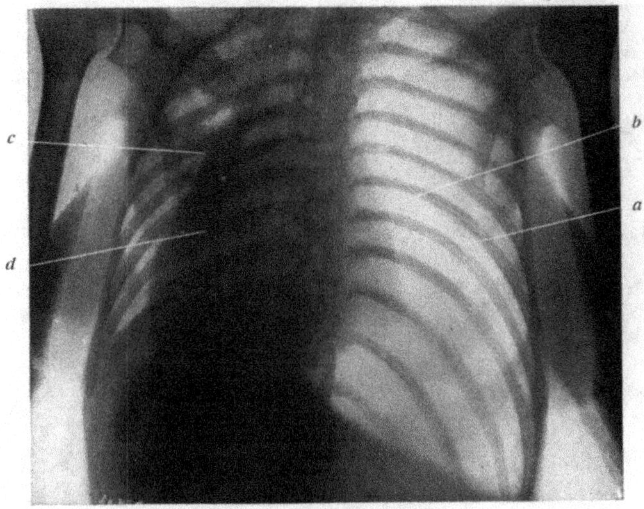

Fig. 24 Adolf Strümpell, *Pneumothorax,* X-ray image from *Lehrbuch der speziellen Pathologie und Therapie der inneren Krankenheiten* (Leipzig: F. C. W. Vogel, 1884), Plate II. Photo in the author's private collection. Image in the public domain.

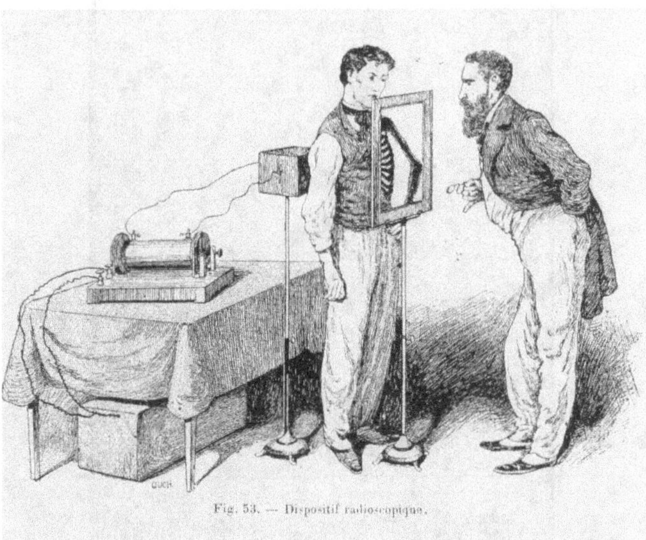

Fig. 25 Guillaume-Benjamin Duchenne de Boulogne, *Dispositif radioscopique* (fluoroscopy), marked "fig.53". Gallica Digital Library. Image in the public domain.

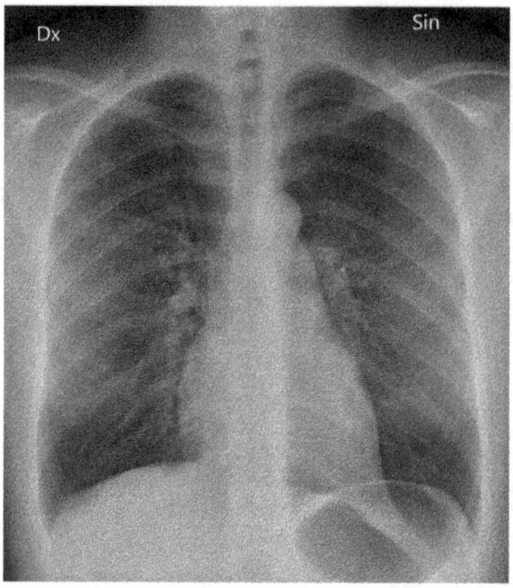

Fig. 26 Anonymous, *X-ray photograph of ribcage and lungs, marked right (Dx) and left (Sin).* Twentieth century.

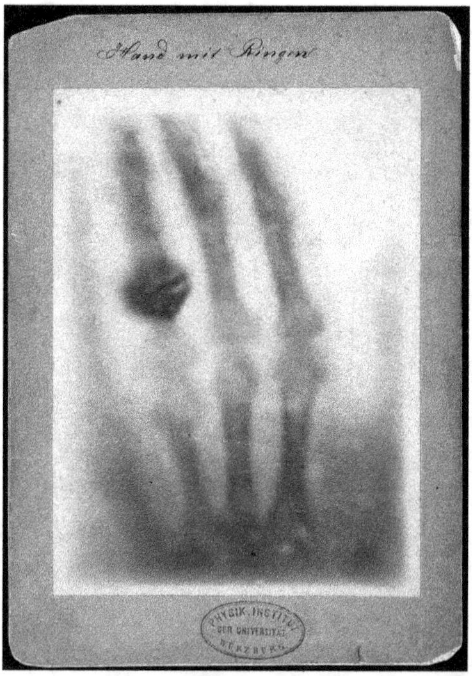

Fig. 27 Wilhelm Konrad Röntgen, *Hand of Anna Bertha Röntgen with Rings* 1895. Physik Institut der Universität Würzberg. Image in the public domain.

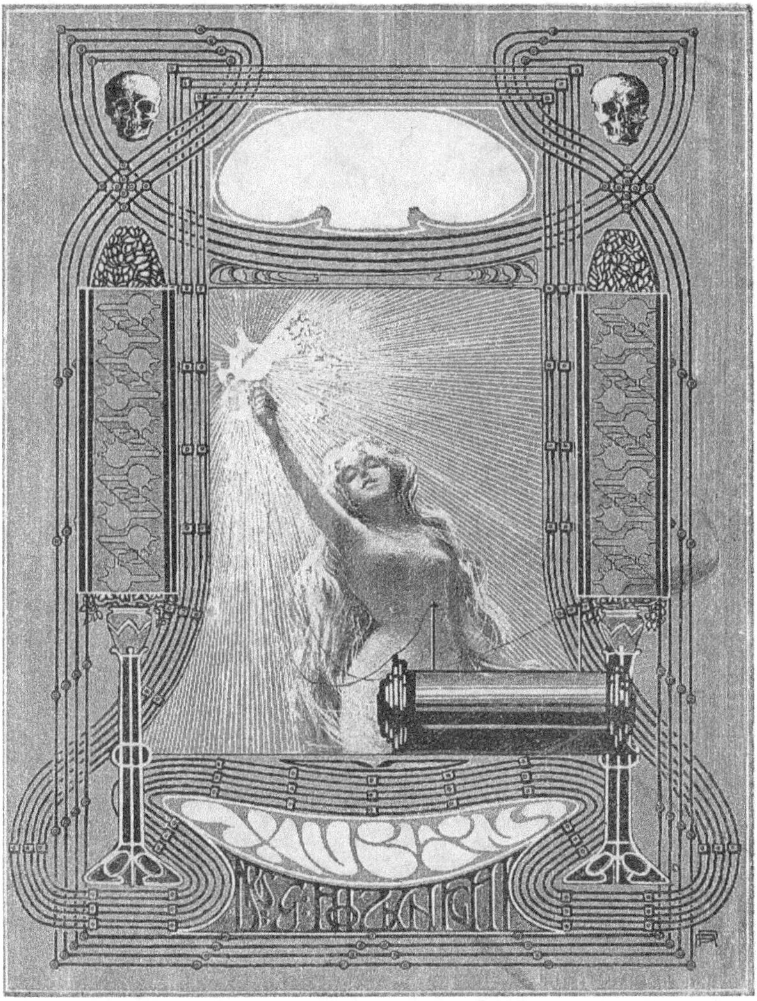

Fig. 28 Designer, *Guido Holzknecht, Ex Libris* Klischee o. 0. o. J. Holtzknecht Nachlass I R print Klischee 5. Stellega D.A. Signed with the insignia AR. Image used with permission from Josephinum—Ethics, Collections and History of Medicine, MedUni Vienna.

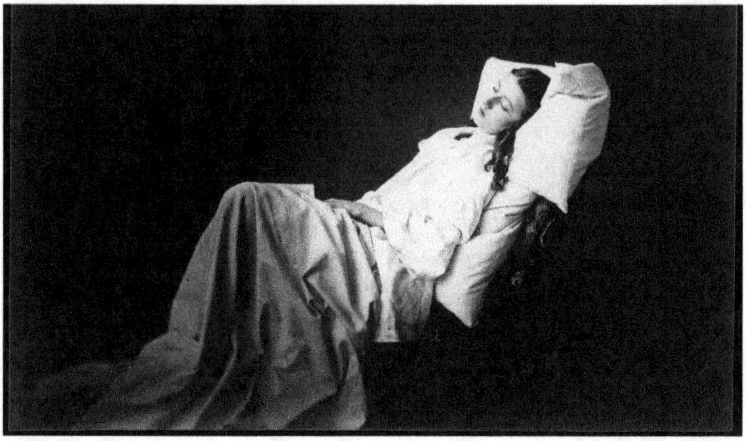

Fig. 29 Henry Peach Robinson, *She Never Told Her Love,* albumen silver print from glass negative, 1857. New York, Metropolitan Museum of Art, Gilman Collection, Purchase, Jennifer and Joseph Duke Gift, 2005. Accession Number: 2005.100.18. Image in the public domain.

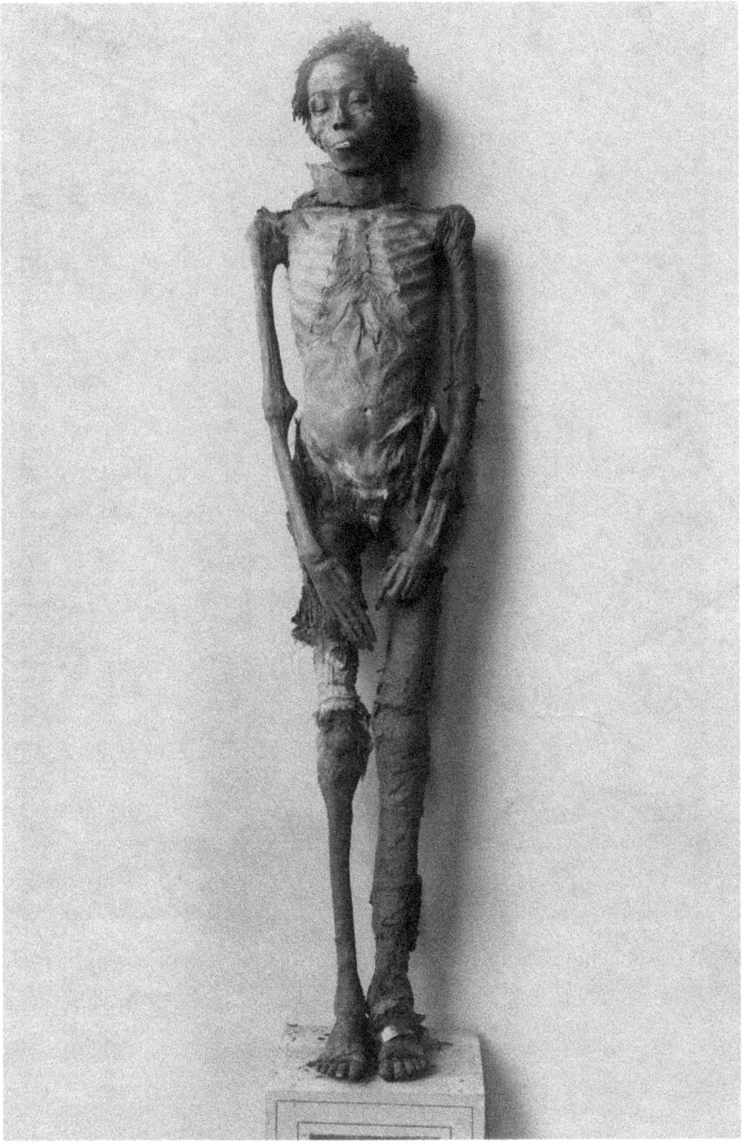

Fig. 30 Anonymous, *Mummy of Mahinpra as installed in Egyptian Museum, Cairo,* 1880s. Image in the public domain.

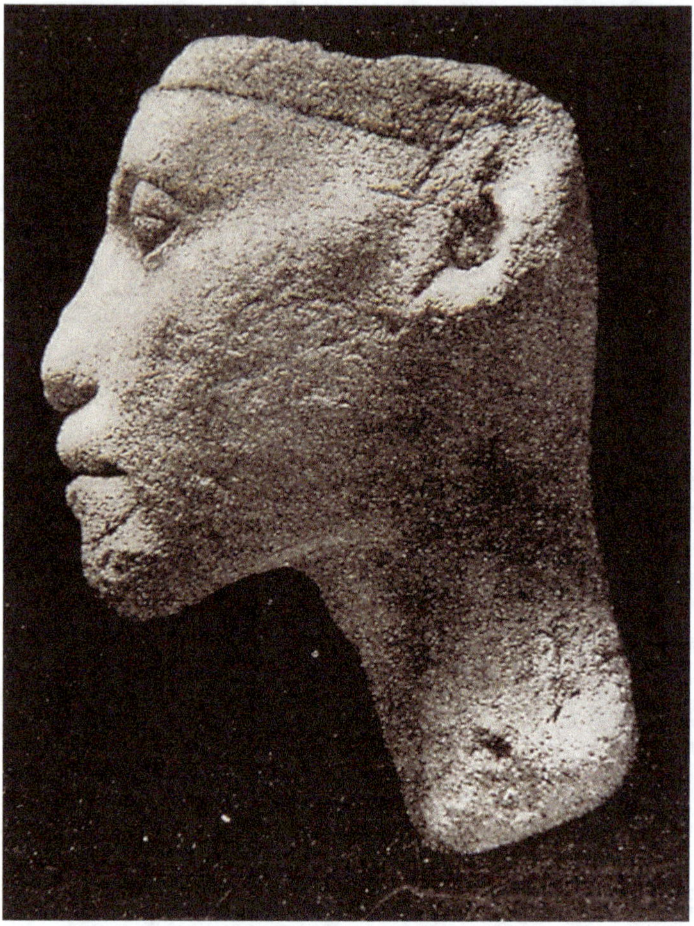

Fig. 31 Anonymous, *Sculptured Head of Amenhotep IV (Akhenaten) from El Amarna,* Egyptian Museum, Cairo. Image in the public domain.

Chapter 1

X-RAY PHOTOGRAPHY AND THE VISUAL IMAGINATION IN VIENNA

"I did not think. I experimented."

Wilhelm Conrad Röntgen

Eros and Thanatos: The Optical Uncanny

X-rays—at once the most visceral and most ghostly of pictures, the most radiant and the most penumbral—were powerful images in terms of function and form. Around 1900, X-ray photographs presented themselves not only for medical inquiry but also for metaphorical analysis in mystical, scientific, and psychoanalytic language. In the scientific news and popular press, the spectacle of X-ray photography prevailed at the turn of the century in Europe and America. X-rays produced new ways of envisioning the body and the world, and photography disseminated these images to a wide public. Fluoroscopy (see **fig. 25**), the most immediate and cinematic X-ray system, was as formative to modern culture as were the still photographs that were generated in positive and negative diapositives and prints after 1839.[1] Although most X-rays and fluoroscopic screens from the turn of the century can be classified as "non-art" images, they belong to a long tradition of sciagraphic representations beginning with the shadows in Plato's cave.

To the extent that abstract concepts, such as truth, verisimilitude, perception, or consciousness, appear in culture as metaphors, Wilhelm Konrad Röntgen (1845–1923) and Sigmund Freud (1856–1939) are inextricably linked. The two researchers emerged from the same scientific *Denkraum*, or intellectual atmosphere, and both men dealt with issues of bringing hidden problems to *light*, and exposing *dark*,

1. Cartwright 1995 and Manon 2007–2008.

disturbing areas inside the human being.[2] Late nineteenth-century Vienna, with its superb medical and photographic institutions, as well as its assortment of innovative artists and designers, was ripe for the creative reception and development of X-ray photography. Richard Panek has speculated that an historical nexus occurred when Röntgen discovered X-rays in 1895, at the same time that sixteen-year-old Albert Einstein (1879–1955) was thinking about space, time, and light, and Josef Breuer (1842–1925) and Freud were changing their way of envisioning human thought in their *Studies on Hysteria*.[3]

With Röntgen's discovery in 1895—"I did not think. I experimented"—the limitations of the visible world were transgressed, breaking through the exterior surface guises of physical objects.[4] Especially poignant were the X-rays of organic bodies, of nature's flora and fauna, whether living or dead.[5] That the living human interior could be observed through the shell of its own "fleshly disguises" with a supposedly immaculate eye, was a fact that shattered Western presumptions.[6] The ability to see the interior of the body was now accessible to ordinary people by way of X-rays, which were photographically illustrated in journals and books. By 1895 a desire to explore the interior of the mind, as we know from the works of Freud and his contemporaries, was already in vogue throughout Europe, and the phenomenon of X-ray photography seemed to validate that quest as well.

The visual possibility of "seeing through" flesh and other matter adumbrated and accompanied Freudian psychoanalysis, allowing individuals to visualize in their own minds what was formerly hidden or dynamically repressed, thus expanding the imagination about the self and the other. By way of psychoanalysis, life above or below the conscious mind, the dark, instinctual, or animalistic desires of human nature—the secrets we keep from ourselves—could appear in consciousness to the release of deep feelings, with a curative effect. Indeed, fluoroscopic and X-ray images are pertinent examples of what

2. Schmidt 1998, 167–76; Blumenberg 2010, 2, 22. Freud's use of figurative language yielded what Blumenberg might call a "surplus of expressive achievement."

3. Panek 2004, 57.

4. Goldberg 1998, 2–27.

5. For X-ray photographs of animals see Eder and Valenta 1896; for plants; Hinterberger 1897, 65–68, figs. 16–17.

6. Goldberg 1998, 41–42.

Tom Gunning has termed the "optical uncanny" of modern vision.[7] Although Freud's essay on *The Uncanny* of 1919 postdated the shock of X-ray photography in its first reception, there is a wide consensus that photography and psychoanalysis struck a chord in Viennese cultural production.[8]

The "sensational discovery" of X-rays by Professor Wilhelm Conrad Röntgen was announced in the Viennese newspaper *Die Presse* on January 5, 1896.[9] The first Viennese scientists to work with X-rays in 1896 included Franz Exner (1849–1926), Sigmund Exner (1846–1926), Julius Tandler (1869–1936), and Albert von Mosetig-Moorhof (1838–1907). As early as 1896 Sigmund Exner and Albert Mosetig-Moorhof used X-rays for diagnostic purposes and for surgery of the hand.[10] Research was continued by Robert Kienböck (1871–1953) and especially by the scientific "hero" Guido Holzknecht (1872–1931).[11]

Freud and Holzknecht were closely aligned in terms of both psychoanalysis and X-ray technology. The latter was professor of radiology and chairman of the Central X-ray Laboratory (Zentral-Röntgenlaboratorium) at Vienna's General Hospital (Wiener Allgemeinen Krankenhaus) from 1905. He was Freud's former patient and a member of the Vienna Psychoanalytic Society. Six years before his premature death from exposure to radiation, Holzknecht helped Freud to found the psychoanalytic outpatient clinic at Pelikangasse 18 in 1922.[12] Electricity, telegraph, and X-rays were among the "invisible" sources of energy that propelled the twentieth century into being, technically speaking, together with an attendant spiritualism that intrigued thinkers like Alexander Graham Bell (1847–1922), Arthur Conan Doyle (1839–1930), Edvard Munch (1863–1944) Paul Langevin (1842–1946), Henri Poincaré (1854–1946), Charles Richet (1850–1935), Camille Flammarion (1842–1925), and Marie Salomea Skłodowska-Curie (Marie Curie, 1867–1934).[13] Radium was used to treat various illnesses including hysteria, epilepsy, muscular atrophy,

7. Gunning 2008b, 68–90.

8. Lippit 2013, 271. Lippit's insistence on assigning the year 1895 an almost mystical importance, however, goes too far.

9. "Eine Sensationelle Entdeckung," *Die Presse* no. 5 (Vienna, January 1896), 1–2.

10. Eder and Valenta 1896, 13–14.

11. Del Regato 1993, 25–31.

12. Molnar 1992, 97.

13. Redniss 2010, 58, 61.

obesity, prostatitis, sexual decline, and senility. Much as radiation killed healthy tissue, it was ultimately used to treat cancerous tumors, as it still is in the twenty-first century to shrink malignant tumors under controlled medical conditions.

When X-ray processes occur in living tissue, photoelectrons destroy the cells of the tissue, and this is why radiation is used in therapeutic treatment to stop the spread of malignant tumors. But in the early days of X-ray technology this property was not fully understood, and constant work with X-rays caused cancer, seriously injuring both of Guido Holzknecht's hands. He died as a consequence of his profession, in the metastasis that followed. Holzknecht's obituary in the *Neue Freie Presse* on October 31, 1931 called him a "modern Mucius Scaevola" referring to the legendary hero from Livy's *History of Rome* who demonstrated his courage to the Etruscan enemies by burning away his own right hand.[14] The idea of the courageous, heroic physician was well received in Vienna, and this notion was current in Freud's circles. Holzknecht's sacrifice of his hands to science echoed that of his contemporary, Marie Skłodowska-Curie, whose hands were seriously damaged by radium, as was her eyesight.[15]

In 1923 Freud began to be treated for his jaw cancer by Holzknecht with a series of "prophylactic" X-ray treatments and local radium applications, and continued to seek Holzknecht's advice throughout the course of his illness. Max Schur (1897–1969), Freud's primary care physician at the time, reported a stirring encounter between the two men when Holzknecht was in the hospital for surgery, having received successive amputations of his finger, hand, and arm. Freud was examined by Holzknecht in the latter's hospital room, both men afflicted by cancer, each having been the other's doctor. In what Schur described as an "unforgettable" moment, Holzknecht advised surgery rather than radiation, and when the men parted, Freud stated, "you are to be admired for the way you bear your fate (circumstance)." And Holzknecht responded, "You know that I have only you to thank for this."[16]

The Viennese psychoanalyst Richard Sterba (1898–1989) remembered a hospital visit on April 22, 1931: he stated that the chief surgeon Dr. Hans Pichler (1887–1949) showed Holzknecht the X-ray of

14. Molnar 1992, 97, 111, 284; Holzknecht 1931, obituaries in *Neue Freie Presse*.

15. Redniss 2010, 70.

16. Schur 1972, 357, 427.

Freud's jaw for a diagnosis. When Holzknecht told Freud that he needed another operation, and Freud refused, Holzknecht simply replied that he himself would be operated upon the following day for the twenty-fifth time. According to Sterba, after Pichler and Josef Peter Weinmann (1896–1960) left Holzknecht's hospital room, Freud stated, "We have visited a real hero. Of course, I will be operated on tomorrow."[17]

Heroic masculinity remained an ideal among physicians in Freud's Vienna. But with the research of Eugen Steinach (1861–1944) the finality of gender categories began to appear more flexible. Steinach was an Austrian of Jewish descent, who was educated at the University of Vienna, and in 1912 became the director of the Vienna Biological Institute of the Academy of Sciences (*Vivarium*). Steinach (whose father had, incidentally, been a pupil of Ernst Brücke) researched sex and gender in animals and humans. At age 67 Freud had a vasectomy together with X-ray irradiation in hopes that it would delay the return of his oral cancer and rejuvenate his youthful vitality of body and mind. Freud was operated on by the urologist Victor Blum (1877–1954) for a "Steinach vasoligature." The results of Blum's intervention on Freud were, however, inconclusive. This procedure on the sex glands, conceived by the neuroendrocinologist Eugen Steinach, was offered to women as well as men, with varying reports of anecdotal observations.

From the point of view of visual culture, Steinach's experiments on animals and humans were also the subject of a film. In 1922 an educational movie directed by Hans Schulze about Steinach's experimentation was aimed at medical professionals. A popular version was made the following year, over the scientist's serious objections.

Steinach's experiments stimulated serious research on glandular functions that resonate even today. He conducted studies on the transplantation of sex glands in animals. He worked with Magnus Hirschfeld at his Institute for Sexual Science (Institut für Sexualwissenschaft) in the area of gender reassignment surgery, a field in which Ludwig Levy-Lenz and Felix Abraham completed the first complete male-to-female transition, on Dora Richter, aged 40, in 1931.

Medical historian Chandak Sengoopta (2000) reports that between 1912 and 1925 testicular grafts from humans, sheep, monkeys, goats, and deer were given to men "for the treatment of a range of disorders, from the debility of old age to schizophrenia."[18] There was, of course,

17. Quoted by Molnar 1992, 97.

18. Sengoopta 2000, 2.

a cultural and social premium on male heterosexuality. Steinach even theorized a medical triumph of human male heterosexuality by removing one testicle of the homosexual subject and replacing it with the testicle of a heterosexual male donor.[19]

Sex-gland transplantation? It seemed to rejuvenate the rats in Steinach's laboratory, but was notoriously unsuccessful on human subjects such as Freud. Nevertheless, Steinach envisioned sexual categories as more mobile and flexible than previously thought, and his hormone research challenged the formerly fixed boundaries between masculinity and femininity.

In our times it has become obvious that Steinach was a pioneer in sexual studies, leaving us—and Freud—the concept that every human being is biologically part female and part male. Steinach bequeathed us the idea of sexual intermediacy, gonad transplantation, and the medical practice of hormone replacement therapy. These concepts and practices are of great importance to transgendered and transsexual people, and many other human beings. The blurring of gender identity has contributed to the way many people now see the world, as well as to their medical well-being. There remains no elixir for the psychological reorientation of a person's sexuality or for regaining lost youth, but for women and men undergoing menopause or andropause, or changing gender, hormone replacement has become a satisfactory fact of life.

As Steinach grew older, he moved ahead with other endocrinological projects. He died in exile and isolation in 1944, but his papers on monosexuality, bisexuality, experimental hermaphroditism, and bipotentiality were important from a scientific and cultural point of view.[20]

X-ray Technology

The shock of the new scientific process of X-ray technology and its potential for injury was fresh in Freud's mind when he wrote about the dangers of psychoanalysis to the practitioner in *Analysis Terminable and Interminable* in 1937, criticizing psychoanalysts who avoided the "critical and corrective influence of analysis" on themselves. "Sometimes," Freud continued, "when we try to understand this we are

19. Sengoopta 2000, 7.

20. Nils Hansson and his colleagues summed things up in a recent paper, Hansson et al. 2020.

driven into drawing a disagreeable analogy with the effect of X-rays on people who handle them without taking special precautions."[21]

Röntgen noticed the shadow of the bones of his hand on a panel coated with fluorescent substance in his laboratory at the University of Würzburg.[22] As his discovery spread throughout the world, the paradigmatic emblem of X-ray photography was the hand of Röntgen's wife, Anna Bertha Röntgen, made on December 22, 1895, where two metal rings seems to float around the phalange of her skeleton (**fig. 27**).[23] This hand appears as a profoundly weighted image in Thomas Mann's great scientific novel *The Magic Mountain* of 1924 (to which I shall presently return). In Mann's description of an X-rayed hand, the protagonist Hans Castorp sees

> the finely·tuned skeleton of his own hand, the seal ring he had inherited from his grandfather hanging loose and black on the joint of his ring-finger—a hard, material object, with which man adorns the body that is fated to melt away beneath it, when it passes on to another flesh that can wear it for yet a little while.[24]

According to both Ernst Jentsch (1867–1919) and Freud, an uncanny, or disturbing, aesthetic (a specific "quality of feeling") occurs when there are doubts as to whether an animate being is really alive, or whether a lifeless object or a cadaver can come to (or return to) life.[25] This ghastly ambiguity between the living and the dead is the signature emotional style, causing the disturbing aesthetic of the uncanny, and has been present in X-ray photographs from their very invention, indicating a living body in the same frame as the bony remains. The X-ray picture conforms to Freud's reference to the German philosopher Friedrich W. J. Schelling (1775–1854) who had stated in his *Historical-Critical Introduction to the Philosophy of Mythology* that "Unheimlich (uncanny) is the name for everything that ought to have remained ... secret and

21. Freud 1937, 249; I am grateful to the late Paul Roazan for having referred me to this passage.

22. Röntgen 1896 in Glasser 1931, 41–52.

23. Frizot 1998, 280–81; Cartwright 1995, 115, has called the female hand X-ray "a fetish object par excellence."

24. Mann 1928, 218.

25. Freud 1919, 219, 225; Jentsch [1906] 2008, 221.

hidden but that has come to light."[26] If the Freudian uncanny comes from the unexpected visual staging of the return of the repressed,[27] then X-rays bring to light literally what has always been covered or buried in the body, as if by some kind of occult magic.[28]

The concept of human mortality has been thematized through the making and reception of X-rays, up to our present day. Among the effects of Guido Holzknecht was his personal "*ex libris*"—a Jugendstil (Austrian Art Nouveau) fantasy of the triumph of X-ray photography (**fig. 28**).[29] X-ray technology is personified by a radiant nude woman with long, unloosed hair. She holds up a dazzling lamp that emanates brilliant, explosive rays. This source of illumination is tethered to a stylized generator by two elusive electrical threads. The border decoration is composed of stylized X-ray lamps, cathode tubes, and generators interwoven in a mellifluous Jugendstil design—a composition that is capped by two human skulls at the top corners of embracing columns. Radiology as truth is able to see through to the bones of the human skull, which in traditional European iconography signify mortality. This was true even in one of the most fertile and optimistic moments of Italian Renaissance art: Masaccio's *Trinity* above the Lenzi tomb at the church of Santa Maria Novella in Florence (ca. 1424–26) is supported by a recumbent skeleton who bears the following inscription: "What you are I once was; What I am you will become."[30] If Guido Holzknecht's *ex libris* is a triumphal celebration of the X-ray, the skulls simultaneously underscore the certainty of death beneath all living flesh. Numerous advertisements for photographic firms and supplies were designed in the Jugendstil style with female figures as allegories or personifications of technology.[31] But it is only here, in the personal iconography of Holzknecht's *ex libris*, that the dark side of radiant illumination is human mortality.

X-rays are skeletal, but X-rays are ghostly too. In X-ray photography the membrane of flesh is reduced to a soft, translucent substance

26. Schelling 2008.

27. Manon 2007–2008, 2–27.

28. Zilcosky 2018, 167–68.

29. The designer of the *ex libris* is unknown, an artist who signed with the stylized insignia "AR."

30. McCarthy 1959, 38–48.

31. See, for example in *Jahrbuch für Photographie und Reproductionstechnik* vol. 14 (1900): "Anzeigen" figures 43, 45, 47, 57, 58.

girding the bones. It is important to remember that the invention of the X-ray was received in a culture that was already immersed in a phantasmagoria of dancing skeletons and ghosts. Luminous miasmas played in the velvety artificial darkness of photographic visual culture. Throughout history, many photographs have derived their impact from the monochromatic palettes of light and dark in contrast and chiaroscuro.[32]

Chiaroscuro and tenebrism are familiar to us postmoderns by their presence in the species of twentieth-century cinema known as film noir, which conveyed a mood of menacing danger and disturbing pessimism. Hugh S. Manon stated that in film noir a chiaroscuro style, with the dark-light palette of an X-ray, conveys the immediate frightening presence of modern criminal activities.[33] Manon's observation that the shadows cast by Venetian blinds as seen so frequently in film noir scenes mimic the X-ray images of the human ribcage resonates distinctly here.[34] We have already acknowledged that photographic medical illustrations, such as Adolf Strümpell's *Pneumothorax* X-ray image, first published in 1884 (**fig. 24**), communicate the *memento mori* of a human skeleton in an uncanny manner. At the same time, however, the cinema spectators of film noir are blind to what is happening before their own eyes, which remains, as it were, unconscious. This looking without seeing (like an eerie psychological knowing without seeing, or its reverse) creates an aesthetic of suspicion and an allusion to undetectable deceits, flourishing at what Manon calls the "thresholds of detectability."[35] Where there is a frisson of fear or the inexplicable uncanny in film noir, there is also a mysterious underlying malady, which initiates a strong feeling (aesthetic) of trepidation.

Although X-ray plates and their photographic prints were vague or exacting to various extents, one quality that distinguished all of them from other kinds of photography was the richness of the black tone when lit from behind or printed in mediums such as photogravure. The presence of this absolute darkness in X-ray photography endowed

32. Lukiesh (1916) demonstrates principles of illumination, shadows, and reflection coefficients of objects using photographs of varied electrical lightings of casts, from simple spherical plaster casts to complex objects such as the head of the Greco-Roman *Laocoön*.

33. Manon 2007–2008, 4–5.

34. Manon 2007–2008, 12.

35. Manon 2007–2008, 6–10.

images with a profound tenebrism, which has enhanced the seriousness of X-ray's demeanor.[36]

Indeed, there is something inverse, negative, and absolute about the darkness of X-rays, so that when directed to the human body they quickly became the heavily laden reminder of death in modern life. This held true throughout the twentieth century: in Woody Allen's film *Hannah and Her Sisters* (1986), for instance, the comic protagonist, who is a hypochondriac, comes face-to-face with his own mortality only when the doctor brings out an X-ray for analysis. Then the frightening truth will be disclosed, for in a fictional movie the harsh information delivered by X-rays demystifies the cause, the time, and even the quality of one's future death. It seems no coincidence here that the character frightened by the sight of an X-ray is a film director—a person who would be intellectually sensitive to radiant photographic images. In another of Allen's films, *Crimes and Misdemeanors* (1989), the character he plays, also a director, is an idealist who has made a documentary about a humanistic psychologist—actually played in the movie by the well-known Freudian psychoanalyst Martin S. Bergmann (1913–2014)—who discourses on the values of life and love, and then suddenly, when the film is about to be aired, commits suicide, leaving the filmmaker to confront a dark void.

The Magic Mountain

The writer who characterized the X-ray most poignantly with all of its mixed implications of morbidity and modernity was Thomas Mann (1875–1955). Mann's novel *The Magic Mountain* (1924) was begun as a memoir of his visit to a fashionable tuberculosis sanitarium in the Swiss Alps (Davos) where his wife, Katja, was confined for a lung problem. X-ray technology is at the center of this gigantic, strangely modern novel, where medical practices and their biological explanations are described in exquisite detail. The protagonist Hans Castorp even falls in love with an X-ray of his beloved Clavdia Chauchat, carrying a small glass negative of her thorax on his person at all times and setting it up on his nightstand when he sleeps as if it were her portrait, even holding it

36. See Elcott 2016a, 17–77.

to his breast and kissing it.[37] Thus the glass X-ray negative is a powerful fetish in Castorp's sex life. When Mann's bourgeois anti-hero Castorp is permitted by Dr. Behrens to look at his own hand through the X-ray screen, "for the first time in his life he understood that he would die." In the words of Thomas Mann, "he looked into his own grave."[38]

Despite scientific claims to absolute objectivity, X-ray photography could be as vague and deceptive as any other "truth-telling" medium. At the beginnings of Castorp's diagnosis he says that "so far there are only acoustic indications [breathing and coughing]; real diagnostic certainty we shall arrive at when I am about again, and the X-ray and photography have taken place. Then we shall have positive knowledge." "You think so?" asks Lodovico Settembrini, the tubercular Italian philosopher, "You know that the photographic plate often shows spots that are taken for cavities when there are none there? Madonna—the photographic plate!"[39] Settembrini, whose rational materialist outlook serves as an accompaniment to all of the diagnostic events on the enchanted mountain, refers here to the ambiguity of what is revealed by the photographic plate; the vagueness of shadows and spots can be as deluding as any other acoustic or visual experience. Far from any concept of immaculate observation, the picture is meaningless without interpretation.[40]

Then there is Castorp's visit to the actual X-ray laboratory. This visit is, to say the very least, transformative. The atmosphere in the laboratory is nightmarish and otherworldly, redolent with the eerie, chthonic melancholy of the Jentschian and Freudian *Unheimlich*. Mann narrates, "Both times, as the door opened, Hans Castorp observed that it was half dark in the X-ray room; an artificial twilight prevailed there [...]. The windows were shrouded, daylight shut out, and two electric lights were burning." One can only imagine what Röntgen himself thought when he visited Davos in the winter of 1898. In addition to photographing the mountains and glaciers, and ice-skating in the sunshine, he must have experienced the profundity of his own invention in one of its most dramatic settings.[41]

37. Freud, too, attributed uncanny powers of sympathetic magic to a photograph of his fiancée, Martha Bernays; see Bergstein 2010, 265–67.

38. Mann 1928, 218–19.

39. Mann 1928, 196.

40. See also Van Dijck 2005, 87.

41. Mann 1928, 214–15; Busch 1998, 33.

Mann's Dr. Behrens is Castorp's guide to the netherworld of shades and bones. After asking Castorp whether he is nervous about exposing his inner self to the gaze of the X-ray machine, he shows him a gallery of images. And like Virgil with Dante,

> He led Hans Castorp by the arm before the rows of dark plates on the wall, and turned on a light behind them. Castorp saw various members: hands, feet, knee-pans, thigh—and leg bones, arms and pelvises. But the rounded living form of the human body was vague and shadowy, like a pale and misty envelope, within which stood out the clear, sharp nucleus—the skeleton.[42]

Castorp lacks the virtue of his cousin and alter ego, the tubercular Joachim Ziemssen. And it is when Castorp observes the X-raying of Joachim that he perceives the fugitive nature of life itself. Ziemssen embodied a healthy-looking young man, as perfect as the Greco-Roman *Apollo del Belvedere*, with selfless intentions and an honorable heart—an ideal European man. But the X-ray process changes Joachim into a ghost of vulnerable organs, tissue, and bones. The making of the X-ray is like the assassination of its soldier-subject on a battlefield, or the transformation of its subject in a lightning storm to a luminous ghostly body. The metamorphosis from flesh and blood to a spectral image made of blinding light is a transformation of form to formlessness, or spirit. It is also, as we hear in the words of Thomas Mann, like an annunciation of death.

> Now, for the space of two seconds, fearful powers were in play—streams of thousands, of a hundred thousand of volts, Hans Castorp seemed to recall—which were necessary to pierce through solid matter. They could hardly be confined to their office, they tried to escape through other outlets: there were explosions like pistol-shots, blue sparks on the measuring apparatus; long lightnings crackled along the walls. Somewhere in the room appeared a red light, like a threatening eye, and a phial to Joachim's rear filled with green glow. Then everything grew quiet, the phenomena disappeared, and Joachim let out his breath with a sigh. It was over.[43]

42. Mann 1928, 214–15.
43. Mann 1928, 215.

Mann's description of Joachim's X-ray picture as it appears on the fluoroscopic screen is shocking in its deadpan description of the strange anatomical spectacle.

> The breast-bone and spine fell together in a single dark column. The frontal structure of the ribs was cut across by the paler structure of the back. Above, the collar bones branched off on both sides, and the framework of the shoulder, with the joint and the beginning of Joachim's arm, showed sharp and bare through the soft envelope of flesh. The thoracic cavity was light, but blood-vessels were to be seen, some dark spots, a blackish shadow.[44]

We may compare Mann's prose with contemporary photographic material such as the photographically reproduced X-ray of a pneumothorax that has become our touchstone (**fig. 24**). This photographic illustration, probably subjected to considerable retouching, was published by Strümpell in his *Lehrbuch* of 1884. The photograph is amorphous in its distribution of light and shadow, but is quite easily understood in terms of Mann's descriptive text, which may have even been written directly from an image like this one.

The most fascinating, if horrifying, moments for Castorp during the entire procedure are not those in which the diseased lungs become visible, but those in which his cousin Joachim's honorable heart can be seen through the fluoroscopic screen. The heart reveals itself thus: "something like a bag, a strange, animal shape, darkly visible behind the middle column, or more on the right side of it—the spectator's right. 'Look at his heart,' and the Hofrat [Dr. Behrens] lifted his huge hand again from his thigh and pointed with his forefinger at the pulsating shadow." Castorp, fixed upon the amorphous image, announces in a suppressed voice to his cousin: "I am looking at your heart." And at this point Castorp gazes "without wearying at Joachim's graveyard shape and bony tenement, this lean *memento mori*, this scaffolding for moral flesh to hang on."

Castorp feels utterly melancholy at the sight of his cousin's heart:

> He was strangely moved by what he saw—or more precisely, by the fact that he saw it—and felt stirrings of uneasy doubt, as to whether it was really permissible and innocent to stand here in the

44. Mann 1928, 217.

> quaking, crackling darkness and gaze like this; his itch to commit the indiscretion conflicted in his bosom with religious emotion and feelings of concern.[45]

Hans Castorp was seeing something that (in Schelling's terms) he should not have been able to see, another man's heart—the heart of a man more valiant than he—at its most vulnerable and animalistic. A sustained act of seeing through to the involuntary beating of another person's heart was neither customary nor bearable in turn-of-the-century Europe. For Thomas Mann the effect is gravely disturbing, causing guilt and remorse. The experience is blinding both in terms of the sizzling lights of the X-ray laboratory and the extent to which a human being is penetrated by another's vision. In psychoanalytic terms it is as though one person were able to observe the Id, or deepest unconscious ideation, of another. Here the Id is configured as a "pulsating shadow" on a fluoroscopic screen, not yet inscribed in cinema or frozen into a still image. Castorp's viewing of his cousin's heart belongs to the realm of the unconscious "optical uncanny," causing the viewer psychic pain when the apperception cannot be repressed.

Here we may turn to Didier Anzieu's idea of *The Skin Ego* (1989), which builds upon Freud's concept of the body ego. For Anzieu the skin ego is a "containing, unifying envelope for the Self; a protective barrier for the psyche."[46] Likewise, Claudia Benthien's *Skin*, a cultural history of the skin, explores the place of skin in figurative speech, concluding that the skin is itself a boundary metaphor for human identity. She cites, among other examples, Robert Musil's (1880–1942) play *Die Schwärmer* (*The Visionaries*) (1921) in which the skin is imagined as a form of self-protection against shame: "You pull your own skin tighter and tighter over your head, like a dark hood with a few eye slits and breathing holes."[47] The most famous pre-psychoanalytic example of the skin ego occurs in classical mythology when the mortal satyr Marsyas with his rudimental playing of the pan's pipes (Id) is punished by the more refined deity, Apollo, who skins him alive. In the *Metamorphoses* of Ovid: "It was visible to count his throbbing organs, and the chambers of his lungs, clearly visible within his breast."[48] If Apollo stands for poetry

45. Mann 1928, 217–18.

46. Anzieu 2016.

47. Schwärmer, quoted by Benthien 2002, 21–22.

48. Ovid 1955, 6: 382–91.

and civilization, or the Ego of human endeavor, the satyr represents the animalistic Id, the primitive and compulsive music played by Marsyas. To see into the body of Marsyas, then, is for rational consciousness to gaze into the forbidden zone of the unconscious mind.

Freud and Thomas Mann had a charged historical proximity. When Mann visited the Freud family on March 17, 1932, Freud had been involved in X-ray and radiation therapy for some years, having had his X-rays read and interpreted by Dr. Guido Holzknecht. By January 1934 a portable X-ray apparatus was installed at Berggasse 19.[49] When Mann spoke in honor of Freud at the Akademischer Verein für Medizinische Psychologie in May 1936 Freud was too sick to attend. A month later, Mann, writing the *Joseph* tetralogy, and Freud, who was working on *Moses and Monotheism*, exchanged views on Moses and Joseph.[50]

Love as a Cause of Death

In *The Magic Mountain*, Dr. Krokowski, one of the sanatorium's staff, who has been characterized by Joseph P. Lawrence as "Freud on his way to becoming Jung," believes love can be the cause of death.[51] Krokowski offers a lecture series for resident patients introducing the theme of "love as a power making for disease."[52] According to Dr. Krokowski, repressed erotic love was never extinguished but rather thrived in dark, secret places in the individual persona, and any physical symptom of illness, such as exacerbations in the thorax, was merely displaced love.[53] In the dialectics of the sanatorium, erotic longing is made visible by looking inside the body with X-rays. Romantic passion resides in X-ray photography for the expiring subject as well as the desiring spectator. The tuberculosis patients' demise betrayed all expectation. Patients seemed to be healthy because of their rosy complexions (in fact a sign of illness) but the reality was the reverse, and people with tuberculosis would soon die.

During the nineteenth century, tubercular illness was romanticized, especially in women, as in Henry Peach Robinson's photograph of 1857, *She Never Told Her Love*, where a young girl languishes with

49. Molnar 1992, 122, 166, 202.
50. Molnar 1992, 122, 166, 202.
51. Lawrence 1999, 7.
52. Meredith 1999, 128–29.
53. Mann 1928, 299.

melancholy and consumption (**fig. 29**). Photography itself was a kind of *spes moribunda* in the portraiture of people with serious illness, and nowhere was this more present than in the romanticized melancholy of consumption.

Séances and apparitions followed closely in the path established by photography, X-rays, visual toys, and cinematic devices in Mann's fictional sanatorium. Of the faddish activities practiced among the patients at the Berghof, amateur photography played a large part, as did cinema: "So for instance amateur photography, always playing an important role at the Berghof, had twice become a perfect mania, lasting weeks and months on end. Everyone saw people absorbedly bent over cameras supported in the pit of their stomachs, focusing and snapping the shutter; and floods of snapshots were handed round at dinner."

In 1895 the Lumière brothers, Auguste (1862–1954) and Louis (1864–1948), patented the cinematograph, showing twenty projected images per second.[54] Patients on the Magic Mountain went to the cinema, too. And in an excursion to the Bioscope Theatre down in the Platz: "Life flitted across the screen before their smarting eyes: life chopped into small sections, fleeting, accelerated; a restless, jerky fluctuation of appearing and disappearing."[55] The Swedish literary critic Sara Danius (1962–2019) determined that the film playing in *The Magic Mountain* was the silent orientalist tragedy *Sumurum* about the favorite slave girl of a sheikh, by Ernst Lubitsch (1892–1947). Thomas Mann himself saw this film, starring Pola Negri (1897–1987), in Munich in 1920.[56] Pola Negri is the dancing-girl femme fatale in this orientalist fantasy, a balletic pantomime in six acts. Frank F. Scherer has observed some typical features of orientalism in this silent film, such as the patriarchal despotic sheikh and his cruel mistreatment of women and eunuchs, and as Scherer says, "in a classic Freudian key," the patriarchal/oedipal struggle between the sheikh and his son over the possession of a charming young harem girl.[57]

54. Mann 1928, 316.

55. Danius 2002, 84, 213, and notes 57, 58.

56. Mann 1928, 635–36. The "cinematographic cylinder" probably refers to Emile Reynaud's Praxinoscope, which by 1882 could be used for individual viewing or seen by a larger audience as a moving projection that appeared to have three dimensions, see Crary 2000, 259–67.

57. Scherer 2011, 93.

Cinematography, especially at the Berghof, had a poignant prehistory and parallel history in apparatuses for various kinds of viewing. When a seemingly miraculous gramophone was introduced to House Berghof it was compared with the visual devices—the stereopticon, the kaleidoscope, and the "cinematographic cylinder" (a zoetrope)—with which the patients typically passed the time.[58] X-ray photography, therefore, was received in an atmosphere of new ways of seeing, from kaleidoscopic images to full-length cinematic productions.

Viewing devices, from X-rays to cinema, all had something eminently natural or "scientific" about them. But as Mann's novel progresses, the residents of Berghof divert themselves with visual phenomena of a supernatural nature: séances, spiritualism, hypnotism, mediums, and ghosts.[59] During one such sitting, in which electric lamps were turned on and off by spirits, something uncanny happened to Castorp: "A light object lay on his lap; he discovered it to be the 'souvenir' which had once so surprised his uncle when he lifted it from his nephew's table: the glass diapositive of Clavdia Chauchat's X-ray portrait. Quite uncontestably he, Hans Castorp, had not carried it into the room."[60] Here, an X-ray not only has "magical" powers of representing the invisible, but the glass photograph itself is moved around by invisible spiritual powers, guided, perhaps, by what we might perceive as unconscious desire. The X-ray image has almost become what Noam M. Elcott and Vera Wittkowsky call a "phantasmagoric *dispositive*,"[61] that is, an image that moves around in space detached from any and all apparati. In Elcott's view, the phantasmagoric must guarantee the highest degree of image detachedness—that is, it must unmoor images from any material support, including screens.[62] The X-ray, Mann's "souvenir" X-ray, is transformed into pure implicit memory. The absent Clavdia manifests herself as an X-ray or memory image delivered directly into Castorp's hands. In this instance the equation of an X-ray image with a spiritual presence is firmly established: X-ray = dispositive as ghost.

58. Mann 1928, 635–36.

59. Mann 1928, 654–70, 666.

60. Mann 1928, 666.

61. Elcott 2016b, 85; Wittkowsky 2021, 15–17.

62. Elcott 2016a, *passim*; Elcott, 2016b.

X-rays and the Occult

Scholars such as Astrid Kury have shown that the invention of X-rays was of considerable importance for modern spiritualism and occultism. X-ray vision proved that invisible essences could be seen by way of invisible rays, even through opaque substances such as closed doors or human flesh.[63] Thus X-ray photography was like the phenomenon of spirit photography, which was meant to depict the radiance of the human soul, or to visualize a person's aura. The uncanny psychic *Doppelgänger* came into sight in photographic images in the wake of the discovery of X-rays. Following the psychoanalytic work on the *Doppelgänger* by Freud (*The Uncanny*, 1919) and Otto Rank (*The Double: A Psychoanalytic Study*, 1926) the concept of the *Doppelgänger* found its way into the social life of the Viennese intelligentsia and bourgeoisie.

The idea of the uncanny, or disobedient, *Doppelgänger* was deeply integrated into the Viennese imagination by the mid-twentieth century. Heimito von Doderer presents the phenomenon in some dialogue in his powerful novel *The Strudlhof Steps* of 1951. In Doderer's retrospective look at Vienna, the troublesome or prankish *Doppelgänger* is a kind of unconscious persona to the conscious individual, and this meaning inspired witty conversation. In a discussion of biological twins, a character called Marchetti says of the amateur pianist Edouard von Langl, "It's a good thing he doesn't have a twin brother. Two of Edoard von Langle? No way! Talk about 'grief made more grievous'!" And then the conversation turns to the identical twin girls, Mimi and Edith Pastré, who took advantage of their identical appearances to play tricks on people, including their own father. "That kind of paired existence as a twin would drive me to despair," cried Buschmann; "a whole life as Doppelgänger to another person! Could that be why [the Pastré sister] ran away?" Von Langl then proclaims that a natural twin brother had nothing to do with a mysterious *Doppelgänger*: "Having a twin brother would seem to me almost purely physical or biological by comparison."

Langl continued to speak. "Doppelgänger—that's the most evil part of us, the part buried deepest, the part that's uncontrolled, and we've lost all power over it. It's broken loose. It's become an entity of its own. It goes around doing things in our name that we *could* do but never would." This is to say that the *Doppelgänger* is nothing other than the unconscious mind that doubles consciousness in an ordinary human

63. Kury 2000, 226; Fend 2005, 311.

individual. Such mysterious prankishness fostered a humorous tone in the "small talk" of Viennese society:

> "How about Edouard here? Look at all he knows," Marchetti said in reaction. "Do you have one?"
> "One what?"
> "A Dopplegänger, I mean."
> "Yes," said Langl. "But I never have any trouble telling us apart. He doesn't know how to play the piano, thank God."[64]

Skin as Screen

Thomas Mann, in his musings upon X-ray technology, the body, and desire, discourses on human skin before he arrives at the more forbidden realms of the viscera and skeleton. Skin—as Didier Anzieu, Claudia Benthien, Mechtild Fend, and other writers have argued—is at once part of the body and its delimitation. Skin is a communicative interface between the bounded exterior of the body and the workings of the hidden interior.[65] As such the skin of a human being shows the inside on the outside. Mann's spokesperson for this lesson is the X-ray specialist Dr. Behrens, who is also a creditable figurative artist and has painted a conventional portrait of the object of Castorp's desire, the mysterious Madame Chauchat. In explaining his portrait technique to Castorp, he discourses on the way to paint skin:

> If a man knows a bit about what goes on under the epidermis, that does no harm either. In other words, if he can paint a little below the surface, and stands in another relation to nature than just the lyrical, so to say. An artist who is a doctor, physiologist, and anatomist on the side, and has his own little way of thinking about the under sides of things—it all comes in handy too, it gives you the *pas*, say what you like. That birthday suit there is painted with science, it is organically correct, you can examine it under the microscope. You can see not only the horny and mucous strata of the epidermis, but I've suggested the texture of the corium underneath, with the oil—and sweat-glands, the blood-vessels and tubercles—and then under

64. Von Doderer 2021, 189–90.
65. Anzieu 2016; Benthien 2002; Fend 2005; Fend 2017.

> that still the layer of fat, the upholstering, you know, full of oil ducts, the underpinning of the lovely female form. What is in your mind as you work runs into your hand and has its influence—it isn't really there, and yet somehow or other it is, and that is what gives the lifelike affect.[66]

Is feminine beauty demystified by biology in this ekphrasis? Or is it expanded in its seeking below the surface? Can one woman's oil and sweat glands, blood vessels, or tubercles cause more loveliness than those of another? And are those organs to be linked with the identity of her individual character? Can the reality of what is under the skin provoke desire? Human skin in all of its complexity, such as the naked flesh painted by Gustave Courbet (1819–77) or Lucian Freud (1922–2011) is evoked in Dr. Behrens's statement.[67]

Such a passage also calls to mind some of the most beautiful scientific drawings made in turn-of-the-century Vienna, those used by researchers such as the great Hungarian dermatologist Moritz Kohn Kaposi (1837–1902).[68] A histological drawing from Kaposi's legacy, attributable to Karl Henning (ca. 1886), is a dynamic pencil drawing labeled in ink, which renders the skin as a crust (**fig. 9**). The epidermal workings are located in the underlying tissue, as a sort of a topographical map, very much like the maps that were used by archaeologists (such as Freud's friend Emanuel Löwy [1837–1938]) in their excavation of particular sites.[69]

The epidermis is like the surface of the earth, with many strata and ducts roiling below. In view of this image Freud's archaeological metaphor comes to mind. The founder of psychoanalysis saw the unconscious mind and past events as being buried below the surface of consciousness; liberating truth could be reconstructed by the "archaeological" excavation of strata in reverse chronological order and the careful piecing together of significant fragments of memories.

66. Mann 1928, 259.

67. "Kaposi's sarcoma" was discovered in 1872. The disease is familiar by way of twentieth- and twenty-first-century AIDS patients.

68. O'Donoghue 2004, 653–71.

69. Cartwright 1995, 50–52; Panek 2004, 181, has stated that although X-rays did not enable scientists to observe hidden thoughts, they paralleled Freud's idea of the unconscious in that they illustrated a delay between cause and effect in the human body.

Indeed, Freud's whole logic of interior states producing external affect and anterior states determining present conditions is compatible with Kaposi's idea of looking under the skin. For Kaposi, skin diseases were in effect symptoms or signs, rather than conditions per se. When toxins were excreted to the surface, it meant that they came from underlying sources (both literally and figuratively), rather than from an ailment of the skin itself. Kaposi's schema is comparable *grosso modo* to Freud's view that somatic conditions such as paralysis could be caused by hidden emotional factors such as hysteria.[70] What troubles the outside comes from the inside.

Now, turning back to the Eros and Thanatos of X-ray photography, we may ask what happens to the female object of desire when we can see inside her body. What happens when the body's natural borders and boundaries dissolve? Let us listen to Mann, who tells us Hans Castorp's thoughts as he observes Clavdia Chauchat's maidenly figure in the waiting room of the X-ray laboratory: "Hans Castorp recalled, suddenly, that she too was sitting here waiting to be X-rayed. The Hofrat [Dr. Behrens] painted her, he reproduced her outward form with oil and colors upon the canvas. And now, in the twilighted room, he would direct upon her the rays which would reveal to him the inside of her body."[71] She will be devoured and her flesh in a certain sense corrupted and consumed by the gaze of the X-raying physician. Certain comments from the doctor to Castorp suggest that it is indeed a desiring gaze with which they apprehend the X-ray of Clavdia's body. Dr. Behrens says, "There is a female arm, you can tell by its delicacy. That's what they put around you when they make love, you know."[72]

An X-rayed thorax when taken on its own is not a "sexy" picture compared to a nude study or even an insightful portrait. Only when the viewer knows what he is looking at—such as Castorp looking at his cousin's throbbing heart or the damaged organs of his lover's thoracic cavity—can the experience become almost unbearably intimate. In an X-ray image the absence of the outer contour of flesh and the absence of constraining skin gives an unbounded view of the primary organs of life. The talismanic significance of these *mementi* is of interest to the cultural historian of the twenty-first century. When Castorp burns with desire for Clavdia Chauchat after she has left the sanitarium, he focuses

70. Mann 1928, 213.
71. Mann 1928, 215.
72. Mann 1928, 348.

on her "X-ray portrait" with the same fervor that a man would gaze upon his sweetheart's face in a photographic print:

> Then he threw himself into his chair and drew out his keepsake, his treasure, that consisted this time, not of a few reddish-brown shavings, but a thin glass plate, which must be held toward the light to see anything on it. It was Clavdia's X-ray portrait, showing not her face, but the delicate bony structure of the upper half of her body, and the organs of the thoracic cavity, surrounded by the pale, ghostlike envelope of flesh.[73]

She becomes an absent presence in X-ray photography—a surrogate of herself, an ultimate documentation of her heart and lungs that not only helped him to remember, but actually brought her body closer to him in the continuum of time and space: "How often had he looked at it, how often pressed it to his lips, in the time which since then had passed and brought its changes with it—such changes as, for instance, getting used to life up here without Clavdia Chauchat, getting used, that is, to her remoteness in space!"[74] The magic of Clavdia's X-ray as a memory picture activated by light becomes the subject of a moving ekphrasis by Thomas Mann as the novel moves deeper into philosophical inquiry and delirium. We may consider Mann's words while looking at a twentieth-century chest X-ray, such as shown in Fig. 26.

> It was a small negative. Held in the same plane with the ground it was black and opaque; but lifted against the light, it revealed matter for a humanistic eye: the transparent reproduction of the human form, the bony framework of the ribs, the outline of the heart, the arch of the diaphragm, the bellows that were the lungs; together with the shoulder and upper-arm-bones, all shrouded in a dim and vaporous envelope of flesh—that flesh which once, in Carnival week, Hans Castorp had so madly tasted. What wonder his unstable heart stood still or wildly throbbed when he gazed at it, and then, to the sound of the rushing waters, leaning with crossed arms against the smooth back of his bench, his head inclined upon one shoulder, among the blossoming aquilegias, began to turn everything over in his mind![75]

73. Mann 1928, 348.
74. Mann 1928, 349.
75. Glasser 1931, 81.

Somehow the real inside of a human being has cast the naked flesh, which he had once "so madly tasted," into a luminous pillow covered by the crust of the epidermis. The outline of Clavdia's heart, lungs, and skeleton makes Castorp's own heart stand still or throb wildly. What happens to sexual identity here? The X-ray "portrait" of Clavdia calls into question the over-cathected subjects of the female face or the female nude in a comical but also tragic manner. There is nothing *zaftig* or contained in a view of heart, lungs, or skeleton, and very little that can even be identified with a specific sex, or a specific individual, even though a ghostly trace of the flesh remains visible. Such an image corresponds with an X-ray from the twentieth century. And still, when held to the light, Clavdia's chest X-ray offers what Mann calls "matter for a humanistic eye," that is, an eye that would typically contemplate a classical female form such as an ancient statue of Aphrodite surprised at her bath, or a photo of a modern woman in the costume (still classical and therefore humanistic) of nudity.[76]

The erotic lure of the X-ray was acknowledged in popular culture almost immediately, as a phenomenon of seeing through clothes. But what happens when we see through to the bone? In *Life* magazine in the United States, for example, a benignly humorous poem about an X-rayed beloved was published on March 12, 1896.

> Around her ribs, those beauteous 24,
> Her flesh a halo makes, misty in line,
> Her noseless, eyeless face looks into mine,
> And I but whisper, "Sweetheart, je t'adore."[77]

With the introduction of X-ray photography, the most mystified areas of the human body, the heart, the sex organs, and the brain, were in fact made to appear in visual documentation.

In her groundbreaking study *Naked to the Bone* of 1997 Bettyann Kevles emphasized that X-rays held a philosophical interest and that spiritualists searched X-rays for evidence of psychic auras and indications of the mysterious fourth dimension, or the passage of time.[78]

76. Bonfante 1989, 543–70.
77. Quoted by Kevles 1997, 26–27.
78. Bergstein 2009, 185–210.

X-Raying Mummies as the Uncanny Other

In 1896 Professor Georg Von Tischendorf conducted X-ray experiments on various materials. He noticed that when X-raying animals, their skeletons stood out like petrifacts, and therefore X-rays were like fossils. Among the precious stones he X-rayed were aquamarine, topaz, opal, pearls, turquoise, and simulated jewels made from glass. Diamonds, Tischendorf discovered, are transparent to X-rays, whereas simulated diamonds were dark.

Perhaps the uncanniest X-rays in Vienna occurred within the sphere of archaeological research. The turn of the twentieth century was a peak moment for archaeological excavations and anthropological photography, and X-ray photography was almost immediately allied with the fields of Egyptology and ethnography.[79] Tischendorf's lecture in 1896 included a section about X-ray experiments he conducted on an ancient mummy from his own private collection, a 5,000-year-old body that his father (the biblical scholar and archaeologist Konstantin Von Tischendorf) had brought back from the pyramid tombs some forty years earlier, around 1845.[80] Tischendorf described the bony structure of the hand of a mummy as photographed through its linen wrapping, and how easily he could discern from the X-rayed foot that the individual had never worn shoes.[81] Western perceptions of Egyptian history tended to be telescoped in such a way that historical time in that culture was considered static; from antiquity to the present, the Egyptians were ancient and changeless in sempiternity. We recall that Ernst Brücke looked at orientalist photographs and noticed "a photograph of a poor Fellah girl, in whom the great toe was conspicuously longer than the second" from not having worn European-style shoes. Photographs of Egyptian peasant women such as those by Pascal Sébah (1823–86) (**see fig. 14**) were commonly collected in the West.

79. Tischendorf 1896, 6. In the course of his lecture, Tischendorf mentioned Herr Professor König's comments from a previous session. König, who was a professor of physics at the University of Frankfurt, was one of Röntgen's earliest collaborators and the first scientist on record to have X-rayed a mummy, publishing his X-ray of the knees of a mummified child. See König 1896.

80. Anonymous 1896.

81. Tögel 2002, 302.

A more shocking Egyptian mummy revelation occurred in Vienna in February 1896, when the X-ray of a human-shaped mummy from the Imperial collection turned out to be not a human body at all, but the mummy of an African sacred ibis, packed in a painted human form. *The British Journal of Photography* of February 28, 1896, reported it thus, under the heading "A Novel Use for the Röntgen Rays":

> According to a Vienna correspondent (but it is not necessary to believe everything written about the latest popular sciences) an application of a very practical nature has been made with the new form of energy. In the Museum of Natural History in that city is stored an Egyptian mummy, which is esteemed as very valuable. In appearance it is like the mummy of a human being, but certain inscriptions upon it suggest that a bird—an ibis—lay beneath the wrappings. It is too rare and valuable a specimen to be subjected to possible injury by unwrapping it, so it was determined to Röntgenate it. It was taken to the School of Photography and operated on accordingly. The sciagraph obtained showed clearly the outline of a large bird.[82]

What was thought to be a human form, morbidly preserved in death, and preserved for millennia in the disguise of a mummy, was actually a large bird (dead and preserved) of spiritual importance to the ancient Egyptians. This revelation belongs to the realm of the Freudian uncanny (*Unheimlich*) only partly because of the human expectation of a human mummy was deceptive. The return from the dead that every discovered (or purchased) mummy represented in the nineteenth and twentieth centuries, and the act of unwrapping a mummy to expose a conserved body, fulfilled certain essential qualities of the uncanny aesthetic as defined by Jentsch and Freud. The "animism, magic, and sorcery" and "man's attitude toward death," described by Freud in *The Uncanny*, are all present in this object and in the X-ray photograph that makes the encounter so much more haunting. Jentsch's emphasis on "intellectual uncertainty" and disorientation in both time and place, the confusion between life and death, and the confusion between human and animal, or human and automaton, or a creature like the Dybbuk of Jewish folklore who lives between two realms, suspended between life and death, created an intellectual uncertainty not only for archaeologists but

82. Howe 1994, 41.

for the public at large. For the Austrian of the *fin-de-siècle*, ancient Egypt already belonged to the territory of the uncanny, via the recession into the deep historical past, and the orientalism of the Western fascination with the East, the "Rêve d'Orient."

Carl Jung (1875–1961) believed that mummies were powerful images of death in Freud's psyche. Directly before sailing to the United States in 1909, Jung chatted with Freud about the natural (accidental) mummification of humans in the peat bogs of northern Europe and in the *Bleikeller* (lead cellar) of the Bremen Cathedral. Jung maintained that Freud resisted the topic, and that in one discussion of these mummies at the dinner table Freud suddenly fainted away, evidently because of the intensity of his own fantasies about such mysterious natural/unnatural objects. Freud had apparently interpreted all of Jung's talk about mummies as a "death wish" against him. Jung may have been right about Freud's mummy obsession, however, because, upon his arrival in America, when Freud visited New York's "China Town," he commented that he was struck by the similarity of older Chinese men to "the mummies of Egyptian kings."[83] In this casual burst of exoticism, confusing China with Egypt, comparing the mummified dead with living bodies, and the disparity of time periods over the centuries and millennia, Freud had slipped into a sort of all-purpose orientalism that was typical of his time and place. I will not subject his slip to analysis, but rather add it to this thick plot, to point out some photographs of mummies that Freud had probably seen.

Egyptologists of the later nineteenth century examined the ancient dead as mummies were unwrapped for study and duly photographed.[84] In a kind of macabre striptease, mummies were unwrapped before spellbound audiences in Europe who witnessed the release of human figures from thick layers of wrapped cloth.[85] I have already pointed to the mummy of a princess-priestess Nessi-ta-neb-asher in the Cairo Museum as photographed by the German photographer Emil Brugsch (1842–1930) before and after the unwinding of her bandages (**fig. 33**). Likewise, an anonymous photograph from the 1880s of the Mummy of Mahinpra (**fig. 30**) represents the unwrapped figure standing erect on a pedestal against a light neutral background in the Cairo Museum.

83. Pringle 2001, 164–65.

84. Eder and Valenta 1896, 14–15; Hinterberger 1897, 118; Glasser 1931, 347; Eladany 2011, 122.

85. philoctetesctr 2009.

The installation of the preserved body on a pedestal for this photograph reinforces the ambiguity between statue and cadaver that so perplexed and enriched archaeological and psychological thinking of the time. The photograph verges on expressing the concept of the dead-come-to-life *and* a statue-come-to-life. This theme brings to mind Freud's essay (1907) on Wilhelm Jensen's *Gradiva*, in which a Roman relief sculpture of a nymph uncannily first becomes a revenant and then a living girl to wed the archaeologist for whom it was an object of obsession. The mummy as cadaver is an uncanny, abject presence, a *memento mori* of the most fascinating order.

Are mummies by their "natural" facture involuntary portraits? If they are received as such, they fit seamlessly into the tradition that governed the interpretation of all portraiture, including statuary, painting, and posed studio photographs of living people.

The head of another important pharaoh from the Cairo Museum appears in Steindorff's *Great Age of Pharaonic Kingdoms* (1900): a stone portrait of Amenhotep IV (Akhenaten) (**fig. 31**) found at El Amarna is presented in a photographic composition that resembles that of the mummified Thutmosis II (**fig. 32**).

The pioneering photochemist Josef Maria Eder announced that Dr. Alexander Dedekind (1856–1940), curator of Egyptian Collections of the K. K. Kunsthistorischen Hofmuseum (KHM), had several mummies X-rayed at the GLV, and that one such mummy, presumably that of a child, had an outwardly human form—but contained the embalmed remains of an ibis.[86] Freud knew of the Egyptian deity Thoth, god of wisdom, with a man's body and an ibis' head, from his childhood exposure to the Philippson Bible, and he subsequently acquired such an Egyptian statue for his personal collection.[87]

The 1896 annual report of the Imperial Egyptian Collection noted that news of the X-ray discovery of a collective ibis mummy (Miramar Gruppe II, no. 6) spread quickly, having great press in European journals and had even elicited an inquiring telegram from curators of

86. I am grateful to Elfriede Haslauer, Egyptian curator of the KHM, for her transcription of this report from the *Jahresbericht* of 1896.

87. A watercolor by Carl Goebel of 1889 shows that at that time the bandaged mummies from the collection in the lower Belvedere in Vienna were shown in vitrines in front of their corresponding wooden sarcophagus cases, which was surely a point of attraction for the public. Satzinger 1994.

the Metropolitan Museum in New York.[88] The X-ray in question, which would have to have been either an extremely large glass plate or a series of glass plates, has not been located in the Egyptian Collection of the KHM nor among the effects of Josef Maria Eder in the photography department of the Albertina, nor has it, to my knowledge, been reproduced in publication.

Freud, who had a keen interest in Egyptian archaeology, certainly read about the ibis mummy and other X-rayed specimens.[89] Guido Holzknecht, who pioneered and developed X-ray technology in the Viennese medical establishment, was also interested in Egypt, and surely knew of Eder's work and its implications for archaeology and anthropology. Holzknecht traveled to Egypt not long before his death from metastasized cancer. During the time he was consulting Holzknecht for his cancer, Freud himself expressed longings to visit Egypt, and the two physicians must have discussed the use of X-rays in Egyptian archaeology including the X-rays of mummies. On March 4, 1923, Freud wrote to Karl Abraham (1877–1925) about the current discovery of the tomb of Tutankhamen and his annoyance at not being able to be there and "at the prospect of descending the Styx without having sailed the Nile." Abraham tried to cheer him up, telling of an uncle who had celebrated his golden wedding anniversary at the age of 75 by traveling with his wife to Egypt, where he even (as most European tourists did) rode a camel in the desert. Freud replied that he could only envy but not imitate the uncle's camel ride in the desert for he had neither the health nor the wealth to travel.[90] A photograph from Holzknecht's journey of 1928, when he addressed the Egyptian School of Medicine in Cairo, conserved in the archive of the Medical University of Vienna, is a typical example of European souvenir photography in Egypt. Holzknecht, his wife, and a guide sit astride camels before the Great Sphinx and Pyramid of Giza (**fig. 34**).[91]

As for Egyptian archaeological subjects in photography, what could be uncannier than a mummy? As the living embodiment of the dead, mummies and portraits of Egyptian kings were well known to Freud from the books in his personal library. Steindorff's *The*

88. Schur 1972, 348–49.

89. This photograph is conserved in the archive of the Medical University of Vienna.

90. Steindorff 1900, 36.

91. Grasset 1896, 257–64.

Great Age of Pharaonic Kingdoms was one of the illustrated books on Egyptian archaeology on Freud's shelves. Its genealogy of the pharaohs as photographed in sculptured portraiture and mummies is of a piece with the medical and archaeological photography that was most familiar to Freud. In Steindorff, mummified bodies and sculptured portraits were brought together within a common format of photographic illustrations. On the one hand, the mummified head of Thutmosis II in the Cairo Museum is photographed according to the same norms as isolated sculptural fragments, as if it were a work of art. At the same time, the portrait resides in the body itself, and it is accompanied (captioned in the text) by a medical diagnosis, concluding that Thutmosis had probably suffered at length from a severe disease that caused him to lose his hair before death.[92] There is a disconcerting superimposition here of the historical human individual with his immortal, eternal self. Where mortality, immortality, and the dead-come-to-life are overlaid in a single image, the uncanny already resides. The explanatory text about the Pharaoh's hair, with its diagnostic assumptions, brings us back quite close to Jean-Martin Charcot and his photographers at the Salpêtrière with their particularly apposite uses of photography of the human body for medical and cultural purposes.

In terms of visual typology, Steindorff's photographic illustration of Thutmosis II has a medical corollary in the photographic illustration of a "mummy man" (photograph attributed to L. Biermann) in Grasset's "Un'homme momie,'" an article published in *Nouvelle Iconographie* of 1896.[93] The portrait of this "living mummy" documents an individual with hereditary syphilis whose congenital condition of atrophied skin, muscle, and bone was meant to be studied for purposes of diagnosis, in a society in which syphilis was a major cause of death (**fig. 35**). This living man's likeness to a body that was already dead and preserved in antiquity invoked an aesthetic of the Freudian uncanny, and is, in Julia Kristeva's terms, an abject presence, an image from which we would happily remove our gaze. Indeed, these two "male portraits," one living and the other long dead, belong to the same family of images. Syphilis (especially in its hereditary form) in France was a source of general and libidinal anxiety, with 85,000 people in Paris infected by 1890. Contagion was mysterious, as were genetic factors, which were also uncertain, as

92. Bernheimer 1997, 234–37.

93. Eder 1886.

various conditions appeared to "skip" a generation. Disease was the societal plot of medical uncertainty in the later nineteenth century that could produce monstrosities and early death, not just for those who had first contracted syphilis by way of sex, but also those who inherited the sickness or those for whom it was communicated by marriage between husband and wife, and from mother to child.[94]

Eder's institute took up experimentation with X-ray photography, and as soon as he and his associate (and brother-in-law) Eduard Valenta (1857–1937) began working they were able to improve upon the effect of X-rays on light-sensitive substances.[95] Eder and Valenta conducted a study involving the X-raying of various materials, the result of which was a breathtaking publication of 1896: a portfolio produced by the Lehr- und Versuchsanstalt including sixteen pages of text and fifteen individual plates. The plates illustrating Eder and Valenta's *Versuche über Photographie mittelst der Röntgen'schen Strahlen* were X-ray photogravures of various objects, natural and human-made, organic and inorganic, living and inert. Looking back from a standpoint in the twenty-first century, with the experience of the many monographs on photography produced throughout the last century, one realizes that it is really the fifteen-page text that illustrates the plates, which can be seen as works of art unto themselves.[96] An original X-ray plate will show, for example, white bones against black flesh; a photographic positive printed from such a negative exhibits dark bones against contrasting white flesh. Eder and Valenta's album featured photographic facsimiles of X-ray negatives, and positive prints made from the negative glass plates.[97]

94. Eder 1889, 466–67.

95. Frizot 1998, 252–53, 255. Eduard Valenta was a photochemist who collaborated with Eder from 1880 to 1912; he was Eder's research associate as well as his brother-in-law.

96. Some plates from this portfolio are illustrated by Dünkel 2016, 226–35, with her perceptive commentary on the images.

97. Each individual plate in the *Versuche* had its own subject. These included the following: 1. *Hand of a Twenty-One Year-Old Woman* (photographic facsimile of a negative); 2. *Hand of an Eight-Year-Old Girl* (photographic facsimile of a negative); 3. *Hand of a Four-Year-Old Child, Which Was Diseased with Rhachitis* (photographic facsimile of a negative); 4. *Foot of a Seventeen-Year-Old Boy with Crooked Toes* (photographic facsimile of a negative); 5. *Degrees of Transparency of Various Substances via X-rays* (positive print); 6. *Three Cameos in Gold*

To call these photogravures effective would be pure understatement. Their aesthetics were captivating, and not just because the images fulfilled the desire to see what was hidden by nature. The printing process of photogravure enhanced the luminescence inherent in the medium of vision (X-rays), making all physical matter seem to glow within a dark atmosphere.[98] In 1896 the content of these images was surprising, even frightening, and the fact that their forms were presented in terms of fluorescence and luminosity gripped observers all the more.

As I view the reproduced images, backlit on my flat-screen computer that generates its own kind of luminosity (liquid crystal display), the pleasure of looking at them is reconcentrated. The computer screen seems to enhance the essence of X-ray photographs, because its own image created by the opacity of liquid crystals blocking the light emitted from the backlit display is an analogue of the X-ray image as first viewed on a film (*pellicula*) and then reproduced as a photogravure.[99] The positive form was in fact created from a negative image, from negative space, from those parts of nature that the X-ray, itself the child of a negatively charged particle, could not penetrate and which on a glass plate coated with silver halide glows from within.

The *fin-de-siècle* X-rays by Eder and Valenta, which were first printed as a folio of photogravures, assume visual authority in the terms of their presentation and illumination on the backlit flat-screen computer monitor of the twenty-first-century beholder. Screen viewing of digital

Settings (photographic facsimile of a negative); 7. *Green Lizard* (positive print); 8. *Chameleon Cristatus* (positive print); 9. *Two Sea Fishes: Acanthurus Nigros and Zanclus Cornutus* (photographic facsimile of negative); 10. *Two Goldfish and a Sea Fish: Cristiceps Argentatus* [missing from folder] (no technique mentioned); 11. *Solfisch: Pleuronectes Solea* (photographic facsimile of a negative); 12. *Frogs Killed by Chloroform in Belly-Up and Belly-Down Positions* (photographic facsimile of negative); 13. *Rat* (photographic facsimile of negative); 14. *Newly Born Rabbit* (photographic facsimile of negative); 15. *Garden (Aesculepius) Snake* (photographic facsimile of a negative).

98. Photogravure had already been selected as the medium for the photography of rare animals at mid-century in France: see "Photographie Zoologique, par M. L. Rousseau et A. Devéria," *Bulletin de la Societé d'Encouragement pour l'Industrie Nationale* (1854), 120, regarding some photographs made by Bisson Frères (French, active 1840–64) and Louis-Amédée Mant (French, 1826–1913). The illustrative photolithographs were by Lemercier and Co.; see Rosen 1987, 307–308.

99. Schultz 2002 in Dowden 1999, 167.

photographs of analog photographs, or X-ray photographs, makes the beholder an active participant, able to see what could not be seen in the original negatives or positives. When viewing a digital image file such as a JPEG photograph, which has a tremendous capacity for digital compression online, the quality of blackness rivals the lustrous black usually associated with hand-printed lithography, or later with velvety darkness of photogravure, as practiced in Vienna by Eder and Valenta, Josef Löwy (1827–1902) and Ludwig Angerer (1827–79). The phenomenon of artificial darkness, as investigated by Noam Elcott (2016) and others, and its attendant opposite glow is still effective in the twenty-first century in the study of visual culture.

Most of the animals (not the humans, of course) in Eder and Valenta's project were killed with strychnine or chloroform before being posed on an X-ray plate, and some had been preserved in spirits for years. Nevertheless, they look alive, and perhaps even more biologically "valid" than when they were living, because great motor action is implied by the vision of the mechanics of skeletons. This lends the luminous frogs, for example, which are posed as opposites, one on its belly and the other on its back, an intrinsic beauty and sense of weightless floating and relaxation (**fig. 36**).[100]

The quality of deep darkness gives the luminous tracing of bones a spectral effect, announcing these images as uncanny ghosts. Just as ghosts were the uncanny dead-come-to-life in art and folkloric superstition, Eder and Valenta's animals and minerals were visual ghosts in X-ray photography.

In the Eder and Valenta album various fishes are suspended in space as though they were swimming, instead of lying dead on a lead plate. They seem to glow with phosphorescence from a dense black ground, in a brilliant chiaroscuro produced by photogravure. The apparent phosphorescence is not native to the fish; nor is it really phosphorescence, but rather *fluorescence*, which is caused by the X-ray medium itself, in concert with the twenty-first-century computer screen. The sunfish that was freshly killed for the imaging process appears as a great oval glow around a precisely articulated spine and tail with the lung of its gills below the head. No swim-bubbles remain in the photogravure, because when preserved in spirits these breath-of-life features disappear (**fig. 37**).[101]

100. This was followed technologically in 1897 by John MacIntyre's investigative X-ray. Motion picture of the movements of a frog's leg, Cartwright 1995, 20–22.

101. Eder and Valenta 1896, 15–16.

Eder and Valenta's newly born rabbit, a bag of soft flesh filled with hard, spikey bones, communicates a pathetic difficulty in distinguishing between life and death as the modest and familiar little rabbit (*Heimlich*) becomes its uncanny opposite, *Unheimlich*.

Never have animals looked quite so "biological" as in these pictures and never have they looked quite so much like spirits. In 1896 a separate off-print by Georg von Tischendorf, *Notices about X-ray Photographs*, was apparently the transcript of an illustrated lecture. Tischendorf discusses the application of X-ray photographs in the physical analysis of various substances, including diamonds, glass, hardstones, porcelain, and various metals. One of the examples he cites is zoological, namely, the X-ray photograph of a bird in full plumage.[102] In this instance Tischendorf observes that the X-ray, in all its bony, explanatory immobility, looks like a fossil. Like a fossil, the X-ray photograph is a trace or imprint of a body. The idea that an X-ray is comparable to a petrifact seems to enhance the absolute authenticity of X-ray photography as an instrument of enduring proof. The fascinating paradox of a natural fossil springs from its origin in geological deep time, versus the seeming freshness with which the image is inscribed. This is about the new discernibility of an ancient artifact, which is an eminently appropriate subject for photography. X-ray photographs of birds, lizards, and fishes communicate a similar intrigue in seeing what should be impossible to see, in other words, an uncanny seeing *through* to the biological essence of an animal, a ghostly being frozen in time. Deep geological time is followed by seeing into ancient historical time in the next photograph to be discussed. Three mythological portrait cameos in gold frames printed in negative belong to the realm of the dramatic photography of sculpture, which separates them categorically from the other plates in this portfolio (**fig. 38**).[103]

Looking through Gems

The cameo X-rays produce the unnerving sensation of looking into the ancient past, at ghosts from antiquity. Cameos are bas-reliefs made through a reductive sculptural process, consisting of striated hard stones, the pure amorphous flint of chalcedony (including carnelian, sard, sardonyx, onyx, chrysoprase, bloodstone, jasper, jade, or agate)

102. Tischendorf 1896, 3.

103. Cf. Bergstein 1992, 475–98.

carved in relief. The cameo sculptor has to choose a naturally variegated stone of at least two strata so that colors are revealed as it is carved. This gives a special polychrome configuration to a figurative, usually mythological, subject, so that, for instance, white figures appear crisply against an amber ground, or a red horse can have a black rider. In an interview in the *New York Times* (2005), the Metropolitan Museum curator of sculpture, James Draper (1943–2019), mused that "[a] cameo is a virtuoso thing to have. You can look at it forever and ever with great happiness. And a cameo is wonderful in the hand, of course."[104] A Hellenistic tradition, classical style cameos fascinated their intimate viewers from ancient Rome through the nineteenth century.

The cameos X-rayed by Eder and Valenta were cut in onyx. The X-ray process demonstrated the increase of opacity of a material with the increased thickness of its strata.[105] Although the cameos consist of striated hard stones carved by human craftsmen, the X-ray photogravure makes the portraits look alive, but in a fleeting, vanishing, manner—again like phantasms. They possess a delicacy of chiaroscuro that makes them look at once more photographic and more phantasmatic, as though their settings contained lenses or "loups" through which one could glimpse fantastic, fugitive personae, shades from the distant past, uncannily returned to life, as in the *Nilus* gem.

All of the gems photographed by Eder and Valenta appear life-sized on the page; they are presently conserved in the Kunsthistorisches Museums and were lent from the K. K. Hofsmuseum by "Sr. Excellenz des Herrn Oberstkämmerers Trautmannsdorff" for the occasion of the X-ray project. Let us read these gems from left to right as photographed on the page. The small cameo to the left was carved and signed by Niccolò Morelli who was born in Rome and worked for the Emperor Napoleon. In 1927 Fritz Eichler and Ernst Kris identified the subject as probably representing "Alexander the Great (?)." The cameo, which is made of pink and white jasper, is displayed in a setting of gilded silver (**fig. 39**).

The large gem at the center of the photograph represents a personification the River God of the Nile, Nilus, and the object is inscribed "PISTRVCCI" by Benedetto Pistrucci (1783–1855) (**fig. 39**). Nilus is portrayed bust-length, bearded, upward gazing, and wearing a crown of reeds. The object is made of white onyx with brownish

104. Quoted by Moonan 2005.

105. Eder and Valenta 1896, 11.

overlay on a darker ground, set in gilded silver. Pistrucci was a Roman artist, trained in the techniques of cameo and intaglio engravings in Morelli's workshop. He was a prodigy: at age sixteen, he had become independent, supplying engraved gems, sometimes resold as ancient, and medals to the dealers Angiolo Bonelli and Ignazio Vescovali. Vescovali maintained his studio in the Piazza di Spagna, where he sold sculpture, gems, and other *objets de virtù*, including some genuinely excavated antiquities, mixed together with some objects made freshly on the premises and patinated to make them look ancient.

Pistrucci made gems that were famous for having been mistaken, or even sold dishonestly, as ancient (Roman) or Renaissance (sixteenth-century) works. In his autobiography Pistrucci claimed that some cameo dealers who had purchased his own signed works "effaced my name and wrote that of some old artist of much renown; and thus, with those in onyx, or other Oriental stones, they either took off my name, and replaced with the name of some [ancient] Greek artist, or sold it as an antique without any name at all."[106] Indeed, for a time, the *Nilus* was set in a conspicuous place of honor in the ancient gem collection of the Imperial Cabinet in Vienna, even though it was engraved with the artist's name.[107]

To the right of Nile in Eder's photogravure is a head of Perseus made after Canova's statue of *Perseus and the Head of Medusa* (1800–1801) that was installed in the Vatican Belvedere in 1801 as an "answer" to the Greco-Roman *Apollo Belvedere* in a neighboring niche. Canova's *Perseus* is transformed into a portrait bust contained in a small gem. Set in gilded silver, the gem is white and reddish jasper; although there is no attribution or signature, the object was probably made by an anonymous Roman artist as a (very expensive) souvenir of the Eternal City for a grand tourist in the nineteenth century.

Classical style cameos were produced and enjoyed widely during the neoclassical period in Italy. Sometimes these handheld gems replicated sculptural models from antiquity in a light-infused material that was far more savory to the connoisseur than a painting or print could be; they were palpable and eminently portable. Although neoclassical gems (from ca. 1760–1840) were considerably less imaginative than Renaissance renditions of ancient gems from the fifteenth or sixteenth centuries were, they had a deceptively faithful likeness to the ancient

106. Pistrucci in Billing 1875, 147.
107. Billing 1875, 87–90, 92.

originals. Considered to be the premier cameo carver of the nineteenth century, Benedetto Pistrucci was properly described in his own time as an "archaeomaniac."[108]

Eder and Valenta stated that they X-rayed these cameos in order to demonstrate the increase of opacity of a material according to the increased thickness of the strata of stone.[109] According to the two photoscientists, the objects in question were cut in onyx, a stone that almost always consists only of silicic acid and siliceous earth, and in this regard is seen to behave almost like quartz. The opacity of the gilded silver settings is a constant solid, against which the fine details of relief carving are expressed in their fully graduated nuance.[110]

The cameos are represented life-size in photogravure, but the application of the X-ray medium transforms them wholly, so that the idea of photographic "documentation" simply vanishes. Although the X-ray technique renders the heads with precision, the sfumato effect of light against dark creates a strange atmospheric delicacy that reiterates the light-on-dark compositions of the gems themselves. Throughout his writings, Eder referred to negatives as "latent pictures" (*Latenten-Bilder*), and here the image, as a negative, is indeed "latent" in every sense of the word. We may contrast the latent River God to a life-size positive (manifest to Eder's latent) photograph by Max Jaffé (1845–1939) published by Eichler and Kris for the Kunsthistorisches Museum in 1927.[111]

Max Jaffé studied photography in Paris (1865) and Hamburg (1868–69). Then he worked for the Hof-Photograph (official photographer to the Austro-Hungarian court) Josef Löwy, who trained him in portraiture. Jaffé was a member of Eder's circle insofar as he was a lecturer at the GLV until 1889, specializing in photographic reproduction.[112] His renditions of the cameos at the KHM are painterly and printed with gorgeous sculptural color in the catalogue written by the classical art scholars Fritz Eichler (1887–1971) and Ernst Kris (1900–1957), who had a double career as an art historian and psychoanalyst.[113]

108. Billing 1875, 92, 99.

109. Eder and Valenta 1896, 11.

110. Eder and Valenta 1896, 11.

111. Eichler and Kris 1927, plate 76, no. 603 and plate 78, no. 628.

112. Eder 1945, 353–54, 407, 628–29.

113. Eichler and Kris 1927, plate 76, no. 603, plate 78, no. 628; Roeske 2001.

Certain historical connections seem too good even to be wished for, such as the concrete connection between Ernst Kris and Freud with regard to ancient gems, both intaglios and cameos. In addition to other small antiquities, Freud collected classical cameos and gems. As of now, Freud's stones and cameos have not been the subject of a full monographic study, which still waits to be written. Freud gave silver rings with carefully chosen inlaid cameo gems to his closest associates, the "secret committee," between the years 1912 and 1928. Whether or not Freud consulted Ernst Kris for the choices of these gifts is yet unknown, but very likely, and the iconographic meanings of these ancient objects also remain to be elucidated. We do know that he consulted Kris with regard to his own cameos and gems in 1924, and we may imagine that Freud owned a copy of the 1927 catalogue of cameos and gems, *Die Kameen im Kunsthistosischen Museum* (Vienna, 1927) for which Kris had achieved considerable fame.[114] Putting Kris's important museum catalogue, with its haunting chiaroscuro photographs, in Freud's hands around 1927 expands our historical imagination in the understanding of cultural history and art historiography.

An earlier photographic illustration of the famous Nile gem was published by Archibald Billing (1791–1881) in 1875 as a photo of a plaster cast of the original—a two-dimensional reproduction of a three-dimensional reproduction—the photograph attributed to "F. Coles of Euston Road, London." This image emphasizes the fine sculptured details of the River God's hair, beard, and wreaths of grain, sculptural details that are easily read in any photograph of a plaster cast, which was an established way of photographing sculpture of any kind in the nineteenth century. It was in the presence of this image that Billing determined that Pistrucci's cameos were seen best in photographs rather than contour-line engravings.[115]

The luminosity of gems and cameos was always an issue in their reception and display. At times the inscription on an engraved gem can only be perceived when held up to the light. At Oxford University, for example, the polymath Nevil Story Maskelyne (1823–1911) (professor of minerology and keeper of the mineral department) was credited with having set up the collection with mirrors behind the gems, which gave "an intensity of light quite charming."[116] This system of display was

114. Eichler and Kris 1927; Roeske 2001, 466–67.
115. Billing 1875, 99.
116. Billing 1875, 110.

deemed effective for intaglio gems, and many museums still illuminate gems from behind, but cameos had to be viewed "with the light upon them, not through them."[117] One can only imagine that the physician-gemologist Archibald Billing, who had a scientific training and was a fellow of the Royal College of Physicians, would have been fascinated to see Pistrucci's cameo in Eder's X-ray photogravure had he only been alive in 1896.

Because we are looking at a printed negative in the Eder and Valenta plate, the direction of the River God's sentience is reversed, and the exquisite sfumato gives the eye and the imagination a greater invitation to search and play. Hard inert matter is transformed first by the sculptor into delicate colored relief, and then by the X-ray medium into smoky wisps—you could, as the late James Draper would say, look at them forever and ever.

The transformative power of X-ray images seems magical, even for physicians who work with them on an everyday basis. In 2020 the medical students Mary Oakley Strasser and Balaji Pandian fell in love over a chest X-ray: "Dr. Mary Oakley Strasser's unhesitating response that she saw Seurat, not Picasso, in a medical X-ray won the heart of her fellow medical student, Balaji Pandian." Thus began their wedding announcement in the *New York Times*: "The pointillist-like dots on the X-ray, shown in a power-point presentation, indicated that the patient likely had tuberculosis." Dr. Strasser was correct, of course. She may have been thinking of a drawing like *Embroidery: The Artist's Mother* (1882–83) seen in the Metropolitan Museum (Gallery 690, Robert Lehman Collection), which is drawn in tonal passages of black with a conte crayon on white Michallet paper.

Such black-and-white drawings are among the most important images in Seurat's *oeuvre*. Their dense blacks echo contemporary photographic prints, and presage the first X-ray images made by Röntgen in 1895. The visual stuff of X-ray photography was duly incorporated into the form and content of abstract and modern art, as Linda Dalrymple Henderson has shown in her work on Francis Picabia and other modern painters, and Astrid Kury has explored in the work of Oskar Kokoschka.[118]

The formal qualities of the images in Eder and Valenta's portfolio create a new aesthetic, a style related to but diverging from that of traditional photographic positive prints. Luminosity is inherent in the

117. Billing 1875, 110.

118. Kury 2000, 219–38; Henderson 1989, 114–23.

new medium of vision and representation, the fluorescent effect of the X-ray. This is enhanced by the printing process of photogravure, which makes matter (living or inert) glow against the contrasting density of a black ground—a field of artificial darkness. But again, what is most novel here is not only the form but the content of these pictures, for they make visible what had always previously been invisible to the human eye.

Georges Chicotot: The Rhetoric of the Breast

The culture of the medical X-ray produced images of visual art in addition to the actual X-ray photographs, as we know from a painting by Georges Chicotot (1865–1921) of 1907 called *The First Trial of X-ray Therapy for Cancer of the Breast* (**fig. 40**), presently conserved at the Musée de l'Assistance Publique, Hôtel de Miramion, in Paris. Essentially a self-portrait of Georges Chicotot, who was head of radiotherapy at the Hôpital Broca, this is a traditional academic painting of an extremely modern topic, by a research physician who was also an accomplished painter.

Trained at the École des beaux arts, Chicotot taught for a time at the School of Practical Anatomy. He earned his medical degree in 1899 and worked on X-ray technology used to treat cancerous tumors at the Hôpital Trousseau. Chicotot's painting is not only unique in its role as a self-portrait of a doctor at work, but it is reportorial to a very high degree. X-rays are focused on the patient's left breast by a glass cylinder, rendered in a masterful passage of luminous post-impressionist oil painting. While the portrait subject (Dr. Chicotot) is heating the vessel that holds the Crooke's tube, he holds a watch in his left hand to measure the exposure time of directed radiation. The upper third of the picture is given over to an imposing electrical apparatus—a transformer with two vacuum valves that stands ominously upon the mantelpiece above the patient. The doctor wears a top hat (a "chapeau de haut forme") and a large white apron as was customary of doctors in their laboratories of the time. The half-draped patient on the operating table is depicted as a classical academic nude, with her clothing, including a pink corset and acid-green dress, piled on a chair next to the bed. She presumes the posture of a healthy artist's model. At a half-century later she is a sister figure to the nude woman, a personification of nature, who inspires the artist in Gustave Courbet's *The Artist's Studio* of 1855 (**fig. 41**).

The doctor himself, seen in a grandiose profile, dominates the scene, almost stooping to fit in the picture space at the right of the painting. The artist/biologist here is represented like God the creating Father in scenes of Michelangelo's Sistine ceiling. A man in contemporary clothing was typically not shown in the presence of nude women in paintings of the time (think of Manet's *Dejeuner sur l'herbe*, where the nude women are pastoral nymphs and not even really meant to be present excepting in spirit). Gerald Weissmann (1930–2019), himself a doctor with multiple métiers, drew attention to Chicotot's magnificent painting in his poetic essay, "The Doctor with Two Heads," about Chicotot, published in 1990.

Weissmann was correct in noticing that the doctor's bourgeois clothing, including the top hat, in a scene with a reclining female nude seems more suitable to a bordello than to a site of medical experimentation, or even an academic painter's studio.[119] In nineteenth-century Europe, painters and physicians, artists and scientists, were uniquely privileged, indeed *required*, to observe nude women in the course of their work. Weissmann also offers the succinct comment that this picture "presents the rescue fantasy of oncology without mutilation." The recumbent woman's body is intact, with her breast, arm, and torso composed in a painterly tour-de-force, in a classical state of repose. Chicotot's painting, oddly overcrowded by its two participants amidst a great deal of assertive-looking equipment, is, as Weissmann says, "charged with Freudian images and touched by death." The doctor's masculinity, underscored by his hat and his position of dominance with regard to the female nude completes the allegorical (or Freudian) duet.

The First Trial of X-ray Therapy for Cancer of the Breast is a monumental work of European painting, unique in its medical and technological content as far as I know. But what is most interesting to me in this study, which is mostly concerned with the role of photography, is that a reproductive photograph of the painting by Neurdein Frères (**fig. 42**) in postcard format was conserved in the picture archive of the Medical University in Vienna, having entered the collection in 1908. The postcard, a black-and-white reproductive photograph of the colorful painting in Paris, ought to be included in any history of visual culture in Freud's Vienna. Although the painterly qualities of the work are not entirely subdued in photographic reproduction, its photographic effect

119. Weissman 1990, 17.

is such that the viewer sees “through” the image to the actual event, as though looking at a photograph of Dr. Chicotot at work.

Photography, with its almost infinitely reproducible “licked surface” or seemingly transparent surface, is the flattest and most transparent of all mediums in the creation of documentary evidence. In the case of this card, reproductive photography imitates documentary photography, to the effect that we are “seeing through” the photograph to the actual medical scene. According to Kelley Wilder, in her book of 2009 about photography and science, “the sheer transparency of photography as a physical object is what is crucial to creating photographic records.”[120] She goes on to claim that transparency “could be called one of the iconographic traits of the photographic record.” Wilder calls this a “photographic disappearing act,” with the help of neutral grounds, measurement indications, create specimen photographs. By isolating the object of the photograph, the observers are encouraged to think they are looking directly at the object, rather than at a photograph of the object. Thus the modest 4” x 6” monochromatic image, made by the technology of industrial photographic reproduction, was actually disguised as a scientific photograph in its physical presence and its visual effect when it arrived (as one of many multiples) in Vienna in 1908.

120. Wilder 2009, 88.

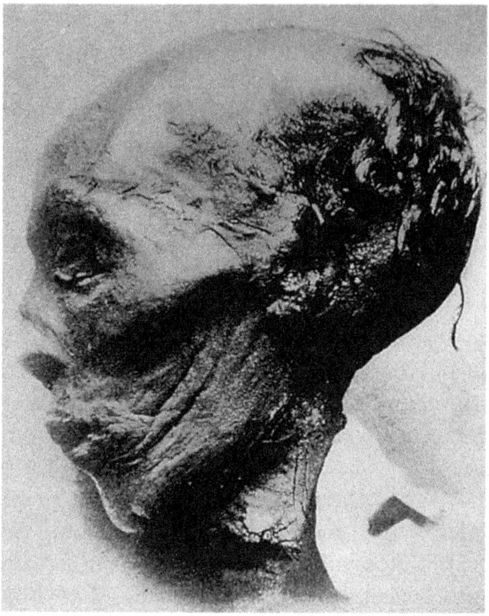

Fig. 32 Anonymous, *Mummified Head of Thutmosis II. Found at Deir el-Bahri Cache,* unwrapped by Gaston Maspero July 1, 1886. Egyptian Museum, Cairo. Image in the public domain.

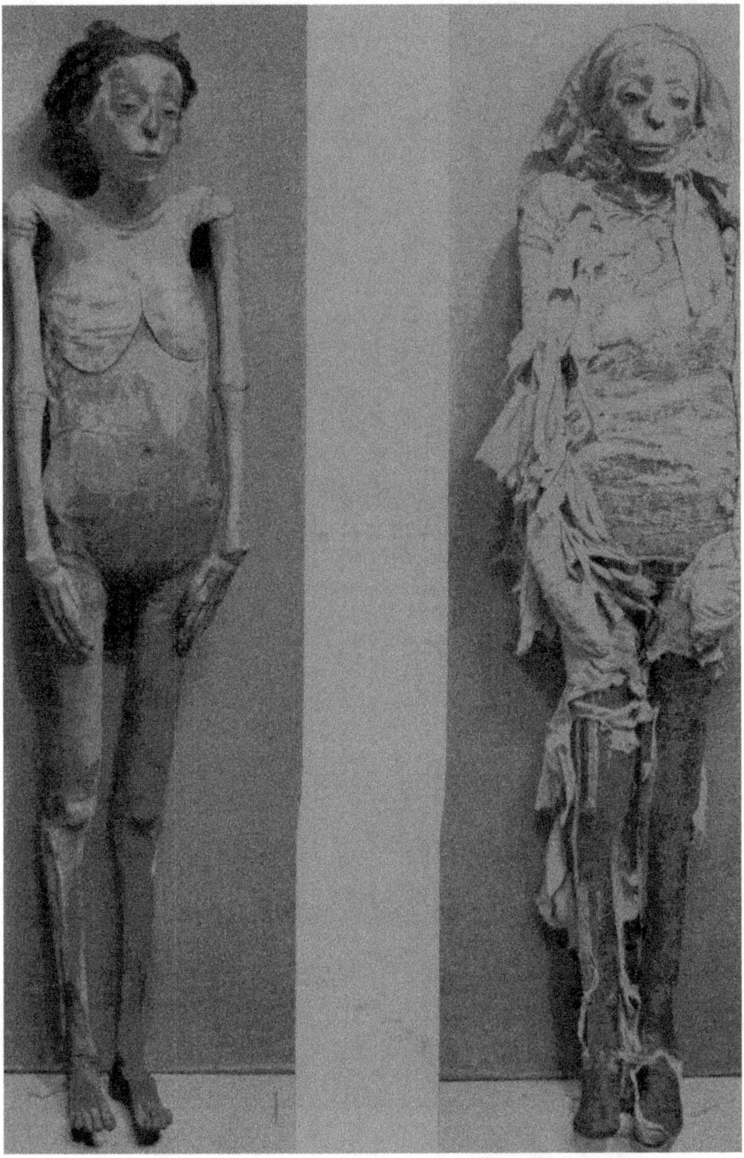

Fig. 33 Emil Brugsch, *Nessi-ta-neb-asher (born ca. 1008 BCE) discovered at Deir-el-Bahri,* now in the Cairo Museum. Image from the author's private collection.

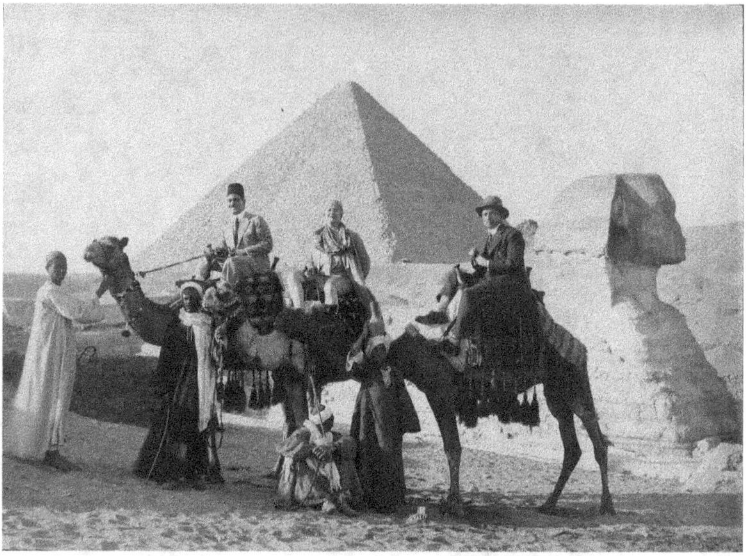

Fig. 34 Anonymous photographer, *Guido Holzknecht, his Wife, and Guides on camels before the Great Sphinx and the Pyramid of Giza*, 1928. Image used with permission from the Josephinum–Ethics, Collections and History of Medicine, MedUni Vienna.

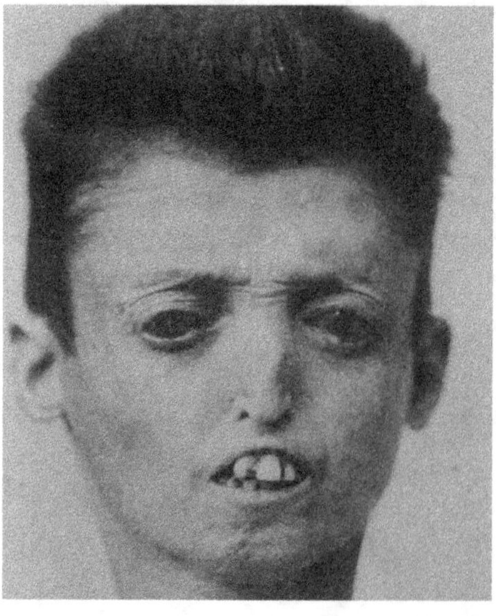

Fig. 35 Dr. Grasset, *Homme Momie Sclérodermie généralisée congénitale*, 1896, p. 258, Nouvelle Iconographie de la Salpêtrière (1896), 257–64, plates XXVIII, XXVIX, XXIX, XL, XLI: original negative by L. Biermann, photographic print by Berthaud. Paris, Masson. Photo by author.

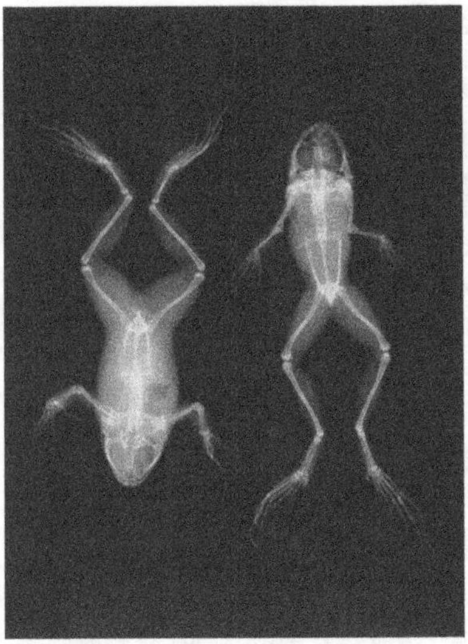

Fig. 36 Eder and Valenta, X-ray photograph (negative), *Frosche in Bauch und Ruckenlage. Versuche mit Röntgen-strahlen. Versuche über Photographie mittelst der Röntgen'schen Strahlung*. With permission of the K. K. Ministerums für Cultus und Unterricht von der K. K. Lehr-und-Versuchs Anstalt für Photographie und Reproductionsverfahren in Wien (Vienna: R. Luchner [W. Müller] 1896).

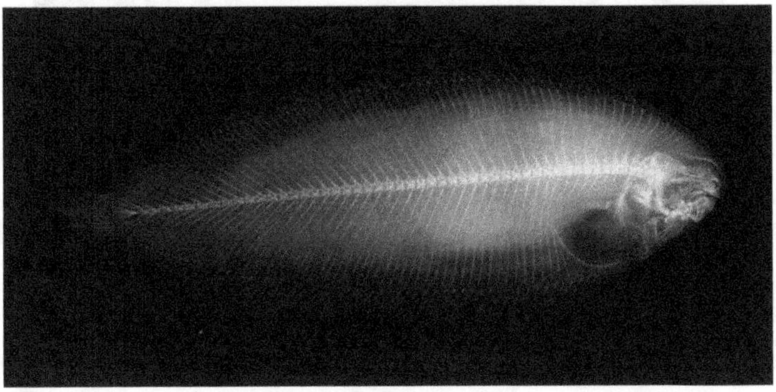

Fig. 37 Eder and Valenta, X-ray photograph (negative), *Solfisch. Versuche mit Röntgen-strahlen. Versuche über Photographie mittelst der Röntgen'schen Strahlung*. With permission of the K. K. Ministerums für Cultus und Unterricht von der K. K. Lehr-und-Versuchs Anstalt für Photographie und Reproductionsverfahren in Wien (Vienna: R. Luchner [W. Müller] 1896).

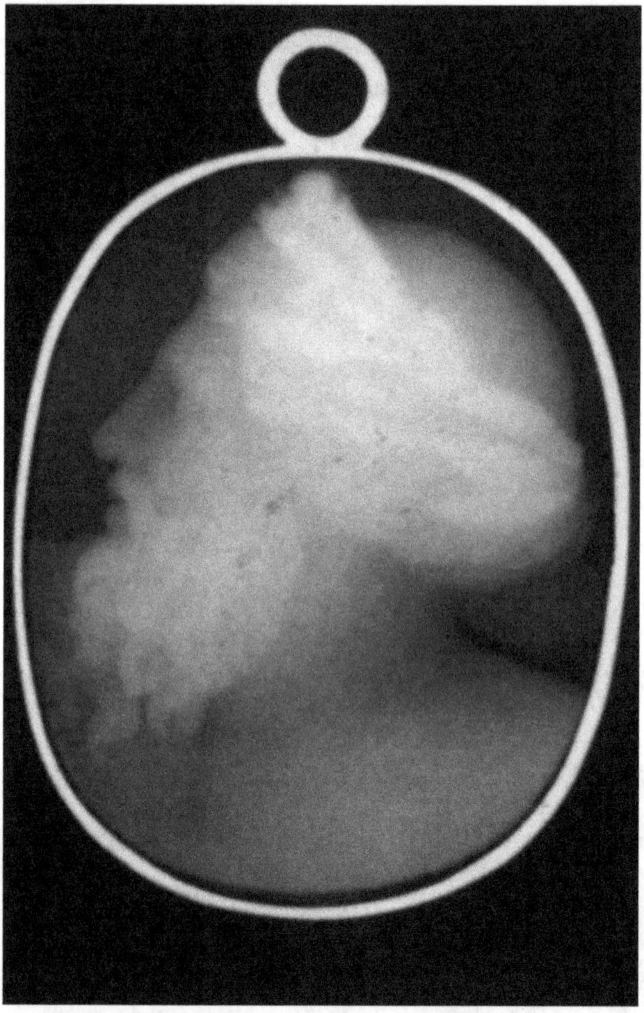

Fig. 38 Eder and Valenta, X-ray photograph (negative), *Cameen in Goldfassung. Cameos in Gold Settings*. Albertina, Vienna. Author's private collection. Image in the public domain.

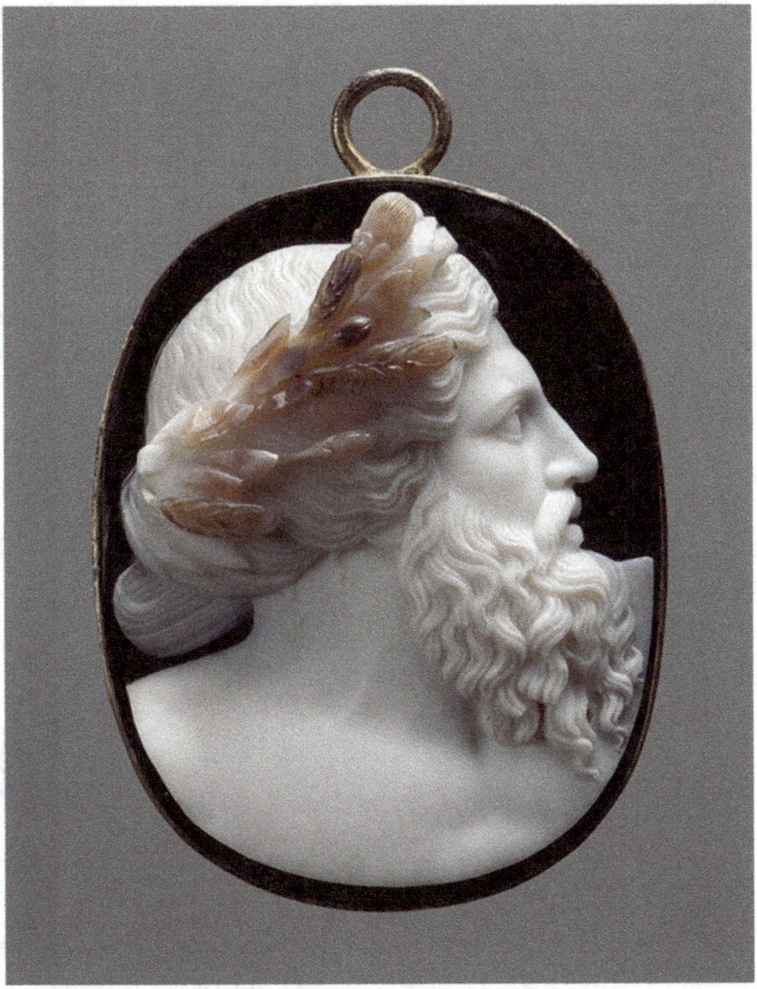

Fig. 39 Anonymous photographer, Benedetto Pistrucci, *The River God Nile*, cameo with intaglio carving, ca. 1800. Cameo – Nile River God. Benedetto Pistrucci: Kameo: Flussgott Nil (ANSA XII 51). Image used with permission from the Kunsthistorisches Museum, Vienna.

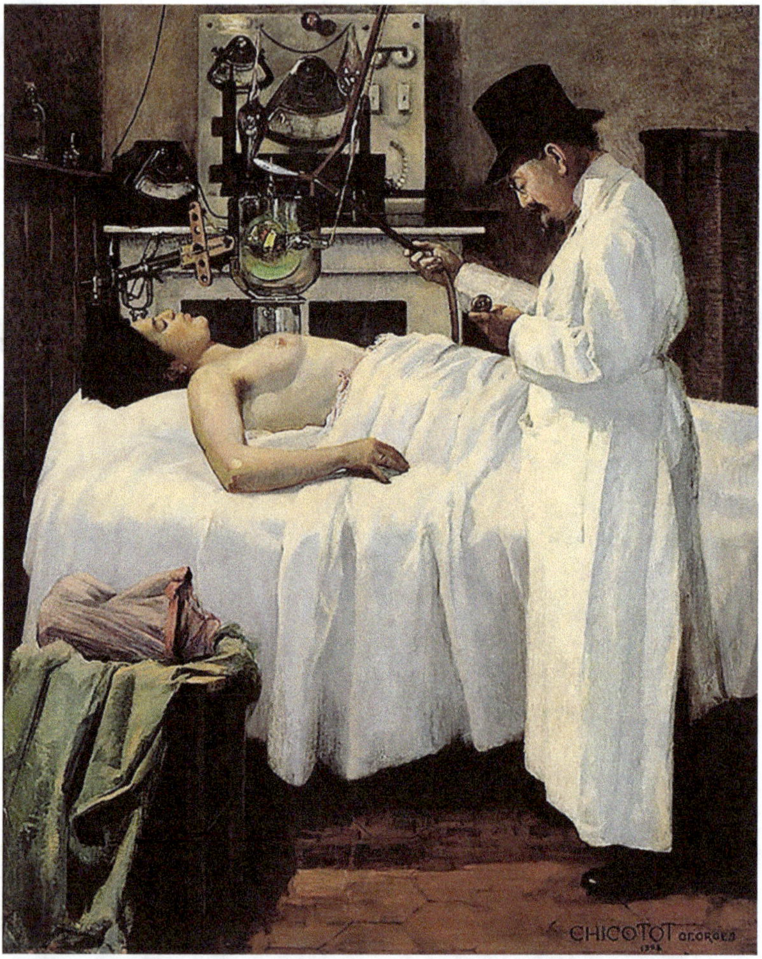

Fig. 40 Georges Chicotot, *The First Trial of X-ray Therapy for Cancer of the Breast*, oil painting, 1907. Musée de l'Assistance Publique, Hotel de Miramion, Paris. Image in the public domain. Courtesy of Wikimedia Commons.

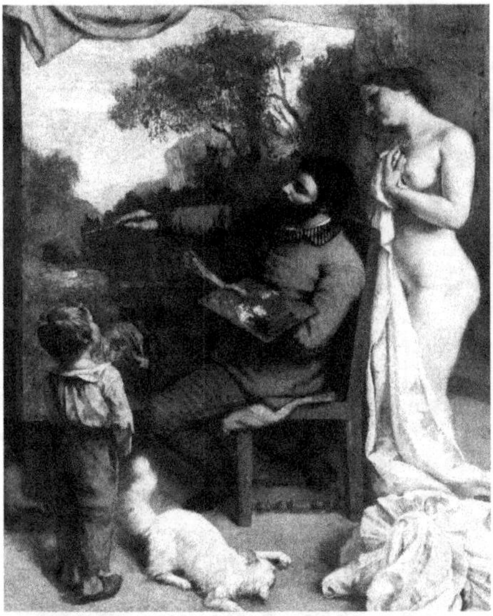

Fig. 41 Gustave Courbet, *The Artist's Studio, a real allegory summing up seven years of my artistic and moral life between 1854 and 1855*, oil painting, 1854/55. Detail of model with discarded clothing. Musée d'Orsay, Paris. Image in the public domain. Courtesy of Wikimedia Commons.

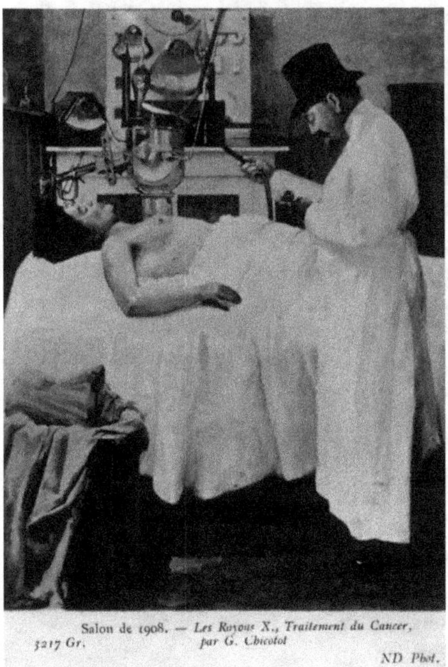

Fig. 42 Neurdein Frères, *Salon de 1908. Les Rayons X., Traitement du Cancer per G. Chicotot. 3217 Gr.* Author's private collection.

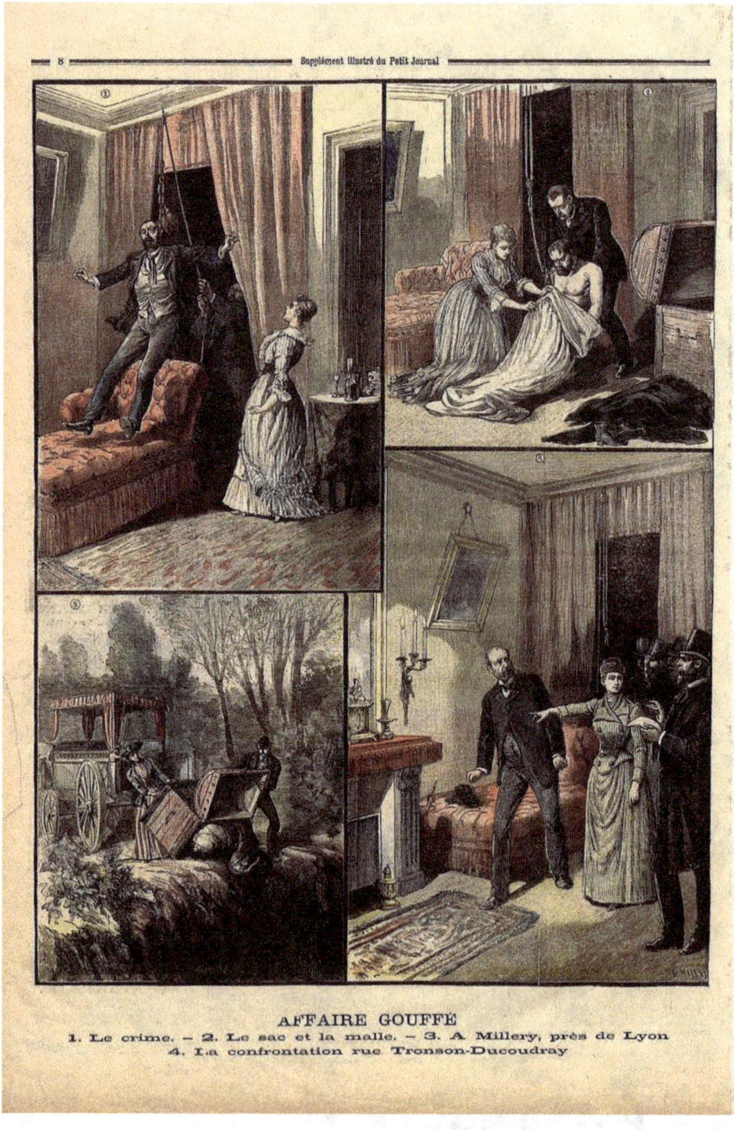

Fig. 43 Ernest Clair-Guyot, *Episodes of the Gouffé Affair. Le Petit Parisien*, June 15, 1890. Image in the public domain.

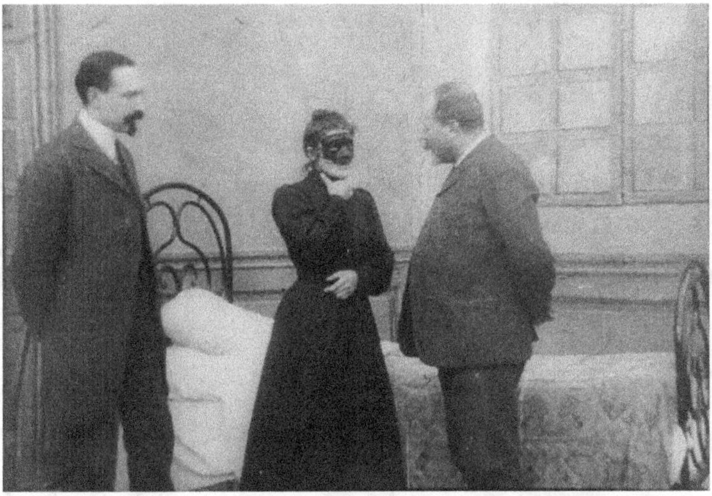

Fig. 44 Camillo Negro, *A Hysterical Crisis,* film still from *Neuropatologia,* directed by Camillo Negro and Roberto Omegna 1908. Cottolengo Hospital, Turin. Image in the public domain.

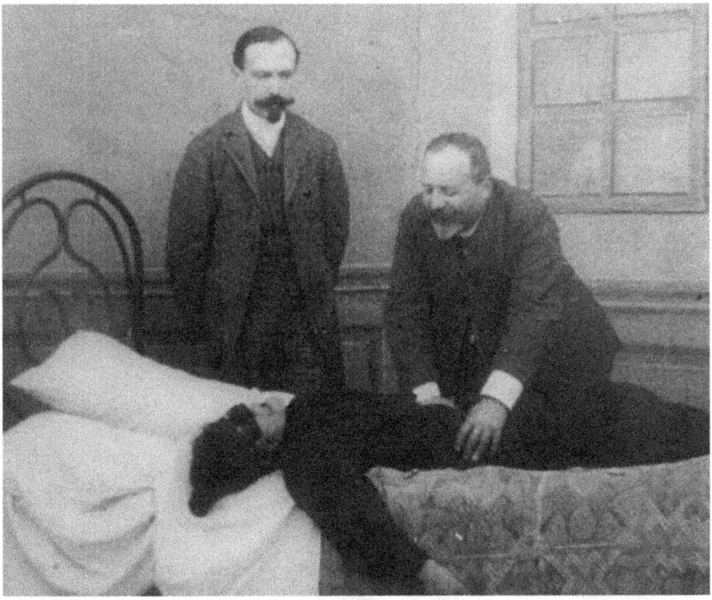

Fig. 45 Camillo Negro, *A Hysterical Crisis*, film still with Dr. Negro demonstrating the manipulation of a woman's uterus to his assistant, Giuseppe Roasenda. *Neuropatologia*, 1908. Cottolengo Hospital, Turin. Image in the public domain.

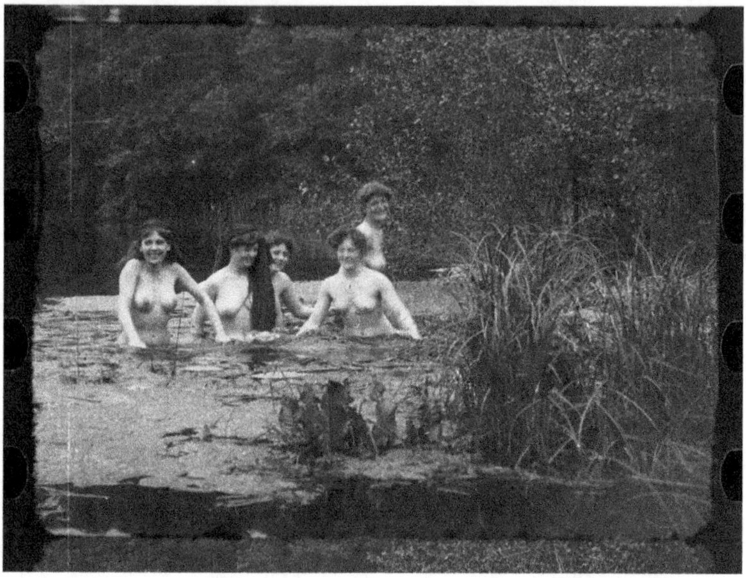

Fig. 46 Johan Schwarzer, film still from *Sklavenraub/Abduction of Slaves,* 1907, produced by Saturn Films.

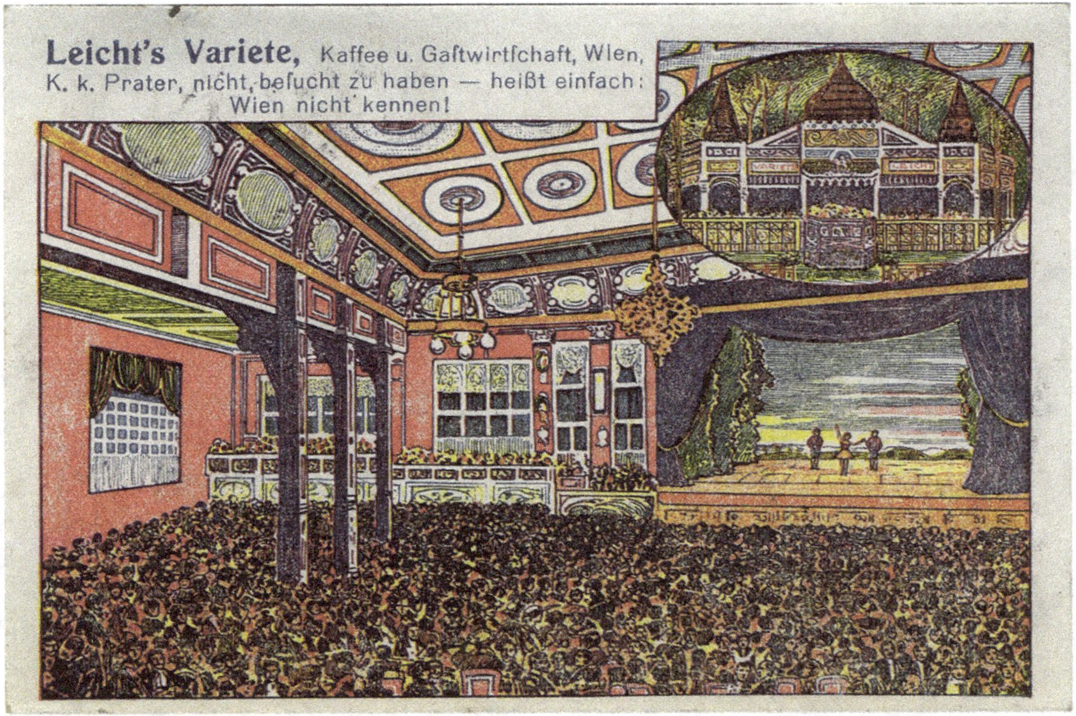

Fig. 47 *Leicht's Variete* (Prater Cafe), illustrated postcard, Vienna. Author's private collection.

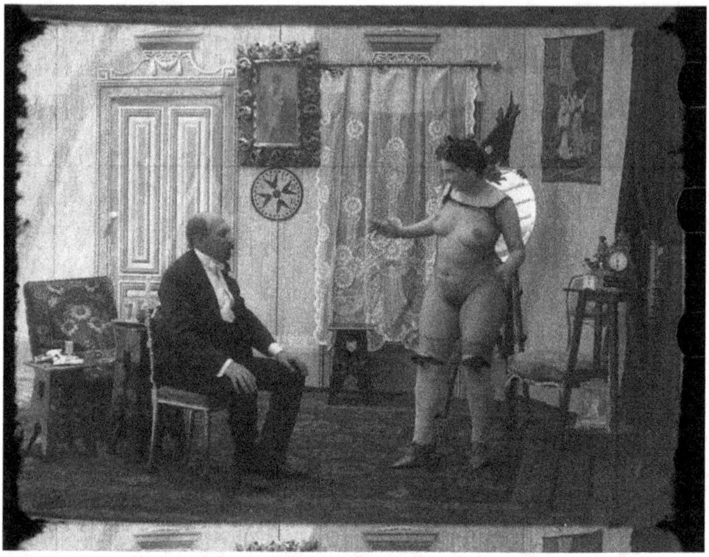

Fig. 48 Johann Schwarzer, film still from *Die Macht der Hypnose/The Power of Hypnosis,* 1908, produced by Saturn Films.

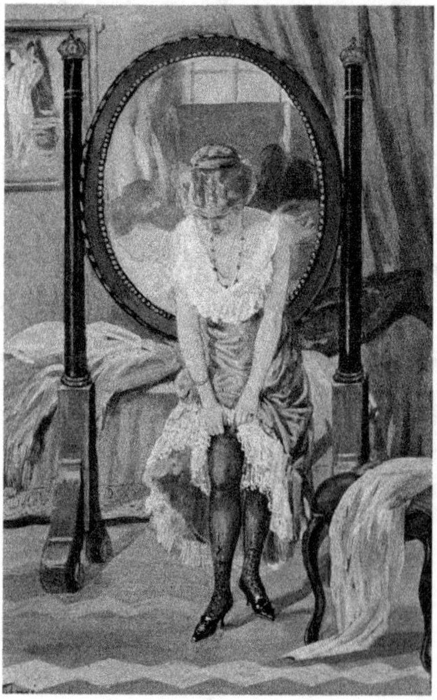

Fig. 49 Illustrator, "Emi." *Das Strumpfband,* postcard.

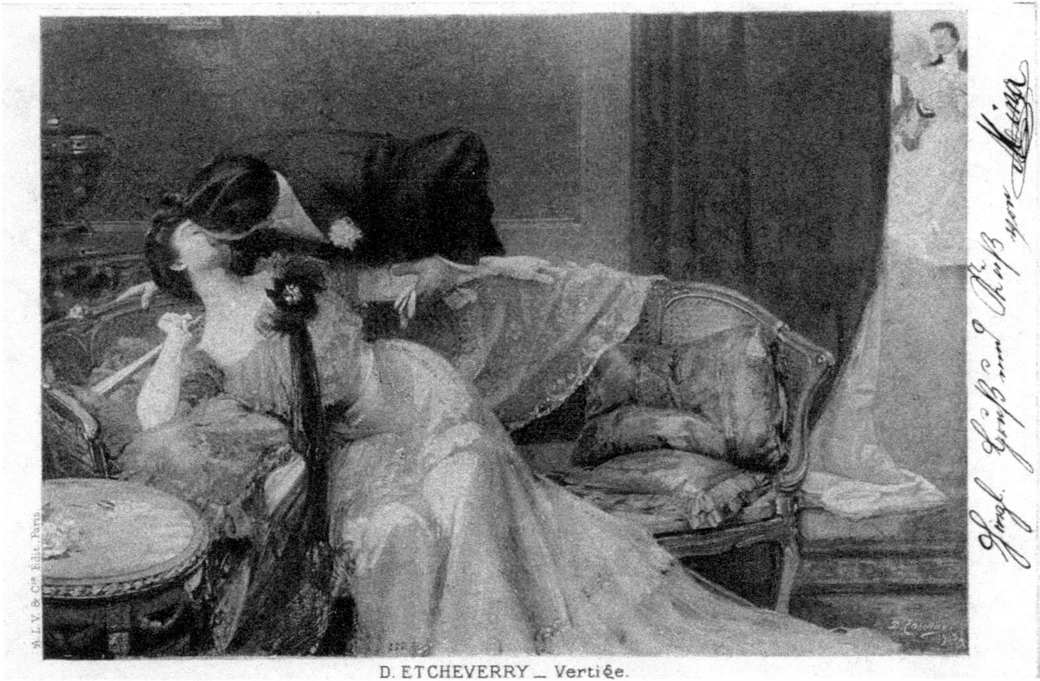

Fig. 50 Hubert-Denis Etcheverry, *Vertige*, 1903. Musée Carnavalet. Photographic reproduction, postcard format, A. L. V. et cie Éditions. Paris, Viennese provenance. Author's private archive.

Chapter 2

FREUD, SATURN, AND THE POWER OF HYPNOSIS

> There is nothing more uncanny than seeing one's face accidentally in a mirror by moonlight.
>
> Heinrich Heine

Interpretation of Dreams

Psychosexual development and adult libido were among the major themes of Sigmund Freud's work. Therefore it is pertinent to interrogate the erotic imagination of Freud's time and place in terms of visual culture. Freud's notion that we dream in visual images, and that these images are never really forgotten, is an important assumption for the visual history of modernism, modernity, and that which followed.[1] In what we might call the "photo-chemistry" of psychoanalysis, images as agents of memory or desire would never simply expire, fade, or disappear, even if they were consciously suppressed or repressed by a dynamic unconscious mind. Fugitive as such fragmented images may be, they may reconfigure and resurface in manifest or latent content of memories (including screen memories), reveries, conscious or unconscious fantasies, and dreams.[2]

As Freud maintained, and subsequent theorists have emphasized, the unconscious realm is a fertile storage place for representation. Visual representations, of course, include signs and symbols, as well as mimetic figuration. When retrieved or reconfigured by way of psychoanalysis, previously unconscious visual content may rise to the surface to engender deep feeling. When such feelings are expressed

1. Freud 1901, 47.
2. Freud 1899, 301–22.

consciously, the individual will experience a curative relief. As light impressions, photographs and cinema closely mimic, at least in a metaphoric sense, the mental phenomena of memories and dreams. As I already mentioned, the carpentry (facture) of photography and film were more or less transparent, as though we were gazing through an invisible skin (or clear filmy substance), or a transparent window, to a primary referent object or scene. Both photography and cinema were considered "truthful," if eerily deadpan, mediums of documentation, therefore their content could operate in the minds of beholders without conscious critique, like unconscious or preconscious material.[3]

In *Mirrors of Memory: Freud, Photography, and the History of Art* (2010) I explored the way photographs and cinema often resemble specters, figments, illusions, or dream images. Such is the territory of "mental images," which have no tactile or material form, and have little real resemblance to photographs. It is, for example, possible to make a photograph of a mirage, which is an optical illusion, and to remember and describe such a photographic image. But projecting or fixing a "mental image" or a "figment" is more or less impossible, all the more so because the screen itself remains imaginary and immaterial, as it were theoretical. Dream images in memory may be the ultimate phantasmagoric *dispositifs*.

Freud's *Interpretation of Dreams* (1900) uses abundant photographic and optical metaphors—microscopes, telescopes, photographic cameras, the refraction of light through lenses, and the latent and manifest states of photographic images (negatives and positives)—to explain dream representations.[4] In Freud's memoirs, his first recorded "Rome dream," a view of the emperor Hadrian's bridge (Ponte Sant'Angelo) is observed from the framed window of a moving train. A concatenation of such views observed from a train slipping slowly out of the station unfolds (at least in the narrative telling) as if it were cinema. Photos and films around the turn of the twentieth century were understood as a kind of living material excerpted from the flow of reality. This visual material is fragmented from (and yet uncannily self-similar to) the comprehensive continuum of time and space, and therefore subject to infinite dynamism and elasticity.

When gazing at an absent-minded individual who is staring into space, mindfulness may well ebb to a distance, and a mildly hypnoid

3. Bergstein 2010, 8–9.

4. Bergstein 2010, 9, 15, 18, 126–30, 146, 185, 189, 261–62, 273–74.

state replaces the stance of factual observation. If we happen to see a person watching events absently, or sorting through an assortment of lackluster advertising photographs (as in an L.L. Bean catalogue), the absent-minded state of the beholder and the state of his or her exterior beholder can provoke what is called autonomous-sensory-meridian response (ASMR) or an involuntary low-grade euphoria.[5] Likewise, certain incidental sounds, such as the crinkling of crisp paper, or the gentle scratching of manicured fingernails on a rough surface, when isolated from their surrounding context, can induce a sensation of tingling or relaxation in what feels like the subject's spine. This response of involuntary low-grade euphoria is one of pleasurable reassurance and detachment. The sense of detachment experienced in looking at photographs and films is not necessarily parallel to an autonomous-sensory-meridian response. But whether it occurs alone or in a social group, the act of glancing at photographs or film in everyday life can (*mutatis mutandis*) replicate the Freudian concept of "spectatorship" within a dream.[6]

Cinema has long been associated with Freud's notions of unconscious memory, vision, and desire. Laura Mulvey's "Visual Pleasure and Narrative Cinema" (1975) points to Freud's *Three Essays on the Theory of Sexuality* (1905) and his later *Instincts and Their Vicissitudes* (1915), where *Schaulust* (scopophilia), or looking at an objectified other, plays a central role in the dynamics of eros.[7] In 2002 the Italian author Luigi Malerba argued that every culture had its own style of dreamscape, and defined the mise-en-scène of twentieth- and twenty-first-century dreams as cinematic—a kind of metaphysical "limbo" that is fluid and without horizon, a space of remarkable mobility and subjectivity.[8] The phenomenon of hypnosis, which had its origins in theatrical spectacle, magic shows, and medical practice, found a sympathetic agent in early cinema. A hypnoid state was an induced trance, which, as in Freudian dream analysis, created flexible passageways in and out of the unconscious mind.

5. Kelles 2019.

6. Bergstein 2010, 130–35.

7. Mulvey 1975, 6–18; Freud 1905a; Freud 1915b.

8. Malerba 2002, 34, 54–55, 61, 77, 87.

Hypnosis and Its Vicissitudes

Hypnosis rendered individual subjects unconscious and insensate, and was used in the treatment of hysteria throughout Europe, where subjects were occasionally photographed and filmed. Cinema itself, of course, is a hypnotic medium, disposed to mimic hypnosis, as we know from early films such as Alice Guy-Blaché's *Chez le magnétiseur* (1897) and the Lumière brothers *Scenes from a Hypnosis* (1898). The themes that I have mentioned—hypnosis, cinema, photography, psychoanalysis, and dreams—overlay, intersect, and thicken one another in the present chapter, which returns to the role of the optical unconscious in hypnotism and hysteria in Freud's Vienna. I shall develop these issues throughout this chapter.

In an attempt to call upon the erotic imagination of Freud's cultural environment, we may consider the work of filmmaker Johann Schwarzer (1880–1914), physiologist Josef Breuer (1842–1925), and hysterical patient and social reformer Bertha Pappenheim aka Anna O. (1859–1936). We shall see that the interrelated phenomena of hysteria and hypnosis produced an erotic (at times even passionate or violent) phantasy about the doctor–patient relationship. This, and related themes including voyeurism, medical examination, and surgery, gave rise to phantasmagoria (imaginary mental images, apparitions, reveries, or their cinematic corollaries) that operated in the visual territory of Freud's time and place.

Let us commence not in Vienna but rather in Paris. The Gouffé Affair (*L'Affaire Gouffé*) was the sensational story of a young woman, Gabrielle Bompard (1868–1920), who committed murder involuntarily while supposedly in a hypnotic trance induced by her devious lover, Michel Eyraud. Bompard claimed that it was under hypnotic suggestion that she lured the wealthy victim, Toussaint-Augustin Gouffé, to her home and seduced him, placing the sash from her peignoir around his neck, so that her hypnotist-accomplice could, by the mere tug on a hidden cord, have her strangle him. Who was responsible for the murder of Gouffé? Bompard's defense was that because she suffered from fits of fainting and hysterical crises, she was especially vulnerable to suggestion, and had virtually no power over her actions when in a sedated-hypnoid (and therefore nonconscious) state.

This complicated, gruesome news story, with its forensic and psychological twists and turns, set forth an effluvium of images, texts, and arguments as to whether a person under a hypnotic trance was responsible for his or her actions. Tried in 1889, the case loomed large at the turn of the twentieth century among medical doctors and the general public. Ernest Clair-Guyot's (1856–1938) illustrations of various episodes of the Gouffé Affair (**fig. 43**) were published, for example, in *Le Petit Parisien* of June 15, 1890.[9]

These illustrations testify to the visual preparedness of the reading public to imagine scenes from the Gouffé Affair. The Gouffé case was representative of an expanded set of phantasies that prevailed in Freud's Vienna and throughout Europe. Such phantasies, rich with the thrilling possibilities of mind reading, telepathy, criminality, and the uncanny, took visual form in live performance, photography, cinema, and in the reveries of the human imagination. All of these salient forms of visual culture were to some extent saturated with the interlocking mysteries of hysteria and hypnotism around 1900.

Hypnosis was always a sex- and gender-laden practice. The idea of criminal hypnosis, including the seduction *of* women and fascination *by* women, was a matter of debate in the medical communities of Paris and Vienna around the turn of the twentieth century. In Europe physicians and psychiatrists diagnosed certain hysterical women as seductive "coquettes," and their receptivity to suggestion was likewise emphasized as a constitutive aspect of hysteria.[10] One fear, of course, was that hysterical women could be hypnotized easily and then seized and raped when in a hypnoid state; but the inverse situation, that men could be entranced by seductive, manipulative women, was also at issue.[11]

Scientific medical culture had long acknowledged the criminal-erotic dangers of the hypnotism of hysterical subjects. Medical doctors routinely hypnotized psychiatric patients, particularly women. Among the most prominent hypnotists were Freud's teachers, such as Hippolyte Bernheim (1840–1919), Georges Gilles de la Tourette (1857–1904), and Jean-Martin Charcot (1825–93). Charcot's photographic team at the Salpêtrière Hospital, headed by Albert Londe (1858–1917), photographed hysterical women rendered unconscious by hypnosis in the 1880s, around the time of Freud's residency in Paris (1885–86). Men at the Salpêtrière hypnotized more or less wretched (sick, impoverished, disenfranchised) young women, as we see in a number of arresting visual representations, and these images were published

9. Levingston 2014.

10. Weygandt 1902, see case no. 26 and *passim* for "flirtatious hysteria."

11. Bogousslavsky, Walusinski, and Veyrunes 2009, 196–99.

abundantly in the *Iconographie photographique de la Salpêtrière* of 1878, a copy of which Freud owned, and the bimonthly journal, *Nouvelle Iconographie de la Salpêtrière*, which was published from 1888 to 1918. As performative as those hysterical episodes may have been—and even in their own time the hysterics at the Salpêtrière were considered "actresses" on par with Sarah Bernhardt (1844–1923)—their now-famous representation in photography was originally dressed up in the guise of scientific documentation.[12] In 1982 Georges Didi-Huberman opened the eyes of late twentieth-century historians of visual culture with his important study, *The Invention of Hysteria*, about the Salpêtrière photographs and the context of their making, bringing medical and psychiatric photography to the forefront of feminist and visual studies.[13] Various photographs by Paul Regnard (1850–1927) and by the socialist neurologist-psychiatrist Désiré-Magloire Bourneville (1840–1909) are now familiar because of Didi-Huberman's attention to them (**see figs. 3 and 4**) and the tendentious reception and replaying of Didi-Huberman's work.

The Salpêtrière photographs speak to us now, not only from the point of view of observant physician-photographers, but also from the minds and bodies of the represented subjects, who are photographed while in (at least ostensibly) absent, nonconscious states. In this way they echo the purpose of the pictures made by Eder and Lenhard at the Kierling-Gugging clinic in Vienna. Freud himself owned a run of the *Iconographie photographique* and issues of the *Nouvelle Iconographie*, which are presently conserved in the August C. Long Health Sciences Library at Columbia University.

Apropos this well-known body of images, we are reminded of Freud's review of August Forel's *Hypnotism* of 1889, and his own writings on the subject from 1891 and 1893.[14] In those years, Freud himself invited a gendered reading of the technique. He stated that hypnosis worked best when conducted *tête-à-tête*, in a darkened room, with the subject's clothing loosened. And he stressed that women were more easily hypnotized by light and ocular fixation than men.[15] Freud theorized

12. Luxenberg 2001, 101–12.

13. Didi-Hubermann 1982.

14. Freud 1893; Freud 1889; Freud 1891.

15. For an in-depth analysis of the transition from hypnosis to psychoanalysis see Mayer 2013.

and practiced hypnosis to a limited extent. But he was always wary of its potential abuses. Much of Freud's speculative work was beset, of course, by historical problems. One such problem for Freud was the eighteenth-century Viennese physician Franz Anton Mesmer (1734–1815), who with his theory of animal magnetism was received by Viennese society as a would-be magician and miraculous healer. Even Mozart spoofed Mesmer's techniques in the character of Despina in the final act of *Così fan Tutte* (1790), where, disguised as a male doctor, she revives sick people by means of animal magnetism, a practice sometimes referred to as "Oriental hypnosis." Mozart and Mesmer crossed paths on occasion, and Mozart and Lorenzo da Ponte (who wrote the libretto of *Così fan Tutte*) were familiar enough with mesmerism to incorporate the phenomenon into opera.[16] Mesmer's dubious activities and association with illusionism left a long trajectory of doubt about the validity of medical hypnotism in Vienna.

Freud must also have been cautioned by images of the fictional Jewish hypnotist Svengali from the popular novel *Trilby* (1894) by George du Maurier, which was also the subject of silent films made in Vienna by Jacob Fleck (1881–1953): *Trilby* (1912) and *Svengali* (1914), under the label of "Wiener Kunstfilmen," as well as several other early *Trilby* films throughout Europe and America. But most importantly, the philosophical concept of illusionism, as opposed to free will, troubled the accepted precepts of religion (Roman Catholic), science, and ethics as they were practiced in turn-of-the-century Austria.[17] In any case, it is well known that Freud rejected the technique of hypnosis in his own psychoanalytic practice in favor of inducing a relaxed, or suspended, state of consciousness in the patient. This condition resembles the involuntary low-grade euphoria that characterized an autonomous-sensory-meridian response (ASMR). Such a relaxation of consciousness was eventually used for Freud's process of "free association" in which recumbent patients spoke about whatever came to mind without losing the dignity of their volition.[18]

The interfacing phenomena of hysteria and hypnosis were spectacles verging on the supernatural that produced a voyeuristic frisson in their

16. Franklin 2004.

17. Perhaps scientific studies in the future will necessitate that people revise those prevailing codes.

18. Mayer 2013, 158–59.

spectators. In *Medical Muses* (2011) Asti Hustvedt explored the way in which the hypnotized hysteric was represented in carnival acts, where nonmedical stage hypnotists reproduced Charcot's demonstrations at the Salpêtrière on the fairgrounds of Europe, for the delectation of the thrill-seeking public.[19] These presentations belonged to the tradition of stage magic acts and illusionism, but here the hysterical subjects (who were supposedly highly suggestible and prone to surrendering their own agency) had a morbid attraction all their own.

Cinema was itself an illusory, hypnotic medium, and thus particularly well suited to the production of hypnotic illusions. Early silent cinema, which was shaped around a special repertoire of themes, thrived post-Gouffé on the drama of hypnosis and its thrilling dangers. Beginning with Georges Méliès (1861–1938) in Paris, silent films were permeated with representations of hypnosis, and hypnosis was a vehicle for introducing hysteria and predatory sex in these early moving pictures. It is significant that Méliès began his career as a "magician" or illusionist, and was therefore familiar with the public's fascination with sensational stage hypnosis. As early as 1897 he produced *Chez le Magnétiseur* (*At the Hypnotist's*).[20] At the same time, films of hypnosis were closely associated with medical cinema, such as it was at the turn of the twentieth century. In one of Auguste and Louis Lumière's earliest films, *A Scene of Hypnotism*, the movements of a female subject under hypnosis bring to mind the photographs of hysterical women under hypnosis at the Salpêtrière.

Medical Cinema: Gheorghe Marinescu and Camillo Negro

The Romanian neurologist Gheorghe Marinescu (1863–1938) made some of the earliest scientific films (1898–1901) about the difficulty of walking due to organic and "hysterical" (psycho-induced) hemiplegia. Hemiplegia is a neurological condition frequently associated with epilepsy. At the end of one of Marinescu's films, men who had been hardly able to walk are seen in a posthypnotic state, skipping along like so many innocent children at play. The naïve lyricism of such medical footage seems to anticipate Henri ("Le Douanier") Rousseau's (1844–

19. Hustvedt 2011, 107–16 and *passim*.
20. Packer 2007, 57; Andriopoulos 2008.

1910) hilarious *Football Players* of 1908 (Solomon R. Guggenheim Museum, New York). Marinescu was trained by Jean-Martin Charcot in Paris and had a sustained interest in the chronophotography of Albert Londe (1858–1917) and Étienne-Jules Marey (1830–1904). Marinescu's medical films have a weird, awkward spirit about them in which representations of moving "actors" (patients) are integrated with documentary drawings to explain symptoms and procedures. In *A Case of Hysteric Hemiplegia Cured through Hypnotic Suggestion* (1899) Marinescu's hypnotic suggestion reaches deep into the unconscious causes of a female patient's psycho-induced paresis, and eradicates the symptoms. For a twenty-first-century viewer, odd, quaint, uncanny details, such as a nurse-assistant dressed in full Romanian folk costume and the whimsical wool knitted gym-suit of the patient, add to the irreal optical dreamscape of this footage.[21]

It is clear that medical films could be as uncanny as fiction or still photography. In Italy, for instance, an episode about hysteria, "A Hysterical Crisis" in *La Neuropatologia* of 1908, portrays two doctors handling and eventually subduing a highly agitated woman patient, dressed in black and wearing a black mask over half of her face, who seems to be experiencing an hystero-epileptic seizure as though her uterus had migrated toward her throat, in line with the classical notion of hysteria.

This film, by the neurologist Camillo Negro (1861–1927) and the camera operator Roberto Omegna (1876–1938), is set in what can be recognized as a ward of the Cottolengo Hospital in Turin. The footage was ostensibly intended as medical instruction, and the action is all about the physical domination of a woman patient by two male doctors, thus gendered according to the default position of medical paternalism. During the course of treatment, the patient is thrown down and pinned to a hospital bed by the physicians, her ovaries compressed by

21. Marinescu's first film was *Walking Difficulties in Organic Hemiplegia* (1898). Marinescu had his patients walk before the camera against a black background in order to analyze their movements before and after treatment. He continued this work to 1901 with his assistants C. Parhon and M. Goldstein, employing camera operator Constantin Popescu, who shot *A Case of Hysterical Hemiplegia Cured Through Hypnotic Suggestion* (1899), and *Walking Difficulties Due to Progressive Locomotary Ataxia* (1900). See Reichert 2007, 26; McKernon 2014.

a repetitive, somewhat violent, pressing and pouncing on her belly by Camillo Negro while his assistant Giuseppe Roasenda looks on (**figs. 44 and 45**). Finally, her body is arranged, immobilized, in a restful position as though she has recovered. Whether this documentary is meant to be "real" or meant to "look real" (a sort of a *fin-de-siècle* docu-drama) is not clear.[22] However, the vigorous manipulation of a woman's reproductive organs as a cure for hysteria is "proven" in this documentary feature. Whatever else "A Hysterical Crisis" may represent, it expresses the male domination of a female body in a clinical setting, bridging misogynistic phantasy with what was apparently the accepted medical status quo—namely, medical paternalism. Following Marinescu, Negro, and Méliès (1861–1938), a spate of films about hypnotism and its effects followed well into the 1920s and beyond.[23]

In refusing to countenance a silent film about psychoanalysis by Georg Wilhelm Pabst (1885–1967), *Geheimnisse einer Seele* (*Secrets of a Soul*) (1926), Freud tacitly announced his resistance to the new medium.[24] Freud was never enthusiastic about cinema as an art. Perhaps he intuited that movies, like the American popular music he so deplored, could ignite human emotions without fueling the intellect. However,

22. Reichert 2007, 25, 26.

23. See Andriopoulos 2008. In my view, the erotic and criminal undertones of hypnosis, suggestion, and hysteria have never been dissociated in the popular imagination—with Mann's *Death in Venice* providing a striking example of this conflation, and adding the associated dimension of contamination. In the mid-twentieth century, for example, Federico Fellini continued this idea in *Le notti di Cabiria* (*The Nights of Cabiria*, 1957) where a heartbreaking Giulietta Masina, as a young Roman prostitute named Cabiria, is preyed upon, seduced, exploited, robbed, and abandoned by a man who has seen her hypnotized in a cheap stage act. The unctuous seducer, who calls himself Oscar, is most certainly an accomplice of the carnival hypnotist rather than the accountant he claims to be. His trickery and violence is predicated upon Cabiria's unconscious revelations (while in a hypnotic trance) that she longed for intimacy and marriage. Cabiria's life is one of poverty and vulnerable abjection, but as we learn from her continuous good-natured will to survive (resilience is a positive aspect of the stereotypical Italian female character) she cannot be classified as hysterical.

24. Packer 2007, 43–48. Instead of Freud, Karl Abraham and Hanns Sachs ended up serving as consultants for this film.

as with Freud's famous indifference to André Breton (1896–1966) and French Surrealism, the cinema seems to have been his unwitting ally whether he liked it or not, especially in the familiar formula: dream = film = unconscious fantasy. It is now taken for granted that cinema constitutes a dream world shared by members of the society at large, with luminous images springing from the unconscious depths of human individual and societal preoccupations.

The Saturn Films

The Saturn films of Johann Schwarzer, which played in Vienna and throughout the Austro-Hungarian Empire, consist of a series of erotic phantasies in which the viewer (as dreamer or audience) is protagonist. These imaginary erotic situations served as mise-en-scènes for scopic desire and fulfillment. Schwarzer's comic narrative strategies, which frame the spectacle of female nudity, catered to a large market for erotica from 1906 to 1911. In their embodiment of obsessional visual phantasies, the Saturn films demonstrate the everyday reveries of the Viennese bourgeoisie, and as such they may be said to "prove" Freud's theoretical work by way of popular culture. In other words, I propose that Freud's ideas on statues come-to-life (Gradiva), hypnotism, transference and counter transference, and scopophilia were all "hiding in plain sight" in the visual culture of Viennese erotic comedy.

Johann Schwarzer (1859–1914) was from Javornik in Moravia (the same part of the world as Freud's hometown of Pribor) and he immigrated to Vienna around 1900. As a photographer-chemist in Vienna his studio seems to have produced the usual fare: portraits, genre scenes, local types, and nudes. Erotica was produced in printed format as well as glass lantern slides. Schwarzer's cinematically precocious Saturn films were among the first moving pictures to be produced in all of Europe, and among the first to be banned, officially suppressed in 1911.[25] But the Saturn season was in any case short: Schwarzer was conscripted into the Austro-Hungarian army and killed on the Eastern Front in 1914, an early casualty of the First World War.

On the surface, Saturn erotica typically stayed within the limits of a few predictable themes, and the images on screen are almost laughably

25. Achenbach and Caneppele 1999, 135.

manifest: women undressing to bathe, nude women dueling or playing croquet, wives betraying husbands, doctors examining patients, and statues come-to-life. These saucy little phantasies belong to the realm of popular culture rather than that of erotica or pornography per se. Although the Saturn films have little or no psychological depth, they resonate visually with certain themes that occur in the early years of psychoanalysis. Such a mental overlay, as in an overlay of photographic transparencies, is not contrived; when we view them in a social cross-section, we see that certain themes were taken for granted in the society that produced them.

Saturn images play in the preconscious mind just as cinema can speak to the fears or desires that haunt any particular culture. It is always pertinent to remember that visual representation (including in the human imagination) and its most effortless understanding occur within the same workshop.[26] This is true in terms of cinema as well as photography, painting, and architecture. In theoretical terms, however, psychoanalysis and visual culture can never "mirror" or explain one another. Nor should one closed system be marshaled to interpret another in a modernist plot, be it art-historical or psychoanalytic. Perhaps the best approach with Saturn erotica is to let these early films and the beginnings of psychoanalysis resonate together in (a fruitfully imprecise) historical perspective.

The voyeuristic embarrassment of female flesh took on a novel dimension in the Saturn films because the medium was able to represent *zaftig* bodies in motion. Some of the movies are filmed outdoors, where "chase" scenes of nude women running away from predatory men show flesh in action as well as natural breezes animating the water and trees.[27] Notwithstanding the novelty of the film medium, a naked woman in nature, *as* nature, is one of the oldest ideas in Western culture, beginning with the biblical Eve and continued in high art by French painters like Jean-Baptiste-Camille Corot (1796–1875), Gustave Courbet (1819–77), and Édouard Manet (1832–83), among others. The Saturn films adhere to essentially conservative themes, such as the romanticization of woman-as-nature, or the idea that women are to nature as men are to culture.[28]

26. Geertz 1976, 1497.

27. Goldstein 2009, 253.

28. See the now-classic essay by Ortner 1974.

For instance, a group of nude women in *Sklavenraub* (*Women Abducted as Slaves*) appear perfectly happy cavorting in the water of a pond; in spite of their fictional status as captives, they act playful and "free" when released into nature (**fig. 46**). The movements of water and flesh are visually absorbing, and Saturn films were truly "photographs come-to-life," complete with moving flesh and captivating ripples of reflective water. In terms of vision, desire, and verisimilitude, Laura Mulvey's "male gaze" is at liberty to consume the buoyant scene from the detached viewpoint of men sitting in the darkened theater.[29]

In a comedic manner, each Saturn fantasy was predicated on fully clothed bourgeois men looking at naked women moving around in the light. This sexual asymmetry presumed an adult male audience, and film showings were known as *Herrenabende*, or "gentlemen's evenings." Sometimes they were advertised as "black evenings" (in Trieste as "*serate nere*") because men in the audience (as well as those projected on the screen) were rigorously dressed in black formal wear. In a more poetic vein, "black evenings" may also refer to the darkness from which the collective gaze emanated, attracted to the radiant moving images before it. Saturn films were screened at traveling cinemas (*Wanderkino*), cinema booths at the Prater, or in large vaudeville theaters. An illustrated postcard advertising Leicht's Varieté at the Prater ("If you haven't visited Leicht's you haven't really seen Vienna!") shows a supper-club theater crammed with crowds of people, suggesting large audiences for novelty acts and films (**fig. 47**).

The Saturn films are good examples of what Laura Mulvey referred to in her signal essay, "Visual Pleasure and Narrative Cinema," as "fetishistic scopophilia." Here in the Saturn films the viewer (as dreamer or audience) gazes from the darkened auditorium even as he identifies with the scopophilic protagonist on screen. Within the Saturn repertory this formula can be played with—momentarily reversed or denied—to create a comic situation, as in *The Power of Hypnosis* (*Die Macht der Hypnose*) (**fig. 48**) from 1908 and *Living Statues* (*Lebender Marmor*) of 1908–10.[30] These movies were predicated on the spectacle of fully clothed men looking at nude women, with similarly clothed men in the cinema audience, and what we might currently call a "trigger warning"

29. Mulvey 1975, 6–18; Freud 1905a; Freud 1915a.

30. Bergstein 2017, 116–19.

("gentlemen only"), no women allowed.[31] Such a warning was ostensibly meant to protect female viewers from erotic material that might upset them, preventing such shocking scenes from creating or reawakening trauma. This way the visual space of virgins and wives would remain uncontaminated. But such proscriptions must have actually served Viennese society as a lure rather than a warning regarding the subject-matter of the Saturn films.

For the most part, these imaginary erotic situations represented scopic desires and their fulfillment, as in *The Abduction of Slaves* (1907) where we come upon some naked women (so-called white slaves in transit) happily bathing in a pond (**fig. 47**). The scene is nothing we don't know from the *plein-air* nudes of French painters like Jean-Baptiste-Camile Corot (1796–1875) or Gustave Courbet (1819–77). Here, however, the medium of cinema itself appeals to the tactile imagination: "capturing" the *movement* of air, water, and bouncy living flesh.[32]

Themes of sculpture come-to-life, and nude women posing as if they were statues, are present in several of the Saturn films. Cinema itself was sometimes known as "moving photographs" or "photography come to life," thereby compounding the analogy of static bodies or images suddenly animated and made palpable in the (sensory) imagination.

Throughout the twentieth century, some movies, especially Hollywood film productions, have constituted a dream world inhabited by society at large, with luminous images springing from the unconscious depths of human desire, projecting societal as well as individual preoccupations on the screen. Beginning with the French Surrealist cinema, many remarkable Hollywood films (such as *The Wizard of Oz* of 1939) are devoted to the topic of dreams and the magical adventures of the unconscious mind. In their embodiment of obsessional visual phantasies, the Saturn films demonstrated the everyday reveries of the Viennese bourgeoisie, and as such they served as an obbligato of popular context for Freud's theoretical work. Indeed, many of Freud's ideas on Jensen's *Gradiva* and other studies were present for all to see in erotic films and pseudo scientific books.

Let us turn to a pertinent Saturn film with an archaeological premise, namely *Lebender Marmor* (*Living Marbles*) of 1908–10. We have already seen that such films use Greco-Roman statuary as surrogate bodies,

31. Gerson 2021.

32. Goldstein 2009, 253.

which sanction the living nude. Schwarzer's cinematic vignettes all have a *locus classicus* and an archaeological plot, but their true realm is that of the Freudian uncanny by way of Pygmalionism in representation.[33] During the time *Living Marbles* was made, a case history of "multiform perversion" was presented by Isidor Sadger in Freud's home the evening of November 3, 1909. Sadger's case of a 32-year-old Swedish archaeologist, who came from a "degenerate" aristocratic family with "hereditary taint," suffered, among other issues, from "an infatuation for statues."[34] His obsession with marbles was not an innocent hobby, but rather a sexual aberration, which was listed among other perversions including exhibitionism, sadomasochistic desires, and narcissism, in a deadpan manner. There is no mention as to whether his uncle, also an archaeologist, who had behaved like a mother to the patient in childhood, was also attracted to statuary as a fetish. In his commentary on Freud's *Delusions and Dreams,* the great Italian divulgator of psychoanalysis Cesare Musatti (1897–1989), coined the term *litofilia,* or lithophilia, for the human sexual attraction to marble sculpture.[35] Musatti's nomenclature carries a positive, mythopoetic resonance in cultural history, and Musatti, as a Venetian Jew who wrote about Freud, brought a sweet cosmopolitanism to all of his writings on psychoanalysis.

In the Saturn film titled *Living Marbles* (1910) four men converse at an outdoor tavern, admiring the waitress. Three of them hire the waitress to pose nude, coated with talc or plaster dust, as a statue of Phryne, for whom nudity was a costume of truth and honor. They set her up as a statue on a pedestal and send in their fourth friend, a dupe we can refer to as "the beholder," to observe the figure. At first, the gazing beholder-protagonist seems to keep to the aesthetic-academic ideal, comparing the statue itself to what is in his portfolio, presumably photographs of classical or contemporary sculpture. The contents of this portfolio remain hidden to the viewer throughout this film. In cinematic diegesis it may be presumed to contain either erotic photographs of girls and women or photographic reproductions of Greco-Roman art, but this is never to be known by the film viewer.

33. These films also play upon the then-expiring tradition of *tableaux vivant* in European culture, see Adriaensens and Jacobs 2015, 6.

34. Nunberg and Federn 1967, 307.

35. Musatti 1961, 9, 12, 230–34.

In a mood of conflicted desire, the designated dupe examines the statue from up close, even touching her. Suddenly, the statue then comes to life and jumps down in a hilarious moment of reveal, laughing with the other men. The duped "beholder" collapses under shock and stress. His phantasy has become a subject of humor not only for his men-friends but also for the desired object herself. He is traumatized and humiliated when his phantasy becomes a reality for everyone on screen, as well as the wider audience, peering forward out of the darkness, to observe.

Although the Saturn films have little or no psychological depth, they resonate, especially visually, with certain themes that occurred in the early years of psychoanalysis. We may recall that for Jensen's Norbert Hanold, the charm of Gradiva is to be found in her flexed foot. A woman's feet and ankles were erotically charged in late nineteenth-century Vienna, as we see, for example, in Otto Schmidt's photograph of a "Graben-Nymphe," or Viennese prostitute of around 1880, one of a series of such specimen-style photographs of urban prostitutes (*Graben-Nymphen*) (**figs. 8, 60**).[36]

Saturn films were phantasies in which the imagining protagonist-subject was the audience itself, doubling up with, and eclipsing, at times, the films' actors.[37] In the reception of Saturn films, the male gaze was collective, focused, and perennially self-referential. Let us keep in mind, too, that the male gaze was echoed by that of female viewers, and certain of the Saturn features were billed as *Pariserabende* ("Parisian evenings") for men and women together. The conscious reactions of contemporary Viennese women to these films have not (at least not yet) surfaced in the historical record, but such films were (obviously) pertinent to their lives, as I shall explore in the discussion of Bertha Pappenheim, who was also known as Anna O. In *The Power of Hypnosis* (*Die Macht der Hypnose*), an erotic film comedy produced by the Saturn company in 1908, the act of voyeurism takes place on screen with the protagonist's gaze redoubled by that of the film spectators. This film was clearly influenced by the Lumière brothers *Scenes from a Hypnosis* (1898) and Alice Guy-Blaché's *Chez le magnétiseur* (1897). With the stilted furniture and lace curtains of a typical Biedermeier interior, Schwarzer's *Power of Hypnosis* is a good place to continue thinking about the vicissitudes of scopophilia. A middle-aged bourgeois visits a

36. Zweig 1964, 74. Conserved in the Vienna Museum, no. 72.601/1.
37. For "phantasy" see Laplanche and Pontalis 1973, 314.

woman (presumably his mistress) in her sitting room, wanting to make love to her. She proceeds to hypnotize her lover, and then undresses to a transparent black-trimmed net gown. Her attire (including the requisite shoes and stockings) is a costume of sexual display, but the gentleman-subject in question is unable to enjoy it, or even to realize his own scopic volition (**fig. 48**). Under her enchantment he has lost his agency for looking (or seeing), which has now been turned over to the cinema audience. In an inversion of the eroticized female controlled by the male hypnotist, the female character in *The Power of Hypnosis* prevails. In the fiction of the narrative the gentleman's eyes are literally closed to his erotic object. But the woman as erotic object is still available, at least in diegetic terms, to the masses of film spectators for their triumphal delectation.

This parody of voyeurism is a trick to be enjoyed, not only by the male protagonist but also by the (presumably male) fantasizing audience, who laugh at a man who cannot perceive the carefully staged nudity that is in front of his own closed eyes, and in front of theirs. While he is under the influence of hypnosis, the woman plays humiliating tricks on him and steals his money. A young butler enters and exits the scene periodically to assist the woman with her trickery, implying that the hypnotized gentleman is also a cuckold. In an ironic moment when the subject is awakened from his trance, the lady appears dressed in a peignoir and the male "victim" takes leave of her with the customary courtly Viennese gesture of "Küss die Hand," that is, kissing her hand.

Schwarzer's *Power of Hypnosis* might be interpreted as a comment upon the extent to which an established turn-of-the-century man could be captivated by his mistress to his own detriment and be made to look ridiculous, or even ruined financially. Indeed, the only passage to actually be censored (cut) from this film relates to a comic reference to Phyllis and Aristotle, where the sexy hypnotist attempts to ride her victim like a horse, reversing the prevailing order of male dominance.

Such an act (familiar to educated viewers of the time from the Hans Baldung Grien woodcut of 1513) must have been considered deleterious to society at large in the Austro-Hungarian Empire.[38] But whereas female flesh and sexuality have a malevolent power in works by Albrecht Dürer, Albrecht Altdorfer, and Hans Baldung Grien, the comedic shocks of the war between the sexes in the Saturn films

38. Achenbach, Ballhausen, and Wostry 2009, 79, 174.

portray women as clever or "bewitching" rather than truly dangerous or evil. Women's bodies, including that of the hypnotist in *The Power of Hypnosis* are to be enjoyed, even consumed, by the eyes of the male protagonist and the group consciousness of the cinema spectators according to popular culture, not feared.

Besides serving as a code to the prevailing *Zeitgeist*, how can we relate Schwarzer's Saturn films to Freud and his patients in cultural history? Let us begin with "Anna O." of Freud's case history. The Viennese physiologist Josef Breuer (1842–1925) used hypnotism in the famous "Case of Anna O.," which for the first time (in the 1880s) established hysteria and its treatment in the German-speaking lands and initiated the "talking cure" for psycho-induced paralyses and other neurotic problems. Certain of the Saturn phantasies can be connected to the life and work of Bertha Pappenheim (1859–1936), known under the pseudonym "Anna O." Anna (Bertha) suffered from hysterical coughing, paresis, hallucinations, and language-loss in the wake of her father's slow death from a tubercular tumor, during which time she never left his bedside.

To the extent that Freud's case histories read like novellas or plays, the mise-en-scène for the case of Anna O. was a sickbed after the fashion of the nineteenth century. And the young Anna's role in this complex melodrama was to be first her father's nurse and then Dr. Breuer's patient. Both of these roles required the enactment of disappointed or frustrated loves. The ingénue is abandoned twice: first by her father's illness and death and then by her doctor's withdrawal and dramatic "return" to his wife and family.

The Pappenheim Family Home

During the course of her treatment, Breuer visited Anna O. at her home. House calls were the procedural norm in medical practice around 1900 and before Bertha fell ill Breuer visited her dying father, Siegmund Pappenheim (1824–81), twice every day. Breuer, who considered the hypnoid state a basic predilection for or symptom of hysteria, believed that a person involved in prolonged nursing at the sickbed of a loved one was subject to some of the same conditions required by hypnotic procedures. Such conditions included crepuscular lighting, the nurse and her bedridden subject's concentration on a single object, such as a ticking clock or a lamp, and a focused attention to the sound and sight of the patient's deliberate breathing.[39]

Ten days after her father's death in 1881 the Pappenheim family called in a well-known psychiatrist for a home consultation with Bertha. This doctor was none other than Richard von Krafft-Ebing (1840–1902), who was a noted expert on sexual disturbances.[40] Krafft-Ebing had written about *melancholia* and criminal psychosis in the years before his famous *summa*, *Psychopathia Sexualis* of 1886. Might Anna O.'s diagnosis appear embedded ("hidden") in the passages on hysteria in *Psychopathia*? There is no record of his interaction with Anna O. or his medical opinion of her case in 1881. We do know that Krafft-Ebing believed in general terms that the sexual life was very frequently abnormal and even perverse to the point of criminality in cases of female hysteria. Still, might he have diagnosed Anna O. not as hysterical at all, but rather as a case of aggravated pathological *melancholia*, or hallucinatory *melancholia*, caused by genuine grief, having lost two sisters and her father within a short period of time?[41] Anna O.'s sorrows may also have included the emotional detachment of her mother, a suffering widow who had already lost two of her children. Distinctions between conditions such as hysteria and *melancholia* were not considered clear-cut before Freud. In fact, Freud's essay on *Mourning and Melancholia* (1917) was an attempt to distinguish conditions of aggravated pathological *melancholia* from that of "normal" grief and its affects.[42] Anna O. may have slipped from a state of mourning into pathological *melancholia* complete with the refusal of nourishment and attendant self-torment.

Reflection as a Strange World

According to the anthropologist Sadeq Rahimi (2021), mirrors play a large part in the hauntology of everyday life. In my view, however, mirrors don't necessarily function as instruments to see the self, or to create a pseudo-portrait as described by Rahimi. My own research on mirrors is for the most part empirical. In practice, flat mirrors (especially

39. Laplanche and Pontalis 1973, 192–94.

40. Rosenbaum 1984, 6.

41. For a typical turn-of-the-century view of *melancholia*, see Church and Peterson 1899, 700–710.

42. Freud 1917.

those again reflecting one or more other mirrors) rearrange space, light, and objects in such a way as to cause the familiarity of the domestic environment to appear distorted and frightening. *Unheimlich* forms are suggested and an uneasy, skeptical quality of feeling. Such views, be they momentary or longer lasting, play with the viewing subject's ocular perception, and cause frightening disorientations, which alienate the subject from the realm of the *Heimlich*. Mirrors, then, create eerie, uncanny spaces, which replace the knowable terrain that the mirror is expected to reflect.

Mirrors make present a strange, alternative reality in much the same way that spirit photography does. Spirit photographs were also revelatory, sometimes including a so-called spiritual "extra." A spiritual extra can be a kind of *Doppelgänger*, a companion to the portrait subject, a person who might have been long dead by the time the photograph print was made—a counterpart (mother, father, sibling, or spouse) shows up from beyond the grave. Séances led by trance mediums, hypnotism, the photography of ectoplasm, psychics, crystals, astrological charts, and various telepathic readings contributed to the lure of spiritualism.

The artificial theatrical darkness we see in glass slides and printed photographs that gives these images a special richness was almost always present in the occult imaginary. Such miasmas appeared in chiaroscuro photographs, the prevailing atmospheres of which were dark and penumbral. Noam M. Elcott's *Artificial Darkness: An Obscure History of Modern Art and Media* (2016), explores the role of absolute, or controlled, darkness in the representation of a three-dimensional space in photography and cinema at the turn of the twentieth century.[43] Darkness was required in order to show the illuminations of X-rays and other film or photographic techniques. Darkness, of course, was a necessary ingredient for the technical development of light-sensitive film in the *Dunkelkammer*, or "darkroom."

During Breuer's lengthy visits Bertha was frequently sedated with chloral hydrate (a "sedative-hypnotic" drug) among other hallucinogenic medications she took, including morphine, which may have induced toxic psychosis, yet another possible diagnosis for Anna O.[44] Under the power of drugs *and* hypnotic suggestion, with the tears in her eyes

43. Elcott 2016a, *passim*.

44. Loentz 2007, 210.

distorting her vision, Anna hallucinated images such as her own arm turning into a frightening black snake. She saw death-heads appear in the mirror, as though envisioning her father's future ghost. It was not unusual for ghosts to abide in mirrors, as we find in the literature of the *fin-de-siècle*, a concept that leaked into the visual culture of the same time. In Anna O.'s family and its environs, the Jewish custom of covering mirrors during *shiva* (the traditional mourning period of seven days) would have been familiar to all, as would the custom of not looking at pictures (photographs) of people during the mourning period. Although Bertha Pappenheim claimed to have dismissed the eastern European superstitions of Judaism, the custom of covering mirrors and avoiding pictorial representations of people would have been practiced even in "assimilated" homes. Mirrors and photographic portraits of people would have carried a certain funereal and ghostly charge in the everyday life of Bertha Pappenheim, especially as her father lay dying—more a melancholic nineteenth-century ghost story than an example of a religious taboo.

In 1945 Josef Maria Eder studied the chemical action of light in his prelude to the *History of Photography*. Eder stated that sunlight reflected from a mirror darkens the mirror's surface.[45] As mirrors age, they produce a patination of black spots and streaks due to environmental dust and humidity. In mirrors, light reaches the reflective silver surface after passing through the glass surface. The glass layer may absorb some of the light and cause distortions due to refractions and reflections on the front surface. Together with various additional reflections, the refracted surface of glass pressing upon the silver backing of a mirror produces "ghost images," which are to a great extent visually suggestive and even pictorial or cinematic. The mirror, especially in an atmosphere of semi-darkness, functioned as a screen that produced and even projected its own images and fragments. Mirrors produced shadows and their opposites, reflections. Since a shadow is more than just an absence of light, its presence is as suggestively productive as a reflection. Such phenomena are investigated by Marina Warner in *Phantasmagoria* (2006) in a subchapter titled "The Danger in the Mirror."[46] Warner declares, "A shadow is similar to a reflection only when it is not a shadow but a shade, but then it shifts toward the nature

45. Eder 1945, 76.
46. Warner 2006, 169–86.

of ghosts—Greek *psyche* covers both."[47] In Warner's analysis, shadows and reflections are "united by a paradox, that their immaterial and insubstantial presence accompanies the being that casts them and gives evidence of that entity's materiality."

The mirror-image and (especially) the shadow-image have spawned a great deal of folkloric superstition in the West. This visual and fictive material was studied in terms of psychoanalysis by Otto Rank in *The Double: A Psychoanalytic Study* of 1925.[48] Such images can come-to-life easily (even by accident) in the imagination of a haunted beholder.

These spirits may have played a significant part in Anna O.'s first hallucinations, triggering sensations and memories of visual illusions. At around the same time that Anna O. was captivated by ghostly hallucinations in her father's sickroom, Henry James wrote about photography as proof of having been there in *The Tragic Muse*, where the painter Nick Dormer says to his muse, "Let me at any rate have some sort of a sketch of you as a kind of feather from the angel's wing or a photograph of the ghost." All of this alluded to spirit photography of the nineteenth century, where ghosts showed up in images produced by mortal photographers.[49]

Looking glasses, of course, have served as transformative, ghostly, proto-cinematic objects in everyday life of the twentieth and twenty-first centuries. Historically, they provided mystical images to medieval European scryers, people who would gaze into crystal balls to see future or past events.[50] In the Christian world, scrying was on par with alchemy and astrology in terms of presumed efficacy and proscription.[51] Black obsidian mirrors, where smoky chiaroscuro was perforce heightened, were especially propitious for divination as well as providing spiritual protection. Looking into the blackness of an obsidian mirror screen provided the beholder with an atmospheric view to the unknown, in which human figures and other images could appear.

47. Warner 2006, 175.
48. Rank 1971, 62–68.
49. James [1890] 1995, 473.
50. Prendergast 2003, 42.
51. Prendergast 2003, 72.

The Looking Glass and the Doppelgänger

In both art and human vision, mirrors and their representations are cathected to a high degree. In our everyday considerations of narcissism, mirrors have been ubiquitous since their technical perfection in sixteenth-century Italy. Sadeq Rahimi, author of *The Hauntology of Everyday Life* (2021), discusses mirrors and the "ocular uncanny" with respect to images of the self, the individual, and self-study of the individual in modern literature and post-Renaissance portraiture (painting and photography). In Lacanian terms, Rahimi states that the visually received reflection of an individual's body in the mirror, once identified by the infant in Lacan's *Stade du miroir* ("the mirror stage"), "functions as a placeholder for the imagined self." Mirrors are thus uncanny objects insofar as they present a (self but non-self) pictorial *Doppelgänger* for the ego.[52] As such, their reflections serve as screened representations. Many individuals mistakenly think of their reflection in a mirror as being reversed from left to right. But it is not true that mirrors reverse images laterally. If a person faces north and looks straight into a mirror, the east side of their face is still on the east side of the image, and the same is true for the west side. The mirror does not reverse the image left to right; rather, it reverses it front to back.

But mirrors don't necessarily function as instruments to see the self, or to create a pseudo-portrait as described by Rahimi. In practice, flat mirrors (especially those reflecting one or more other mirrors) rearrange space, light, and objects in such a way as to cause the familiarity of the domestic environment to appear frightening. *Unheimlich* forms are suggested and constructed in shadow and light, creating a skeptical quality of feeling. Such views, be they momentary or longer lasting, play with the viewing subject's ocular perception and cause frightening disorientations that alienate the subject from the realm of the *Heimlich*. Mirrors, then, create eerie, uncanny spaces, which replace the knowable objects that the mirror should reflect.

Mirrors are important in the theory and practice of psychoanalysis, and not only in cases of narcissism. Mirrors play together with sources of illumination to produce effects of a disorienting Freudian uncanny in human vision on an almost everyday basis, and mirror images address one another in the production of suggestive visual material, for anyone

52. Rahimi 2013, 1–24, 13.

who chances to observe them. Early in the nineteenth century (1826) the German Romantic poet Heinrich Heine stated in *Die Harzreise*, "There is nothing more uncanny than seeing one's face accidentally in a mirror by moonlight."[53]

It is noteworthy that the style of suspended oval-shaped (or long rectangular) mirror that was most common in nineteenth-century bedrooms was called a "psyche" (**fig. 49**). A full-length psyche was typically present in bedrooms such as that of Bertha's father, Siegmund Pappenheim. The reflective surface of the psyche provided a cinema-like surface for the screening of hallucinations, particularly at night.

According to Dr. Joseph Grasset, hallucinations and illusions (termed "less serious hallucinations") were said to arrive at night to people who were "semi-insane" or merely neurotic, from light sources emanating from mirrors or gas lamps. Just as such overly imaginative people found music or words in the accidental sounds of everyday life, certain of these individuals experienced "cinematographic hallucinations." These were hallucinations of sight that appeared at night with rapidly changing movements, according to Dr. Grasset in his *Marvels Beyond Science* of 1910.[54] Such pseudo-cinemas, created by accident in the minds of the observers, were considered marvels "beyond science" that belonged to the realm of the occult.

No one can forget that in the course of her intimate treatment Bertha (in the role of Anna O.) supposedly formed an amorous attachment (or transference) to her doctor, even hallucinating (and performing an episode) that she was pregnant with Breuer's baby. At this point the doctor apparently demurred, leaving Vienna to go on vacation with his wife. He narrated the case to Freud, however, who published it in 1893 (articles) and 1895 (*Studies on Hysteria*).[55] Bertha Pappenheim's false pregnancy is considered an "hysterical pregnancy" in the psychoanalytic writing of Freud's time.[56] But women's menses and pregnancy had long been legible in mirrors: Aristotle wrote that, "If a woman chances during her menstrual period to look into a highly polished mirror, the surface of it will grow cloudy with a blood-colored haze."[57]

53. Quoted by Rank 1971, 43, n. 19.

54. Grasset 1910, 101.

55. Freud and Breuer 1895.

56. Prendergast 2003, 57.

57. Prendergast 2003, quoting Aristotle, 57.

The literary and social culture of *fin-de-siècle* Vienna put great emphasis on "impossible" romantic love and its transformative power. In popular visual culture, for example, Denis Etcheverry's highly romantic painting *Vertige* (**fig. 50**) from the Parisian Salon of 1903 was circulated as a favorite black-and-white postcard in Vienna, like the one addressed to Fräulein Hilda Hüttmann at Währingerstrasse 83, with "Grüss und Küss" from her friend Nina.

It is likely that both Anna O. and Josef Breuer were susceptible to, or even protagonists of, this overly romantic mentality. Their mutually mirroring cases of "transference" and "countertransference" became among the most accepted principles of Freudian psychoanalysis from this first instance of the "talking cure" to psychotherapy in the present day. The extent to which this melodramatic "novella" of Anna O. is fact or fiction in the medical record is less important than its resonance in cultural history as one of the founding narratives of psychoanalysis.

The Family Doctor

A doctor's romantic entanglement with a patient, which took place in a domestic setting, among nightclothes, chloral hydrate, morphine, and mirrors, could give rise to erotic phantasy in the visual imagination. Such imaginings are played out in a Saturn film of 1908–10: *Der Hausarzt* (*The Family Doctor*) is a phantasy in which a malingering patient deliberately seduces her doctor during a series of house calls. The patient reveals more of her body as the examinations go on, all the while insisting to the doctor that she is not well and needs further physical examination (**fig. 51**).

The Saturn doctor's medical technique, like that of Freud and his contemporaries, consists of a morphological (visual, audial, and tactile) examination of the patient. The seduction takes place in two episodes in the patient's home: first on a couch in the parlor and then in a bed in the lady's boudoir. Next, after the doctor reads the lady's bedside diary, he realizes that she desires him, and they fall into each other's arms. Such popular phantasies provide a cultural context for Anna O.'s psychological adventures with Josef Breuer.

Bertha Pappenheim recovered from her illness some years after her treatment, if not because of it. She became a social reformer who dealt with Jewish issues and women's rights. If Anna O. was hysterical about sex in her youth, she developed into an accomplished feminist in her later years. We may once more tighten the Freudian association with Saturn films in terms of Pappenheim's further biography.

In 1903 Pappenheim (the former "Anna O.") visited Polish Galicia and western Russia to examine the abject condition of the Jewish populations. And in 1911–12 she traveled east to the brothels of Salonika, Istanbul, Jerusalem, Cairo, and Alexandria to find Jewish girls abducted from eastern Europe and rescue them from the sexual slavery into which they had been sold.[58] Here, one can turn to Schwarzer's orientalist films of sexual slavery (*Sklavenschiksal*, *Sklavenraub*, *Am Sklavenmarkt*, *Im Harem*, and *Die Sklaverei im Orient*) for an equivalent in popular culture. These erotic film phantasies were contemporary with the campaign against "white [Jewish] slavery" by Bertha Pappenheim.

Pappenheim's *volte-face* from youthful hysteria to her eventual status as a highly esteemed social worker is legendary. In a simplistic interpretation it might appear as though Bertha consciously realized that what had actually ailed her as a girl was the ruling law of the prevailing patriarchal system. Her interest in women's issues was unprecedented in the German-speaking world, and at the same time she was a practitioner of the noblest principles of Judaism. Meanwhile, Pappenheim's problematic personal biography seems to have had a happy ending: she escaped from the stifling paternal order of her father's sickroom and the sustained talking-cure attentions of Breuer. Her womanly know-how allowed Bertha Pappenheim to command the social horizon of Jewish life for others as well as herself. But, as wary of happy endings as all historians should be, I'd like to problematize Pappenheim's position a little further.

Apropos slavery and racialism, Pappenheim sometimes wandered onto a slippery slope: she applied one of the most common brands of Jewish orientalism, claiming that Jews from Polish Galicia were "half-Asian," lazy, dirty, uncivilized, and depraved. And she was especially hard on the Jewish women from these regions, referring to their supposed "hot blood" and "moral insanity."[59] In blaming these victims for their own misfortunes, despite her conscious unwillingness to do so, Pappenheim designated Western Europe as a colonial superego to be

58. Bristow 1983, 4, 6, 39, 51, 70, 72, 102, 218–19, 232–35, 253, 257, 260–61, 263–64, 266, 269, 273, 276, 279–80, 284, 299–391, 304–305, 323.

59. Loentz 2007, 133–34, 141, 143.

imposed upon the impoverished Jews of the East, who were, not unlike the hysterics of the Salpêtrière, amoral and out of control. Similarly, when Alfred Döblin (1878–1957) sought his Jewish roots in Eastern Europe, he felt as though he had come upon an "exotic tribe" of men who all looked alike.[60]

Furthermore, not unlike hysterics, these eastern European Jews had been deeply traumatized. Among the eastern Jewish women aided by Pappenheim were those rendered homeless by violent events such as genocidal pogroms. Other women had acquired the marginalized status of *agunah*, still "shackled" to their marriage vows, having been abandoned by husbands who had emigrated to America or elsewhere. Bertha Pappenheim's particular style of Jewish orientalism cast her as a quintessential protagonist of Austria and Germany, educated according to the precepts of her own society. A peculiar irony of Pappenheim's rescue work is that some of the Jewish girls who were abducted as slaves believed they were actually on their way to Germany or America to live as married women in a more modern, industrialized, bourgeois society.

In terms of Jewish orientalism and sexual slavery, we may turn our attention once more to the *Slave Market* phantasies by Johann Schwarzer. These films reverted to orientalist themes such as life in the *seraglio* and young women inspected for sale as slaves. Here the thrill of illicit looking was enhanced by the exotic lure of the East, at least in its fictitious European representation of a "sultan" with numerous women in his entourage. Bertha Pappenheim probably did not see these movies, but she may well have known about them by way of her brother Wilhelm Pappenheim (1860–1939) or friends, and seen them advertised in the daily newspapers.[61] Freud, Breuer, and their fellow physicians may or may not have seen these phantasies at the Prater, a *Wanderkino*, or elsewhere. I am not suggesting any precise causality here, but rather I propose letting these phenomena resonate in the cultural moment.

It is well known that the oriental harem and slave phantasy was an erotic staple of nineteenth-century European painting, as in Jean-Léon Gérôme's *Slave Market* (1866), and that photography was the modern medium of colonial adventure. The orientalist phantasy willingly undermined the bourgeois husband–wife relationship that prevailed as an ideal in newly industrialized Europe. The non-European women

60. Döblin 1991, 175.
61. Loentz 2003, 79–102.

who were sexualized in exotic scenarios provided a reactionary phantasm for men whose wives, daughters, and even mistresses were evolving in a rapidly changing European society. The conjugal situation as such is satirized in Johann Schwarzer's *Eine Moderne Ehe* (*Modern Marriage*) (1907) in which a bourgeois husband, tricking his wife, goes to his mistress rather than to his office or his club. As soon as he leaves the house, however, the wife summons her own lover, who shows up immediately for an illicit tryst. As in *The Power of Hypnosis* (1908) (**fig. 48**), with its accommodating manservant, the young parlor maid seems not altogether innocent, but rather complicit in the intrigues performed by both husband and wife. Young housemaids and manservants are rarely innocent in the Saturn films, but rather co-conspirators of the women or men wealthy enough to employ them. In *The Vain Parlor Maid* the young servant takes the initiative to undress and mimic (or indeed compete with) a seductive recumbent marble sculpture. This episode seems to surprise the maid herself, who, ironically, comes from the same class of women who actually performed as actresses in the Saturn films.

Viennese Modernism

Side by side with all of the visual material under discussion here, a single question hangs in the air: what about Viennese modernism? Modernist art in Vienna was contemporary art for Sigmund Freud and his circle. Although such art did not particularly interest Freud, Johann Schwarzer, or Bertha Pappenheim, it lends itself, in an almost interminably overdetermined stereotype, to psychoanalytic appreciation and critique. This cultural configuration of anxiety-ridden and highly expressive art comes under the umbrella commonly known as "Vienna 1900."[62] Paintings by artists such as Egon Schiele (1890–1918) and by amateurs such as the avant-garde atonal composer Arnold Schönberg (1874–1951) were radically modernist and anti-classical in their effect. Schiele's nudes, female and male, were awkward, anxious, physically afflicted, and ill at ease, both physically and mentally. His pairs of lovers (heterosexual and homosexual alike) are tormented rather than joyful in the act of loving (**fig. 52**).

62. For the concept of "Vienna 1900" see Kandel 2012.

Schönberg painted too, and his images of the human visage, as in *Der rote Blick* (*The Red Gaze*) of 1910 express the power of the gaze in terms of a stunned, horrified consciousness. The experience of scopophilia, or pleasure in looking, has gone awry and turned to absolute *Angst*.

In the realm of avant-garde Viennese art, Egon Schiele rejected "normative" sexuality in favor of what art historian Gemma Blackwell has called "the spectacle of the pathological body."[63] This documentary spectacle of disease was current in photographic illustrations of sick people in hospitals, and departs far from the romantic concept of illness that is seen in films such as *Der Hausarzt* (*The Family Doctor*) (**see fig. 51**). In this regard, the Saturn films were still "old fashioned" in their treatment of the nude and in the psyche of the on-screen beholders, as well as the film's audience of spectators. Schwarzer's films do not necessarily disclose any real sexual anxiety, or dark side, or unhealthy alternative to the prevailing "natural" order. In fact, in one Saturn episode a female slave is actually *rejected* by the sultan for being too slender and adolescent looking. The sultan apparently valued an aesthetic opposite to those uncomfortable extremes that were adopted by Kokoschka or Schiele.

I introduced this chapter by way of early films of hypnotism and hysteria, and proceeded to analyze *The Power of Hypnosis* and other sexual phantasies from the Saturn films. Apropos pathology, I'd like now to complicate the issue, and conclude by pointing out that Saturn erotica, innocent as it may initially seem, was compounded by serious humiliations of the flesh in the conditions of its reception. This is in part because Saturn screenings were not necessarily single-feature events. Macabre slides of medical oddities and films of gruesome medical procedures and surgery frequently accompanied them.[64] In 1903, for example, Louis Geni exhibited a traveling "anatomical museum" as well as cinematic erotica with screenings and views designated "for men only" together with the Saturn features.[65]

63. Blackshaw 2007, 377–401.
64. Achenbach and Caneppele 1999, 131.
65. Achenbach and Caneppele 1999, 131.

A Difficult Treatment

Around the turn of the twentieth century, the ostentatious French surgeon Eugène Doyen (1859–1916) was the first to film his operations for documentary purposes. In 1898, for instance, Doyen paid a camera operator to film him performing hysterectomies and a craniotomy in his private clinic in Paris. These films, which paralleled Marinescu's efforts in Bucharest and Negro's in Turin, made a hero of the doctor, who was now a film director and actor. He is a surgeon protagonist who performs seemingly impossible feats on screen.

Doyen maintained that he never meant such documentaries to be entertainment in the fairgrounds of Paris or Vienna. In one of Doyen's textbooks about surgery, he illustrates a well-appointed patient's room, as photographed by C. Ruckert (**fig. 55**). We see a hospital bed for sleeping and also a daybed, meant for relaxing in convalescence. The chaise longue seen here, at the viewer's right in the photograph, is a poignant and elegant predecessor, in style and also perhaps in function, to Freud's analytic couch.

In the same spirit, Doyen meant for his films to be methodological instructions for surgeons. He stated that "The double necessity of adopting a surgical method and of applying it in operations can be most convincingly demonstrated in the cinematograph."[66] Nevertheless he enjoyed great fame from these little movies, and Doyen's productions were eventually smuggled into public viewing for sensational entertainment.[67]

They, like Louis Geni's so-called Panopticon films, were commonly shown for gentlemen in tandem with erotic films like the Saturn features in the Austro-Hungarian Empire. If Vienna was the most medically advanced city in Europe around the turn of the twentieth century, the scopophilia associated with medical procedures and anatomical oddities thrived apace. In March 1907, Charles V. Burke of *The Medical Times* described a report from Dr. Kurt Torkel of Breslau, who witnessed a "kinetescope show" of a vaginal total hysterectomy performed on a naked woman at the Bioskope Theatre at Freiburg-im-Baden Württemberg.[68]

66. Doyen 1917, 7.
67. Lefebvre 2004.
68. Burke 1907, 156.

The film of the operation included extensive hemorrhaging, and Dr. Torkel remembered that "several persons" fled the theater in horror. Torkel believed that such films of major surgery were public spectacles that were degrading to the camera operator and demoralizing to the spectators, as well as disrespectful to the patients who were filmed while unconscious. Some of this footage was misogynistic on conscious and unconscious levels. The *Journal of the American Medical Association* of March 1907 termed the hysterectomy film as "Surgery as a Vaudeville Show."[69] Around the same time, silent film comedies about surgical procedures performed with saws and icepicks were in vogue. Georges Méliès (1861–1938) directed *Up to Date Surgery*, a zany comedy of dismemberment and reconstitution in 1902.[70]

Such scientific medical documentaries seem to have inspired a film called *A Difficult Treatment* (*Eine Schwierige Behandlung*) that has been attributed to Johann Schwarzer, but may be by Doyen himself, or perhaps by an anonymous director, satirizing Doyen's surgical films (**fig. 53**). It features Doyen's patented operating table known as "Doyen's bed" ("*le lit de Doyen*") (**fig. 54**). Was this movie really an info-mercial for a newly designed operating table? I would propose that it was probably not. In this film, of Austrian provenance and now conserved in the Austrian Film Archive, the doctors and female surgical patient appear to be actors. Is the nude woman on the operating table to be understood as unconscious? Is she understood to be dead? Her body (nude except for shoes and stockings) is objectified, inspected, handled, and operated on by the pair of surgeons. Will they cut into her flesh? Will these doctors perform one of the vaginal or abdominal hysterectomies that were Doyen's specialties as filmed in 1898?[71]

Although it remains possible that this film was intended as a scientific introduction to the value of a new kind of operating table, many twenty-first-century viewers, including a group of visually savvy students at the Rhode Island School of Design, interpret these images as dark and even bordering on pornographic.[72] Apropos the humiliation of female flesh

69. Burke 1907.

70. Catalogued by the Star Film Company cat. 422–25, presently conserved in the George Eastman Museum, Rochester, New York.

71. Doyen 1899; see also Cohen 2006.

72. Burke (1907) of Newark, NJ, reported on his residence in Paris during winter 1905–1906. My most sincere thanks are due to all my students from

(as seen in the Saturn films) here we're introduced to a more morbid and intrusive kind of misogyny. The actress playing the patient was probably conscious in the filming of this episode, as certain aspects of her body posture would indicate. But in the cinematic representation, or phantasy, a woman's unconscious body becomes an object to be manipulated by men for a fetishizing (male audience) beholder. The woman's body is looked at, examined, touched, and perhaps incised by the two male doctors. All the while she is (in the fiction of the film) in a state of oblivion induced by hypnotism, ether, or chloroform.

Adding to the perplexity of the meaning of *A Difficult Treatment*, the operating table filmed there is clearly identical to the one invented by Doyen and illustrated in Doyen's official textbook *Technique chirurgicale* of 1897. The Doyen operating table is also to be seen in a photograph by C. Ruckert in Doyen's "position of the patient for a nephrectomy" (kidney removal) in the same volume (**fig. 54**). In this photograph the nurse and surgeon have turned the patient on her side to face them during the course of the operation. The viewer of the photographic illustration observes the nude patient (gendered as female?) from behind, bringing to mind some of the zanier sketches from *A Difficult Treatment*.

Are the images in *A Difficult Treatment* in fact involuntary or "unconscious" by-products of scientific technical culture? No matter what the film's original purpose may have been, there is a perplexing slippage here between medical and erotic (even pornographic) cinema. The pathologized female body had a fetishistic lure as a focus for the male gaze. *A Difficult Treatment* hovers between categories, and this condition of sliding between medical science and the phantasy realm of misogynistic sex may apply to many other art and non-art images in this culture, whether consciously or not. Due to the presence of certain photographs and films, whether imported or local, erotica did its cultural work in combination with medical voyeurism in Viennese society. It becomes pertinent for future study to look into the realm of factual, deadpan, documentary medical imaging and its relation to the subjective phantasy world of what was visually forbidden.

Rhode Island School of Design in my seminars about "Visual Culture in Freud's Vienna" from 2013 and 2014 for their valuable feedback on the issues addressed in this chapter.

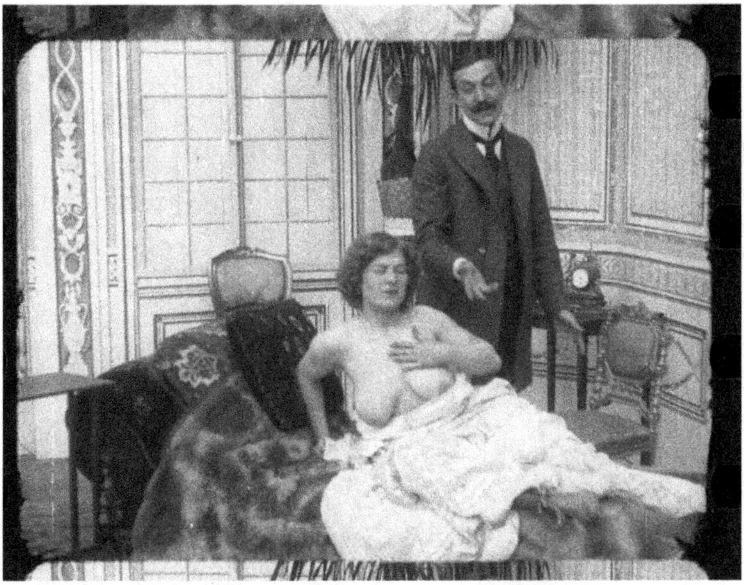

Fig. 51 Johan Schwarzer, film still from *Der Hausarzt/The Family Doctor*, produced by Saturn Films, 1908–10.

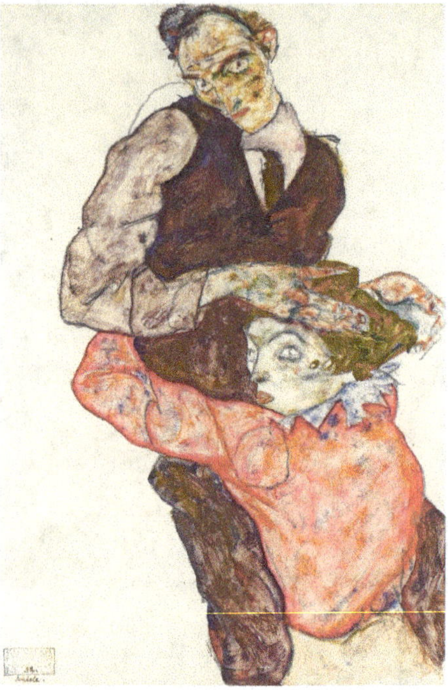

Fig. 52 Egon Schiele, *Lovers: Self Portrait with Wally,* watercolor and pencil drawing, 1914. Leopold Museum, Vienna. Image in the public domain. Courtesy of Wikimedia Commons.

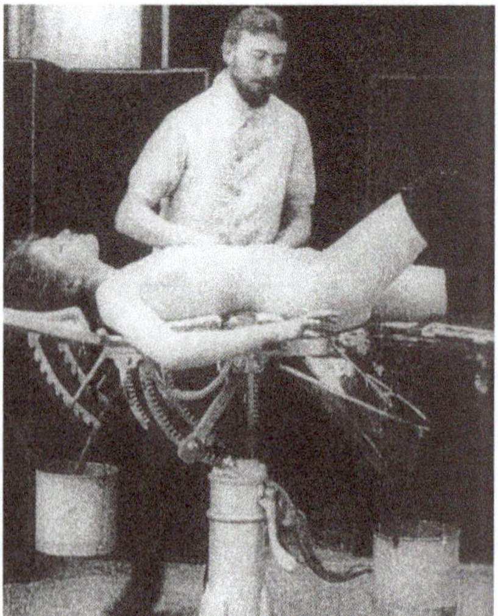

Fig. 53 Anonymous director, film still, *Eine Schwierige Behandlung/A Difficult Treatment.*

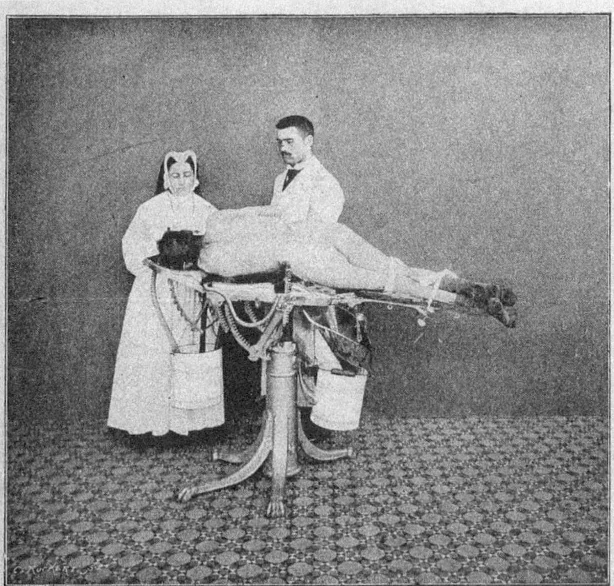

Fig. 56. — Position du malade pour la néphrectomie.

Fig. 54 C. Ruckert et cie., *Doyen's Operating Table.* Image from the author's private collection.

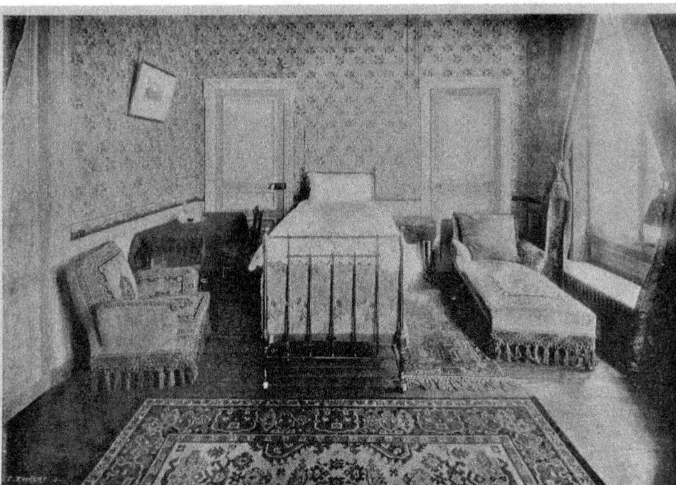

Fig. 55 C. Ruckert et cie., *Patient Hospital Room of Dr. Doyen.* Image in the author's private collection.

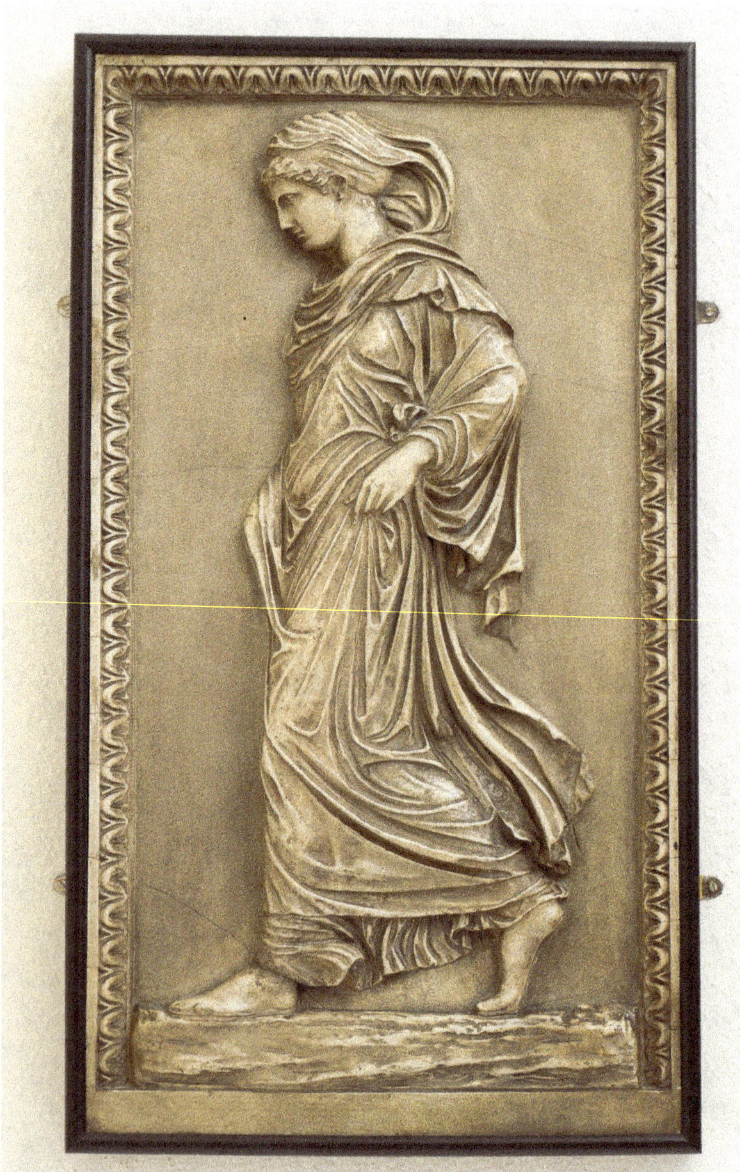

Fig. 56 Freud's plaster cast of Gradiva. HP 20. © Freud Museum London.

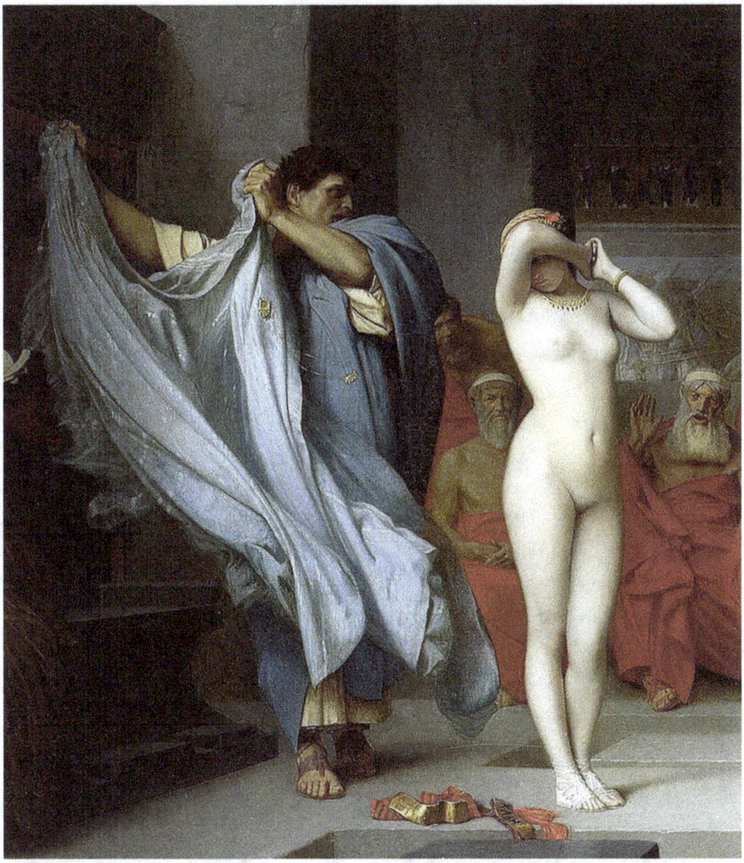

Fig. 57 Gérôme, *Phryne* (detail). Image in the public domain. Courtesy of Wikimedia Commons.

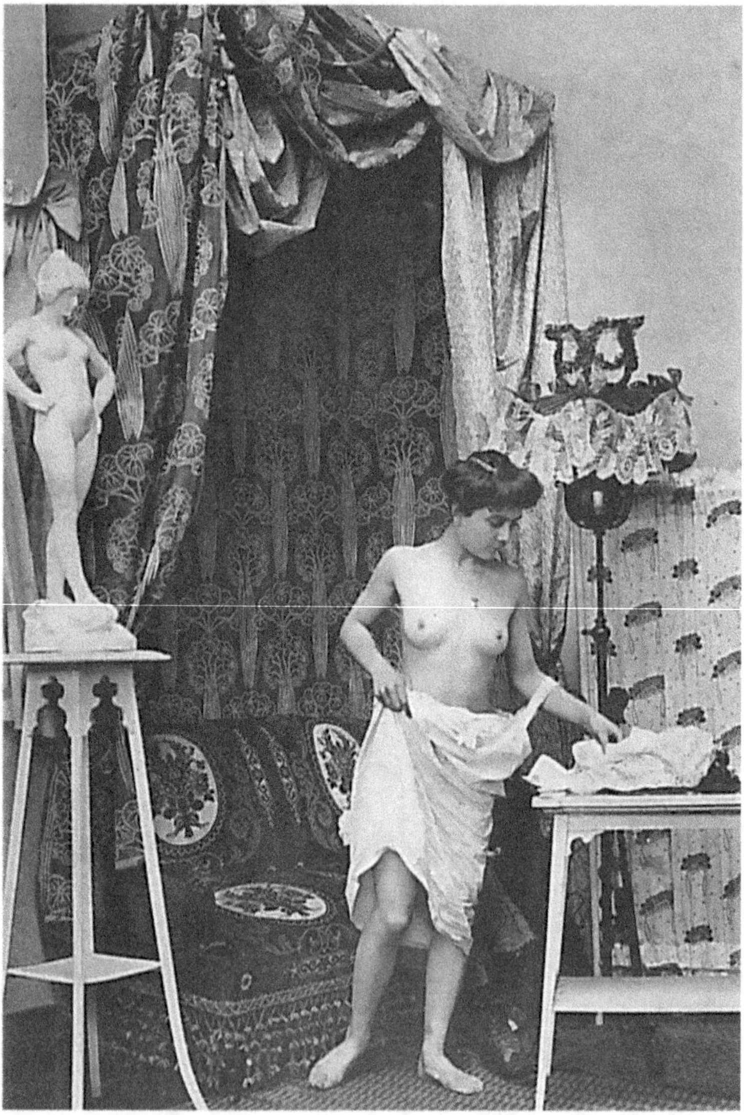

Fig. 58 Johann Schwarzer, *Woman Undressing in a Viennese Interior with a Statue of Phryne,* ca. 1912, photograph in postcard format. Author's private collection.

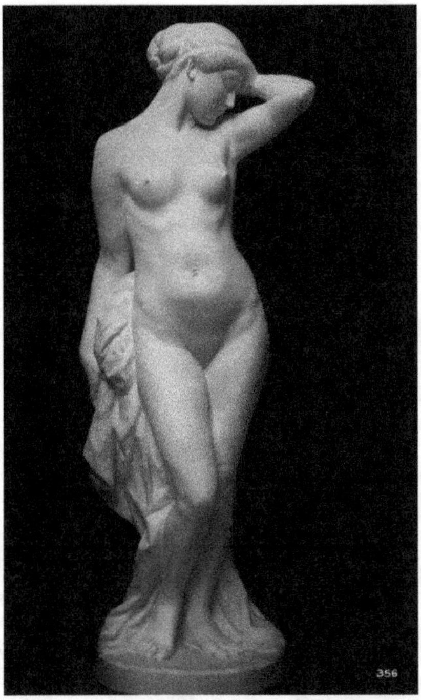

Fig. 59 Max Valentin, *Phryne*, plaster cast, ca. 1910. Postcard format. Photograph by Friedrich O. Wolter, Berlin. No. 356. Author's private collection.

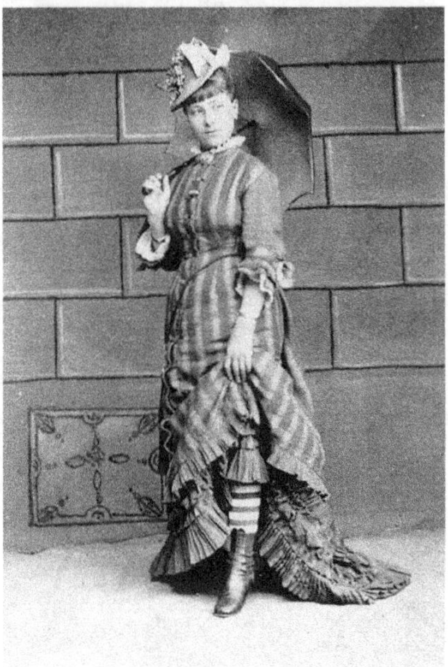

Fig. 60 Otto Schmidt, *Graben Nymphe*. Cabinet card format. Author's private collection.

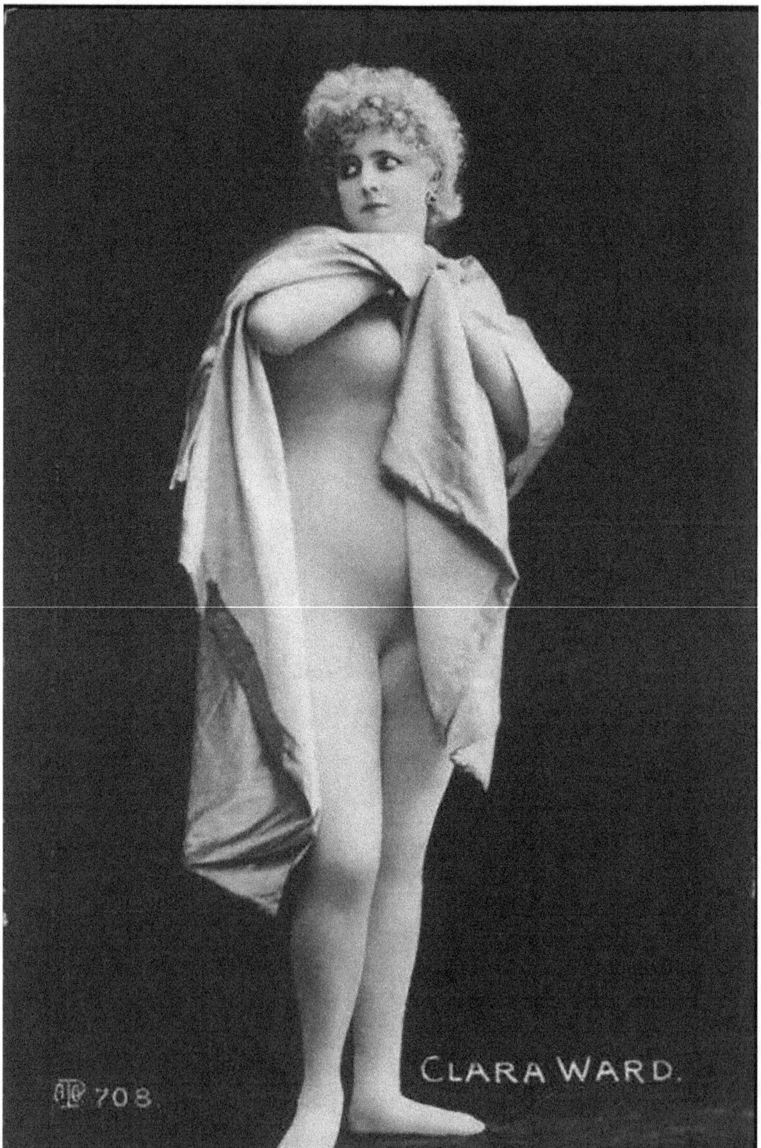

Fig. 61 Anonymous, *Clara Ward as Phryne*. Postcard format (no. 708). Author's private collection.

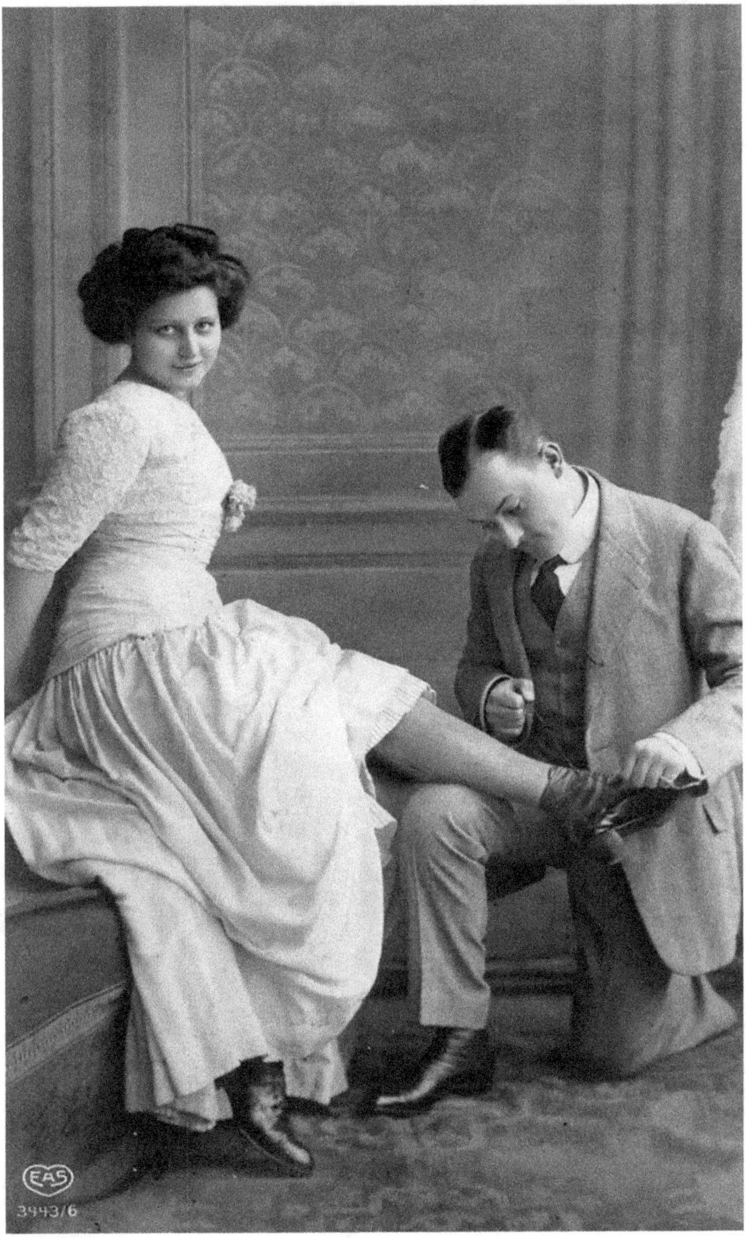

Fig. 62 Anonymous, *Shoe Fitting*. Postcard format, 1910. Author's private collection.

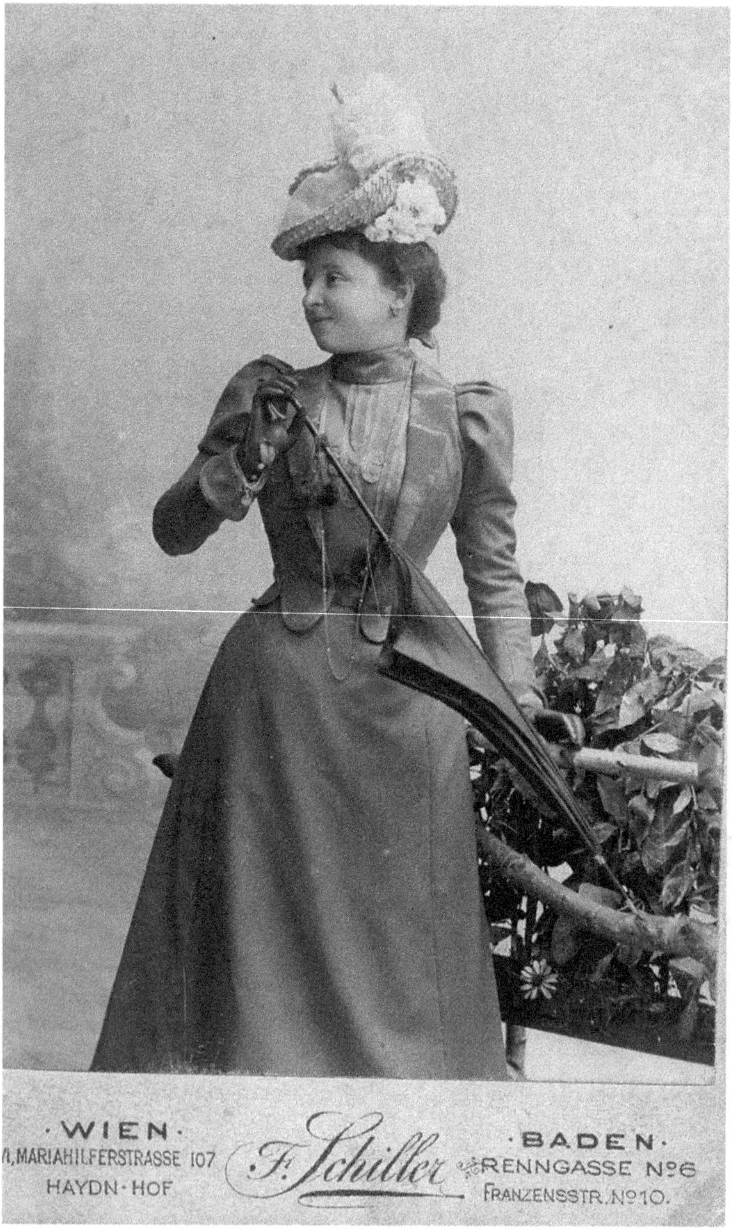

Fig. 63 Franz Schiller, *Portrait of a Young Woman*. Cabinet card format. Author's private collection.

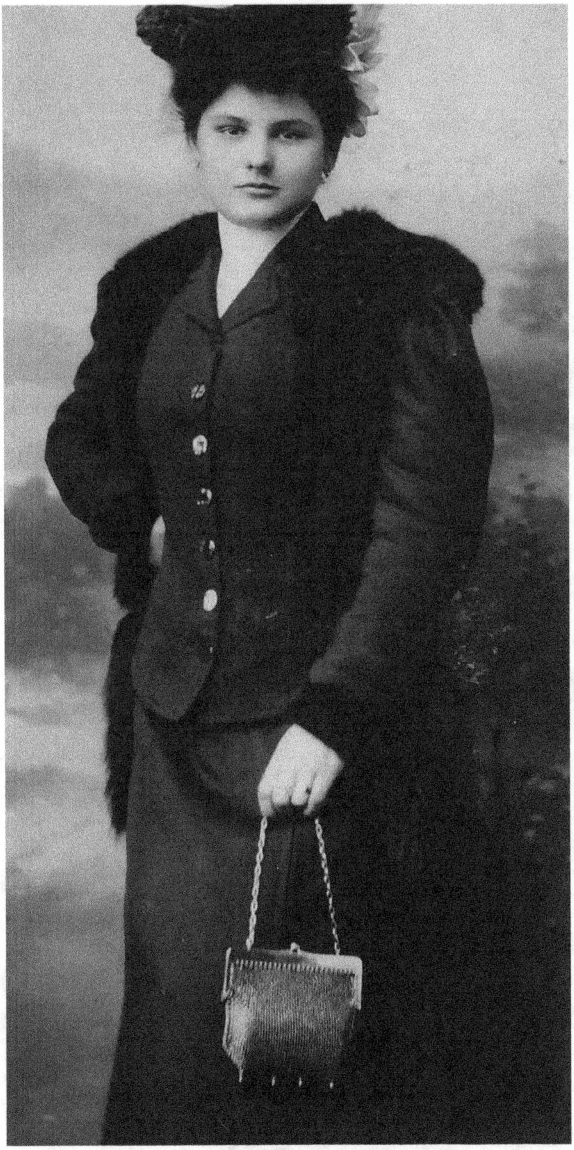

Fig. 64 Atelier Kral, *Portrait of a Viennese Woman with Reticule*, 1907. Author's private collection.

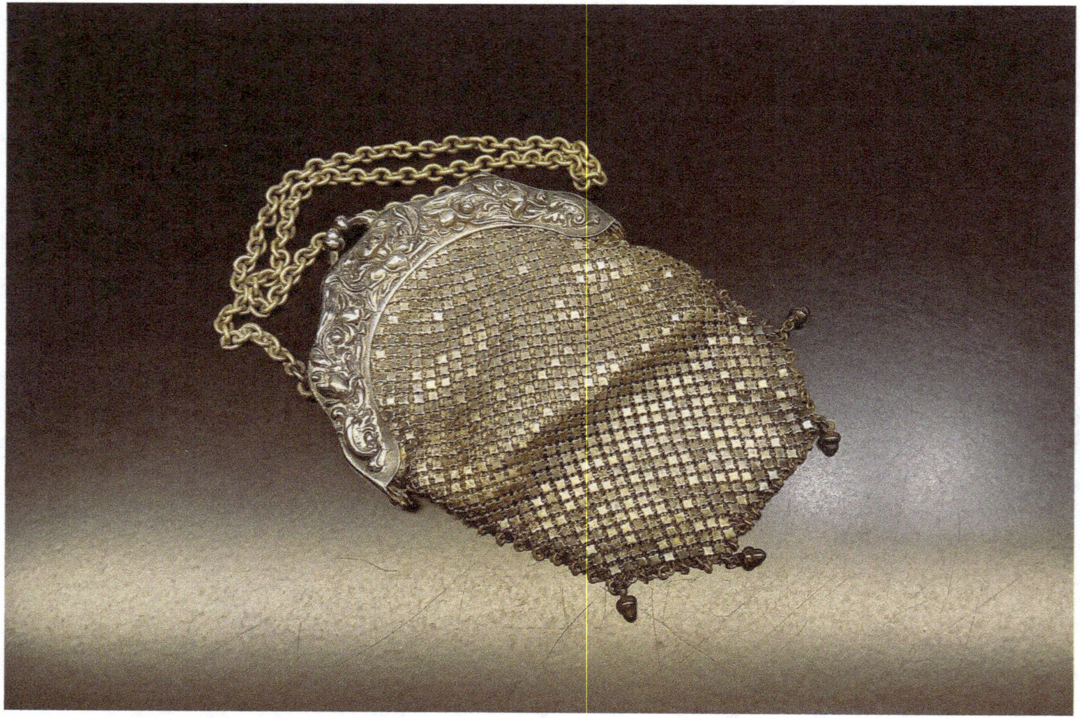

Fig. 65 Reticule of Viennese provenance, ca. 1910. Gilded metal. Photo Marcin Gizycki. Author's private collection.

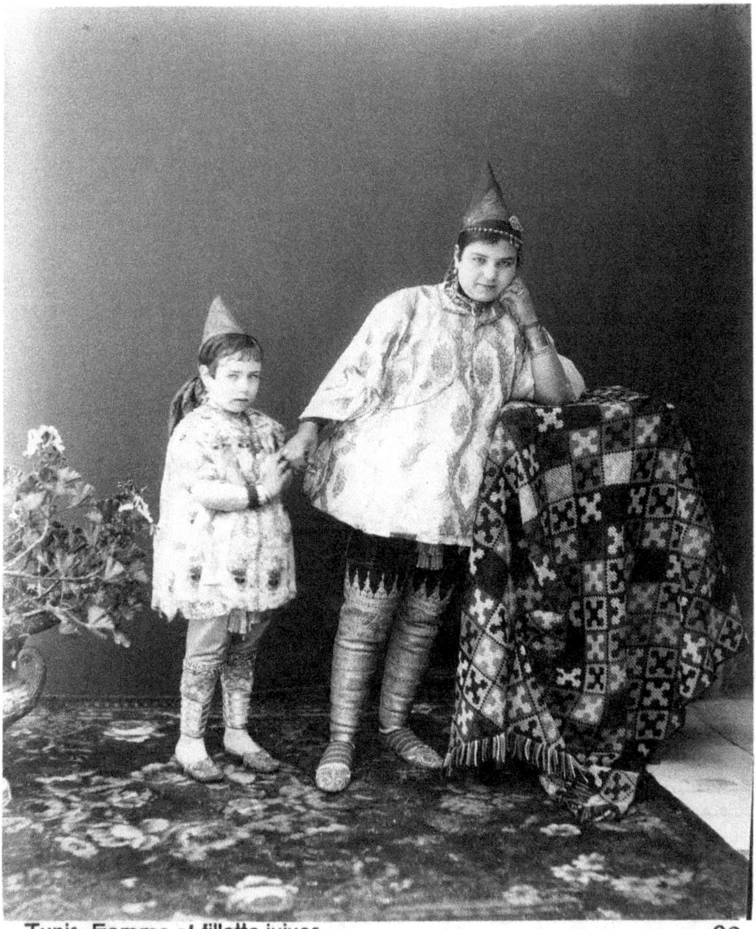

Fig. 66 *Portrait of Two Girls* (Tunisian Jews) from Stratz, *Was Sind Juden?* Image from the author's private collection.

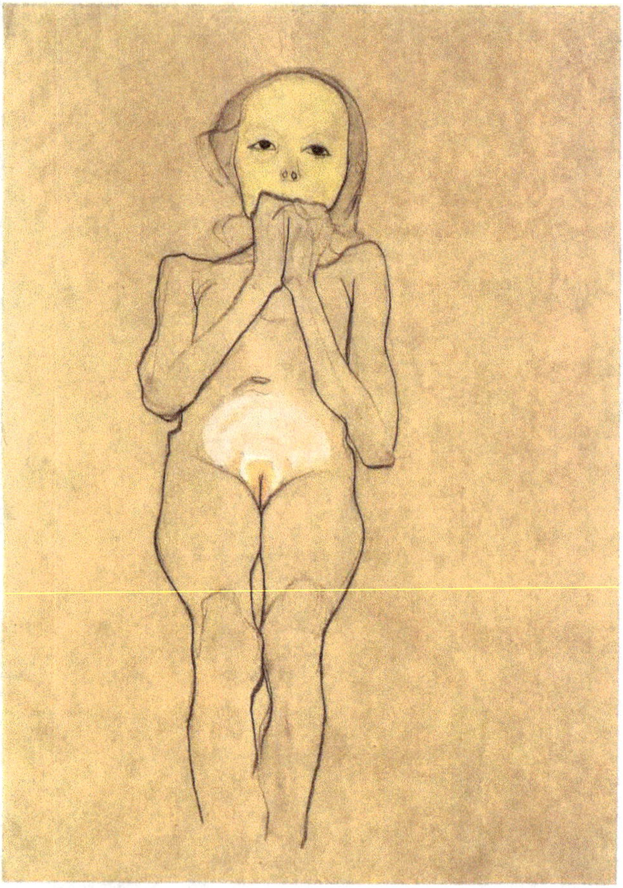

Fig. 67 Attributed to Egon Schiele, *Seated Sick Girl*, black chalk and gouache on prepared paper, 1910. Size: 44.9 × 31.3 cm. Leopold Museum, Vienna inv. 1454. Image in the public domain. Courtesy of Wikimedia Commons.

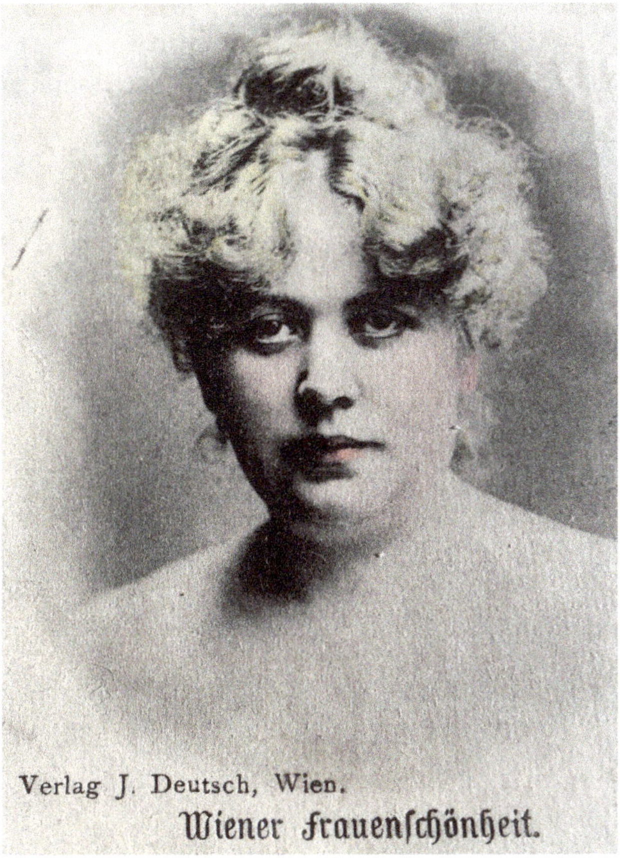

Fig. 68 Anonymous, *Wiener Frauen Schönheit*. Verlag J. Deutsch, no. 32. Author's private collection

Chapter 3

DELUSION AND DREAM IN VIENNA: GRADIVA, PHRYNE, AND THE CHILD-WOMAN

> Sometimes I am so weary that I think I'm not going to live much longer. I look wretched, so wretched that I have had to take to rouge, which I hate, for rosy cheeks don't suit me.
>
> Margarete Böhme, 1905
> *The Diary of a Lost Girl*

Pygmalion Unbound

At the threshold of the twentieth century, the erotic lure of the "statue-come-to-life" prevailed as a Romantic ideal in Europe's classical tradition. The theme of "living sculpture" was expressed in archaeology, psychoanalysis, photography, cinema, daydreams, and dreams around 1900. The Pygmalion myth flourished in 1903, when Wilhelm Jensen published the novel *Gradiva: A Pompeiian Phantasy*, about a repressed archaeologist, Norbert Hanold, whose libido is awakened by a sculpture come-to-life, whom he meets in the ruins of Pompeii. Freud glossed this novel in 1907 with his famous study of *Delusion and Dream in Jensen's* Gradiva.[1] In Freud's psychoanalytic text, he claimed that Hanold's archaeological interests acted at the service of a complex hysterical delusion, serving as an intellectual pretext for unconscious erotic desires.

When Freud examined the fictional Hanold's case history he located several pathologies, among which were voyeurism and fetishism. The famous *Gradiva* relief (Vatican Chiaramonti) come-to-life awakened the libido of the repressed archaeologist, who was otherwise stifled and numbed by the aridity and obsessive focus of academic life.

1. Freud 1907.

Freud identified closely with young Hanold's dedication to professional study, and his particular association of Italy with erotic love. A plaster copy of the *Gradiva* relief was installed in Freud's office, placed so that she is walking toward the patient on the analytic couch and the doctor seated behind the couch (**fig. 57**). It is pertinent to Jensen's *Gradiva* story that German-language writers on health and beauty, called "life-reformers" (1890–1930), consistently expressed a bias *against* academic studies. The novelist Wilhelm Jensen (1837–1911), who was trained as a medical doctor, and Freud too, must have noticed that for these social critics, neurasthenia was a direct result of too much thinking, and delusions resulted from the scholar's conscious mind being occupied with too much esoteric study.

In *Mirrors of Memory* (2010) I discussed the Freudian reception of archaeological photography, addressing the classical pretext for erotic images, and concluded that although the pretext was one of graphic technology in the service of classical humanism, the image frequently arrived as a sensual and romantic instrument of subjectivity. It is always useful to remember Larissa Bonfante's famous observation that in classical antiquity nudity was always a costume. Male statues wore nudity as a costume of virtue and power, whereas female nudity in Greco-Roman art was a costume of sex and vulnerability.[2] How did this formula play out in "Vienna 1900"?

Johann Schwarzer was a Viennese photographer who turned to filmmaking around 1906. His films, as discussed in Chapter 2, were erotic comedies, called "Saturn Films," advertised "for gentlemen only." One of Schwarzer's earlier still *photographs* shows a woman undressing in a Secessionist style interior (**fig. 58**). She is accompanied by a small-scale plaster statue (her classical counterpart) that appears to be one of the many copies of the sculptured *Phryne* by Pierre Etienne Daniel Campagne (1851–1914). Campagne produced numerous versions of his *Phryne*, originally inspired by the figure of Phryne in Gérôme's famous painting of the subject (**fig. 57**). These objects were reproduced in various materials including marble, plaster, and bronze, and dispersed widely. Thus the figure of Phryne entered popular visual culture: the American socialite Clara Ward, for instance, for whom nudity was a badge of honor, had herself photographed as Phryne for posterity (**fig. 61**).

According to mythological sources, Phryne was an Athenian *hetaera* whom Praxiteles used as a model when creating the *Aphrodite of*

2. Bonfante 1989.

Knidos. When Phryne was brought before the judges of the Areopagus for the crime of impiety, she bared her breasts in a plea for mercy. In Schwarzer's photograph, the presence of ancient sculpture, fused as it is with a classical theme *about* female nudity—that is, the nudity of Phryne dazzling the Areopagus—legitimates the view of a contemporary Austrian woman taking off her chemise. "Phryne" and "Olympia" were names commonly taken by French or Viennese prostitutes working in brothels.[3] Taking names of the great courtesans of ancient history burnished the reception of these women by their client-base by alluding to the ancient Greek aesthetic tradition in which courtesans were credited with "charm, *esprit*, and unrivaled intelligence."[4] Schwarzer's photograph synthesizes the classical sublime with the ever-present quotidian condition of the contemporary moment, the Greco-Roman ideal serving as a pretext for the everyday erotic imagination.

Arthur Schnitzler (1862–1931) recalled his youthful experience with young prostitutes. In Schnitzler's recollection (dating from about 1879), young men were conflicted about their experience (or lack of it) with prostitutes such as those walking in the Kärntnerstrasse: "We gave the more startling of these females in the Kärntnerstrasse the names of Greek goddesses, and it was Venus, Hebe, and Juno who inflamed out imaginations most."[5] At age sixteen, Schnitzler (who would become a leading novelist, dramatist, essayist, and diarist) followed the blonde Venus of his choice to her place in Stock-im-Eisen Platz, at the corner of the Graben and Kärntnerstrasse. Schnitzler, still a teenager, assumed the role of a more mature man here, as he was torn between exploiting or rescuing this "Graben-Nymphe," who was about his own age but more worldly and easily bored by her clientele. Schnitzler recalled, "While the pretty thing reclined naked on the divan," he urged her to find "a more decent and promising profession than the one she had chosen," thus installing himself firmly in the patriarchy, in a higher social position than that of the young woman, who merely shrugged at his callow advice. This episode was one of several that initiated the presumptuous young writer into the paternalistic treatment of women in late nineteenth-century Vienna.[6]

3. Jerusalem 1909, 48, 106; Klein 1904, 222.

4. Sullivan 2003, 175–77.

5. Schnitzler 1970, 69.

6. Schnitzler 1970, 69.

A similar theme is played out in a Saturn film called *Erotik des Schuhwerks* (*The Erotics of Footwear*) (1908–10). A traveling shoe salesman arrives at the home of a bourgeois lady to assist her in trying on a shoe. He gazes at her ankles and fondles them, as her skirt is pulled up to more revealing views. The erotics of footwear were also displayed throughout the early years of "low culture" or popular Viennese modernism, as we see in an Austrian postcard from my personal collection postmarked 1912 (**fig. 62**). On this subject the always acerbic Karl Kraus mixed fetishism with misogyny in the famous statement, "There is no more unfortunate creature under the sun than a fetishist who yearns for a woman's shoe and has to settle for the whole woman."[7] Freud wrote about fetishism in terms of inanimate things, body parts, or particular conditions as substitutions or "stand-ins" for the living sexual object: "No other variation of the sexual instinct that borders on the pathological can lay so much claim to our interest as this one [fetishism], such is the peculiarity of the phenomena to which it gives rise."[8]

In *Photography and Anthropology* (2011) Christopher Pinney spoke of the "internalization" of photography into the protocols of cultural anthropology: "So fully had photography infiltrated anthropology's codes of authority that it was invisible, like a drop of oil expanding over the surface of clear water."[9] This was certainly the case in the pre-Nazi literature of race, gender, and anthropology. During these years, a group of men called "Life-Reformers" established cults of health and beauty in the German-speaking lands. These men wrote about gender aesthetics and racial aesthetics, calling upon classical sculpture and documentary photography as anthropological "evidence." Such material was meant to demonstrate, for example, the notion that Nordic (German) women had the most Greco-Roman (or Mediterranean) bodies and therefore came closest to the classical ideal of beauty. Such absurd racialist ideals persisted throughout the 1930s, as is seen, for example, in a painting of *Aphrodite* for a Nazi audience by Oskar Graf (1873–1958). This oil painting was installed in the Haus der Deutschen Kunst in Munich, a Nazi museum constructed from 1933 to 1937 according to the plans of

7. Zohn 1997, 137.
8. Freud 1905a, 153–55.
9. Pinney 2011, 62.

Paul Ludwig Troost (1878–1934). The building itself was a neoclassical design typical of the style favored by the Third Reich.

In a similar vein, we have already seen that architect Paul Schultze-Naumburg (1869–1949) was a proponent of what he considered "classical" Aryan art. For Schultze-Naumburg, "racially pure" German artists could produce human figures that displayed Greco-Roman ideals, whereas non-Christian or racially "mixed" modernist artists showed their essential corruption by producing human figures that were distorted or highly abstracted. Degeneracy in biology served as evidence of the "degeneracy" in modernist art.[10] In his *Kunst und Rasse* (*Art and Race*), published in Munich (1928), Schultze-Naumburg reproduced examples of modern art next to photographs of people with deformities and diseases as proof positive of his nationalistic theories of aesthetics. His pseudoscientific book *Die Kultur des Weiblichen Körpers als Grundlage der Frauenkleidung* (*Culture of the Female Body as the Basis for Women's Clothing*, 1901) presumed to introduce the cultivated reader to the hygienic advantage of women's reform dresses (*Reformkleider*).

In Schultze-Naumburg's view, when the corset is removed, the woman is healthier and more beautiful, more like classical statuary, as is signaled in the photo of a girl in reform dress who is accompanied by a copy of the torso of the *Knidian Aphrod*ite (**fig. 13**). The idea, of course, is that she should be entirely comfortable in her simple but elegant dress, designed for freedom of movement. A typical photo-portrait of a fashionable Viennese lady by Franz Schiller (**fig. 63**), however, shows the opposite, a woman cinched into a restrictive *tailleur femme*. She nevertheless looks at her ease, whereas the model in *Reformkleid* enacts a dour, unyielding demeanor. Since photography is a system of representation, it is obviously impossible to extrapolate a sitter's affect from facial expressions in photographic representation. Nevertheless, in book design, certain photographs are selected and others omitted, according to the judgment of the author and/or the graphic designers.

Whether in spite of or because of its ostensible anti-corset position, Schultze-Naumburg's book circulated in Vienna as erotica during the twentieth century, its graphic strategy by the German designer Johann Vincenz Cissarz. Whereas mid-twentieth-century capitalist advertising

10. For a good introduction to Schultze-Naumburg and his racialist views, see English 2021, chs. 8, 9, and 10. Especially 75–103 and *passim*.

photography has been opened to critique by sociologists, anthropologists, and psychologists, turn-of-the-century graphic design is rarely queried for its psychoanalytic or unconscious content. Here, however, we have seen that the ensemble of images doesn't just "illustrate" the ideas written in the text, but constructs meaning—which is consciously or unconsciously received by the reader. Schultze-Naumburg's book is telling us one thing in the text, but *showing* us something else in the pictures, as would a subject in a psychoanalytic session. Or indeed, any "civilized" person whose "repressed wishes and secrets" come to the surface of his or her everyday life by way of *Fehlleistungen* (linguistic slips), pictorial representation, pathological forgetting, bungling ordinary phrases, or the performance of inadvertent gestures.[11]

The linguistic slips that Freud called *Fehlleistungen* are now commonly known as "Freudian slips" in everyday conversation or writing. Among such unconscious giveaways was that of Freud's "Dora" in the "symptomatic act" of playing with the clasp of her reticule, which the doctor decoded as an unconscious mimicking of female masturbation.[12] A reticule was a small purse, either beaded, or knitted metal mesh, with a clasp at the top. Such an object is present in the portrait of an anonymous woman by the Viennese photographic studio Atelier Kral from about 1907 (**fig. 64**). A reticule of Viennese provenance in Jugendstil design (**fig. 65**) comes down to us in the twenty-first-century as a sensuous flexible little object—an animalistic vaginal sort of container with feminine shapes, its interior usually not seen.

Medicine, classicism, and pederasty also corroborated each other in published or private photography at the threshold of the twentieth century. Medical photography thus overlapped with the photography of ancient sculpture once again in putting bodies on display. Dr. Theodore Beer, professor of medicine at the University of Vienna, was a case in point. Dr. Beer was tried for homosexuality in 1905 for having supposedly seduced and photographed two adolescents, called "adult boys" in the *Neue Freie Presse*.[13] The nude photographs, which were considered indecent, shocked the general public. But Beer's legal defense was that the photograph was to serve as an illustration for a book he was writing about "the history of ideal human beauty." Such a

11. Freud 1901; Freud 1905b, 3–122.
12. Freud 1905b, 77–79.
13. *Neue Freie Presse*, October 27, 1905, 11.

lofty, academic sounding topic, with its allusion to the history of art and classical aesthetics, could serve as the cover to a whole Pandora's box of homosexual erotic themes.[14] If the author's interest in photographing pubescent boys was motivated by scientific or cultural research, as his credentials would lead the reader to assume, then his book could take its place beside the illustrated works of Schultze-Naumburg and Carl Heinrich Stratz, whose ostensible topics (health, medicine, and, again, the history of aesthetics) were vehicles for material that could be subjected to pornographic and racist gazes.

The German racialist and anti-Semitic writer Carl Heinrich Stratz (1858–1924), a gynecologist and contemporary of Schultze-Naumburg, used photography as his primary medium too, as in *Die Rassenschönheit des Weibes* (1922) and *Die Schönheit des Weibliches Körpers* (1898). Stratz's approach to Jewish ethnography and anthropology, for example in *Was sind Juden? Eine ethnographisch-anthropologische Studie* of 1903, was strongly orientalizing.[15] Stratz's book on the aesthetics of the female body, *Die Schönheit des Weiblichen Körpers* (*The Beauty of the Female Body*, 1898), also used a pointed strategy of photographic illustration.[16] In a disingenuous manner Stratz dedicated his book to "Mothers, Doctors, and Artists." Corsets were among Stratz's topics too.

At the turn of the century Jewish orientalism was a subject of much attention in Austria, Germany, and France.[17] In Stratz's study of the Jewish racial imprint, he published ethnographic photographs of Tunisian and Algerian Jewish women, whose striking costumes, with pointed hats and silk, and bandage-like trousers, were displayed as exotic (**fig. 66**).

These engaging pictures, ostensibly ethnographic and informational, were made in large numbers by such Western colonial photographers as Marcelin Flandrin (1889–1957) and Rudolf Lehnert (1878–1948) depicting Jews as exotic non-Europeans. What are Jews? Stratz used photographs to construct his argument that Jews were non-Europeans of an exotic caste. It scarcely beleaguers the historical imagination to bring these illustrated books that were circulated in Vienna into the purview of the Freudian psychology that was emerging there at the same

14. Vyleta 2012, 135–44.

15. Stratz 1903.

16. Stratz 1898.

17. Bergstein 2014, 149–72.

time, especially since we know that in 1911 such photographic essays were brought under consideration by Freud's Vienna Psychoanalytic Society.[18]

The kind of visual material I've been discussing here can be brought to bear on Freud's famously unfinished analysis of a hysterical young woman, Ida Bauer, whose medical pseudonym was "Dora." Using the vocabulary of archaeological retrieval, Freud called his case history of "Dora" a fragment. Or, perhaps more artistically speaking, in a word Freud would have understood through his studies of Michelangelo, it should have been designated a *nonfinito*. Rather than a fragment of a finished work from the past, which was subsequently degraded by time, "Dora" was an unfinished attempt, an essay always underway, an adventure never to be finished in its author's lifetime, ripe with possibility for completion.

Who was Dora? Ida Bauer (1882–1945) was the daughter of bourgeois Jewish parents in Vienna, living on Berggasse, the same street as the Freud family. Ida's father, Philipp, sought help from (the fatherly doctor) Freud first in 1894 when he experienced partial paralysis and pathological confusion as a result of premarital syphilis, a disease that he had also communicated to his wife. Ida's mother, Katharina Gerber, apparently suffered from "housewife's psychosis," a neurotic compulsion to constantly clean and organize the home. By the time Ida herself was twelve, she developed a persistent cough, a *tussis nervosa*, which manifested together with aphonia, debilitating migraines, and chronic depression. She coughed and smoked her way through these anguished adolescent symptoms. When Ida showed signs of becoming suicidal, she was diagnosed with hysteria and brought to Dr. Freud by her father in 1898 when she was seventeen years old.[19] From this point on, Dora's case was chronicled by a symphony of male voices: father, doctors, and other authority figures.

Ida Bauer was involved with the "K" couple (pronounced "kah" in German), named for the final syllable of their family name, Zellenka. Frau K. was Peppina (Giuseppina) Zellenka née Heumann (born in Ancona, Italy, as Bella Peppina Neumann), who died of tuberculosis in 1912. She was the recipient of sexual attention and love from Philipp Bauer, Ida's father. Her husband Johann ("Hans") Zellenka, known

18. Nunberg and Federn 1967, vol. 3, 194–200.

19. See Mahony 1996 for an important study of Ida Bauer and her family.

in the psychoanalytic literature as "Herr K." died in 1913, also from tuberculosis.

Tuberculosis, as we know from Thomas Mann (1875–1955) and more recently Susan Sontag (1933–2004), possessed its own erotic charge.[20] Sontag stated that to nineteenth-century people, tuberculosis was seen as "a vehicle of excess feeling." It was the disease that made manifest intense longing; that disclosed, in spite of the reluctance of the individual, that which the individual did not want to reveal. The contrast is no longer between moderate passions and excessive ones, but between hidden passions and those that are brought into the open: "Illness reveals desires of which the patient probably was unaware."[21] Tuberculosis, as the disease that makes manifest intense desire, and thus reveals unconscious wishes, was therefore like psychoanalysis itself. What better diagnosis for Peppina and Hans Zellenka, whose desires and entanglements were so troublesome to one another, as well as causing difficulties for Dora, her father, her mother, and Freud?

If illness is a metaphor, then this case is doubly perplexing, because Dora's father, Philipp, was both tubercular and syphilitic. Philipp Bauer was unwell, infected with a chronic infection from tertiary neurosyphilis, as well as gonorrhea, and sometimes suffered from paralysis and mental confusion. Philipp's romantic involvement with Peppina Zellenka began at his sickbed, when his wife Käthe Bauer apparently became withdrawn and unwilling or unable to care for her husband. As Andrew W. Ellis has stated, "a mutual attraction between Philipp and Peppina flourished in the darkened room."[22] In the melodrama of Breuer's case history, this phenomenon echoes the darkened sickroom of Siegmund Pappenheim (d.1881), Anna O.'s father, where Bertha Pappenheim's and Josef Breuer's mutual fascination ignited among hallucinations and ghosts. Indeed, the "darkened room" (camera obscura) provided a place that could be "captured" by photography and haunted by apparitions.

To further complicate the issue, Herr K. was a mutual family friend of the Freuds and Bauers, who knew each other from the spa town of Merano in Alto Adige (then part of the Austrian Empire) as well as from Vienna. Herr K. made sexual advances toward Ida Bauer on more than one occasion, first when she was only thirteen and then when she

20. Bergstein 2020, 36–51.

21. Sontag 1978, 13, 21, 25, 29, 39, 45; Sontag 1989, 45.

22. Ellis, Raitmayr, and Herbst 2015, 9.

was sixteen. Ida underwent hydrotherapy and electric shocks as cures for hysteria possibly occasioned by these sexual traumas before being interviewed by Freud.[23] Meanwhile Ida had developed and harbored a kind of a "gynaecophilic" (as Freud called it) fascination, or same-sex "crush" on Peppina Zellenka, praising her beauty as she imagined the Italian woman's lovely white skin, her "adorable white body."[24]

At the turn of the twentieth century a woman's skin, which presented what Mechtild Fend recently called "a constellation of issues," served as a sort of erotic magnet to the admiring male gaze. The dermis was imagined as what Fend calls a "communicative membrane," and at the same time a boundary of the individual person.[25] Henry Havelock-Ellis wrote about the psychology of skin in terms of sexual attraction, noting that snow, alabaster, ivory, milk, and cream were all called in as similes when praising a woman's skin.[26] Whiteness, as we well know, was an important criterion in the valuation of a woman's beauty in Europe. This indicates that Dora may have taken (consciously or not) a male position of desire toward Peppina, and Freud states that such language ("adorable white body") spoke in "accents more appropriate to a lover than to a defeated rival."

But Ida seems not to have been a rival to Peppina for Herr K.'s affections, which she never sought but rather repulsed. Nor did the two women (Dora and Frau K.) seem to have a balanced lesbian relationship. Dora was the admiring lover to Peppina's maternal figure, and even took care of Peppina's children as required for Peppina to have time alone with Dora's father. As such, Ida's same-sex fascination for Frau K. was underscored, consciously or not, by the fact that her father, too, had a largely unhidden romantic relationship with Peppina. As Jacqueline Rose explained in her essay on the Dora case, Freud set out not to "classify Dora as a homosexual in any simple sense," but rather "to acknowledge the homosexual factor in all feminine sexuality."[27]

Ida Bauer finished her analysis with Freud in 1902, having left the case history in a "fragmentary state," and went on with her life. In 1903 she married the aspiring musician Ernst Adler, who had been raised by

23. Mahony 1996, 18–19.

24. Freud 1905b, 61.

25. Fend 2017, 311–12.

26. Havelock-Ellis 2018.

27. Rose 2005, 28–47.

his uncle, the actor Adolph Ritter von Sonnenthal (the famous "Jewish Jupiter" of the Viennese stage). The couple had a prosperous and glamorous lifestyle, attending the theater and opera on a regular basis. Ernst Adler, however, lost his health and well-being: injured fighting on the Eastern Front in 1914 Adler went deaf in one ear and for the rest of his life suffered from physical and psychological difficulties.[28] Meanwhile, Ida Bauer acclimated herself to the theater world and became a working stage actress.

Bauer died in New York in 1945, having fled Paris in 1939 before the Nazi occupation, by way of Casablanca in Morocco. Her son Kurt Herbert Adler (1905–88) was born in Vienna but left Europe in 1939, spending the rest of his life in the United States as a celebrated opera conductor. Bauer had a career as an actress, was photographed in a number of different roles, and maintained a close and trusting friendship with Peppina Zellenka throughout her life. Peppina ("Frau K.") was deported from Vienna in 1942 to the concentration camp Theresienstadt, which she survived against considerable odds: she was found alive with 168 others at the liberation. She died of natural causes in Mayrhofen in 1949 at the Hotel Pension Kumbichl (still operative as a resort in 2021). Peppina never disclosed to anyone that she was Freud's "Frau K." Perhaps after Theresienstadt, the Freud episode and her close relationship with Philipp Bauer, who had after all died more than thirty years before, had dimmed in importance.

Girls diagnosed as hysterics, as in the case of Ida Bauer, were always burdened by gendered viewpoints that were the product of medical paternalism. Already early in his career Freud, citing Anna O. and Josef Breuer, announced that a patient's transference love for the physician was a vital part of psychoanalytic treatment. In Freud's essay of 1914 *On Narcissism* he proclaimed, "The majority of hysterical women are among the attractive, and even beautiful, representatives of their sex."[29] Dora had apparently been one of these. She'd had several adult male admirers since the age of thirteen. The Bauer family was affectively entangled with the Zellenka family in ways we would now consider unhealthy or at least, as we would say in 2023, "inappropriate." Hans Zellenka gave Ida numerous compliments and gifts, and a love affair

28. Ellis 2015, 14.
29. Freud 1914, 99.

developed between Peppina Zellenka and Philipp Bauer, who were in any case each other's long-term confidants.

As we have seen, family systems were troubled in these unwieldy constellations, and now in the twenty-first century we might find that networks, rather than individuals, were ailing. In other words, these disorders were not necessarily due to the neurosis or neuroses of any of the individual players who presented themselves for medical psychoanalysis. From a standpoint in 2023, the entire family system would have to be interrogated in historical, anthropological, or sociological as well as psychological terms rather than seeking hysterical pathology only in the young woman called Dora. Although Freud was excellent at social observation, he still concerned himself, first and foremost, with medically oriented case histories of individual suffering, frequently cast in melodramatic terms with reference to "darkened rooms" and unconscious ideation (ghostly memories) from the past.

Freud registered surprise at Dora's reluctance to feel flattered at Herr K.'s sexual advances. This reaction was, of course, cultural. Beginning with Erik Erikson, we later critics tend to be shocked that anyone would *not* be upset by the situation.[30] Hans Zellenka was an adult married man, and Dora still a girl at the age of thirteen when Zellenka let his intentions be known. She first came into Freud's office at age seventeen before the turn of the twentieth century (1898). Freud retold the story in print in 1901 (1905) when Ida Bauer was still a young woman. Recent critics have seen Freud as a patriarchal enabler intent on covering things up for Dora's father and his friend Zellenka, while at the same time harboring a transferential (or countertransferential) love for the young woman. Nobody would deny that the emplotment of Dora's case history is fraught. These are fascinating propositions, training the light of psychoanalytic critique on Freud himself. But who loved whom within Freud's inner circle must remain a question for a more informed historical speculation than I can offer.

My query now is rather to ask: how would a middle-aged Austrian man envisage his love affair with a Jewish teenager like Ida Bauer? What were the mental pictures that accompanied such a fantasy? The answer, I believe, can be found in the visual culture of the turn of the twentieth century. In fact, we can see this mode of exploitative and misogynist

30. Gay 1988, 686.

thinking in the production and reception of photographs in Vienna around 1900. Much of this material was coated in sugary classicism in publication. Again we turn to the photography of Carl Heinrich Stratz. Stratz, in his treatise on the beauty of the female body, *Die Schönheit des Weiblichen Körpers* (*The Beauty of the Female Body*), compared a photograph of a fifteen-year-old Viennese Jewish girl (labelled as such) with the ancient *Esquiline Venus* in Rome.[31]

The *Esquiline Venus* was excavated in 1874, together with other marbles buried under the Esquiline Hill, in Piazza Dante. The charming *Venus* was probably made around the middle of the first century CE, most likely a copy of a Greek original from the first century BCE. The statue may represent (under the guise of the goddess Aphrodite) Cleopatra VII Philopator (69–30 BCE) of the Ptolemaic dynasty. If not a Jewish girl with eastern European origins like the model on her facing-page, then at least Cleopatra (whose name meant "glorification of the Father" and Philopator "love of the father") was from the east: an Egyptian adolescent from Alexandria. Cleopatra was a figure of great interest in the "Egyptomania" of nineteenth-century Europe and was represented in an academic painting by Jean-Léon Gérôme, *Cleopatra and Caesar* (1866), where she is represented as a beautiful young brunette emerging from an unfurled carpet to confront Julius Caesar for the first time, at age fourteen, during the Roman expedition into Egypt.[32] In the photographic illustrations that supported Stratz's text on the beauty of the female body, a model's age and ethnicity are frequently mentioned in the captions. Most of the model-subjects were underage; copies of classical statues were used as props to validate the pictorial content of the photographs.

We may well ask: How did the author/photographer engage his models? And how did an author like Stratz gather his illustrations? Because Leipzig was a center of the book-publishing industry, I suspect that there would have been an abundance of photographs at hand. This is a topic that deserves more research in such Leipzig archives as may remain. Meanwhile, in Vienna we know from Stefan Zweig that photographs of nude girls and women were sold under the table at cafés and by professional studio photographers, such as the ever-prolific

31. Stratz 1898, 18–19.
32. Ackerman 1986.

Otto Schmidt (1849–1920).[33] Why did established Viennese photographers like Schmidt, whose output was tremendous, undertake to sell voyeuristic photographs of young girls? The corpus of Schmidt's work comprised a kind of *omnium gatherum* of photographic topics of his time: from his *Wiener Typen* (Viennese street-types) cabinet cards published in 1886, to sentimental family portraits with an emphasis on motherhood, to classical nudes, to voyeuristic pictures of little girls.

These last photographs, including one of a seated girl by Otto Schmidt, prurient and degrading, were not only permitted, but also legitimized and published under the modern auspices of health, nature, beauty, or art. In terms of anxiety, however, such photographs were eminently comparable to some drawings of similar subjects attributed to Egon Schiele around 1910 (**fig. 67**). Schiele's *Seated Sick Girl* in the Leopold Museum, for example, is close enough to have been based on the offensive *Photograph of a Young Girl* by Otto Schmidt, which, because of its exploitative content, could not be reproduced on the pages of this book.

Whence the models and the pictures? These were among the "Susse Mädeln" of Viennese life; they came from the same class of women that were prostitutes in the brothels and the streets of Vienna, as well as the numerous waitresses, governesses, actresses, and domestic servants who engaged in covert or part-time prostitution. Such women were chronicled in *The Red House* as those who worked during the day in poorer-paid jobs of the "better sort," including governesses, models in department stores, reception clerks in offices, dressmakers, and even married women whose husbands traveled for work, who would hire themselves out for half a night to a brothel for a percentage of their earnings.[34]

Covert prostitution within family circles, what we would now term sexual predation, was sometimes expected or required of young poor or middle-class women in Viennese society. The tragedy of covert prostitution is best chronicled in literary fiction by Arthur Schnitzler in his novella *Fräulein Else*, where the nineteen-year-old Else is asked to prostitute herself (to show herself naked in private) to a friend of

33. Zweig 1964, 75–76.
34. Jerusalem 1909, 76, 86.

the family, Herr von Dorsday, who had long admired her in erotic expectation. In the context of a family visit, when she was just twelve or thirteen, Dorsday had stroked her cheek and declared her to be already a young lady. Later, when Else's father faced a crushing debt, he advised her to approach Dorsday to request a sizable loan. This action would be absolutely repulsive to her, as it was already understood that the collateral would be her young body, as well as the innocence and honor that had thus far guaranteed her relative mental freedom. On the road to her destruction, Else's ability to think is eroded at a manic pace and replaced by the negative fantasy of taking her own life. Her suicide, a performance of self-annihilation in which she falls, naked, to her death before a crowd of onlookers, scandalized her family and everyone else involved. This vengeful spectacle of a suicide is both the climax and denouement of the story. *Fräulein Else* is thus a tragedy in the full meaning of the word.

Daria Colombo (2010) and Diane O'Donoghue (2019) have both written on the low social status of female domestic servants, whom Freud characterized, in a capitalist conflation of poverty and immorality, as "people of low morals," or what his patients referred to as "worthless female material."[35] These young women from the working classes, including Jewish girls from Lemberg (Lviv), were frequently hired by bourgeois families primarily for sex with the men in the household, and especially to initiate the younger men.[36] At Lemberg in 1909 police reported that two-thirds of registered prostitutes had been domestic servants previously. Richard von Krafft-Ebing, whom Edward Bristow refers to as "the Newton of sexual deviance," concluded that the sexual pursuit of maids was related to "apron fetishism."[37] These days, historians such as Bristow and others would see cause and effect as having worked the other way around: domestic servants were socially powerless and isolated, and therefore likely victims of sexual assault in bourgeois households. The societal habit of exploiting maidservants as prostitutes *ad hoc* could have established the apron (and the role of maidservant) as an automatic sexual fetish for men of the entitled classes. This stereotype of the sexy, clever housemaid was reified

35. Colombo 2010, 835–59.
36. O'Donoghue 2019, 63–64.
37. Bristow 1983, 98.

in the erotic Saturn films and elsewhere. Such was the golden age of photography that in Vienna, as elsewhere, portraits of servants were made by local photographic studios, as in a sympathetic portrait of Frau Frorst by Dr. Székely.

Was urban Vienna truly the "Sahara of morality" that Else Jerusalem documents in *The Red House*?[38] The same idea of an overpopulated moral desert occupied by a dying prostitute was expressed in the familiar aria "Sempre libera," sung by the doomed courtesan Violetta in Giuseppe Verdi's *La Traviata*, composed by the librettist Francesco Maria Piave (1810–76).

Povera donna, sola, abbandonata
In questo popoloso deserto
Che appellano Parigi

The *anomie* of nineteenth-century urban life was defined by Émile Durkheim in 1893, to refer to the disappointing dissolution of moral codes and expectations when people feel alienated (or dissociated) from their social environment. This concept had been romanticized in the opera *La Traviata*, which literally means "girl who went the wrong way." Verdi's *Traviata* premiered in Venice at La Fenice around the middle of the nineteenth century (1853) and had an enduring impact in cultural history. Let us jump to the turn of the more recent *fin-de-siècle* when the twentieth century expired. If the popular television series *Sex and the City* (1998–2004) had been styled as a tragedy rather than a comedy, its profligate female characters might have suffered from disquiet, even regretting some of their empty or materialistic concerns, concerns that they had in common with the supposedly self-seeking *lorettes* of a hundred years earlier in Paris.

Photography had an important role in the business of prostitution, as provincial girls and their panders sent photographs to the brothels of Vienna as applications for work there. In fact, part of the fictional Mrs. Goldscheider's work at the Red House was to review packages of photographs that came in the post from procurers and traffickers from the outlying regions.

The urban anomie of the nineteenth-century European metropolis was played out, both in fact and fiction, in the lives of unmarried

38. Jerusalem 1909, 110.

girls and women struggling to survive. Girls and young women were destroyed as the "good and pious" people of the monied classes implanted an undertow of self-contempt and self-immolation in these girls.[39] Such societal ills were abetted by commercial photography in the production and circulation of thousands of photographs of naked women and girls.

Photographs were part of the everyday business of prostitution, and in the reception salons of brothels there were photographic albums containing pictures of young women in the nude or in negligée, who were available for clients to choose from.[40] But such exploitation of girls existed not only throughout the working and criminal classes of society. Within the coterie of Viennese literati it was considered "modern" or socially unconventional in an artistic way ("Bohemian") to keep young girls, also known as "child-women," as mistresses. In visual culture this infatuation with, and empowerment of, the "child-woman" was apparent in the work of Dominik Stahala, Otto Schmidt, and others.

In a literary example, it is well known that the poet Peter Altenberg (1859–1919) collected photographs of young girls and decorated his room in the Graben Hotel with them. And let us remember that, when he was forty-five, Altenberg's (Czech-born) mistress, Albine Ruprich (1890–1920) was only fourteen years old. A nude photograph of Ruprich by Franz Xavier Setzer (1886–1939) (unpublished in its own time) is exquisitely pretty, bringing the sexual exploitation of young girls into the fashionable milieu of Viennese culture. A standing nude photograph of Ruprich by Hermann Clemens Kosel (1867–1945) now conserved in the Historisches Museum der Stadt Wien, bears the following inscription by Altenberg: "Deine Seele, Albine Ruprich/14-Jährige, ist so vollkommen/wie Dein geliebter Leib!/Peter Altenberg." (Your soul, Albine Ruprich, fourteen-year-old, is as perfect as you beloved body (flesh) Peter Altenberg.) Andrew Barker, in *Telegrams from the Soul* (1996), stated that a "disturbing head and torso shot of the naked fourteen-year-old Albine Ruprich, her gaze brimming with reproach, betoken a side of Altenberg's sexuality which is far from wholesome."[41] It is not clear which image of Albine Ruprich Barker was referring to, but the "gaze brimming with reproach" is not perceptible to me in any

39. Jerusalem 1909, 110.
40. Wingfield 2017, 134.
41. Barker 1996, 154–55.

of the photographs I have cited. Furthermore, as stated above, since photographs are essentially opaque representations, it is never possible to know what a portrait subject is thinking from his or her photograph, although a great deal of tendentious thinking has gone into such interpretations.

The concept of "Das Kindweib" or the child-woman, which announced a theory of precocious female adolescent sexuality, was introduced by Fritz Wittels (1880–1950) in a lecture of 1907 to the Viennese psychoanalytic society.[42] According to Wittels's memoir, he also read the report to Freud in private. The subject of his discussion was his young lover, Irma Karsczewska (1890–1933), whom he referred to as a precocious *hetaera*. The report was then published as an essay by Wittels in *Die Fackel*, the widely read literary magazine edited by Karl Kraus (1874–1936).

Kraus had also had a romantic involvement with Karsczewska, and had intervened in her relations with Wittels, as though such relations were a sort of social entertainment or game. In Karczewska's diaries she recalled in 1930 that Kraus had first taken her from her home at the age of fourteen and a half.[43] Karl Kraus drew Fritz Wittels into his vortex, and explained to Wittels that in modern times women were expected to live "against their nature," insofar as they were all basically *hetaerae*, or whores, whose lives should be given over to the sexual entertainment of men.[44]

In Else Jerusalem's anthropological novel, *The Red House*, a philosophical former teacher, named Horner, states, "The harlot is the symbol of Nature. What we call life is naught but the vibration of her lustful, insensate, vain, body, offering itself to anyone."[45] Clearly, Else Jerusalem's world was also that of Kraus and Wittels, and Jerusalem had a gimlet eye for the exploitation of women. Such psychosocial pronouncements by adult males like Wittels or Kraus (or the fictional Horner) justified affairs with girls of fourteen and younger, who were thought to be sexually charming and precociously available. These networks of men who at once adored and condescended toward young girls were entrenched in prevailing social systems.

42. Wittels 1995, xi.
43. Wittels 1995, 166.
44. Wittels 1995, 55.
45. Jerusalem 1909, 110.

The official age of maturity for a woman in the Austrian Empire was twenty-four.[46] But the ideal love object, as perceived in the erotic photography and literature of the time, seems to have been a good ten years younger. Felix Salten (1869–1945) was the presumed author of the pornographic memoir said to be by Josefine Mutzenbacher, *The Story of a Viennese Wench as Told by Herself* of 1906. In the story of her life, this young prostitute tells of having been photographed in graphically sexual positions, with and without a male partner, at the age of fourteen. The age of fourteen was apparently the "ideal age" for females in Viennese erotica, as it comes up time and again in photography, reportage, and literature as the age when girls, at their most desirable to adult men, lost their innocence.

Grete Lainer's diary (*A Young Girl's Diary*) was endorsed in a letter by Sigmund Freud in 1915 before its publication: "Never before, I believe, has anything been written enabling us to see so clearly into the soul of a young girl belonging to our social and cultural stratum."[47] The diarist alludes several times in this memoir of her childhood to the age of fourteen being the age of erotic awakening for girls in Vienna. On the day the diarist herself turns fourteen, she considers herself no longer a child. This is especially noticeable when, from a younger age, she described the behavior and attitudes toward her older sister, Dora. When Grete's father is enraged by the fact that Dora may have flirted at the tennis courts, Grete states, "What upset her more than anything else was that father said in front of me: 'This little chit of fourteen is already encouraging people to make love to her.'"[48] The father's anger may have been a response of personal anxiety to his realization that his elder daughter had come of age, and henceforth her sexuality would have to be kept under control. She was now at risk, and an unspecified anxiety and sorrow followed in the daughters as well as the father. Another personage in *A Young Girl's Diary*, a friend called Hella, cannot be officially engaged to her fiancé until the following year because "she can't be engaged until she is fourteen because her parents would not allow it."[49]

The psychoanalyst Hermine Hug-Hellmuth, herself a pupil of Isidor Sadger, became a member of the Vienna Psychoanalytic Society

46. See Wingfield 2017, 51.

47. Lainer 2006, 1.

48. Lainer 2006, 10–11.

49. Lainer 2006, 113, 125.

and wrote about adolescence in the conscious wake of psychological literature by G. Stanley Hall. She was one of the first psychoanalysts to deal with children, and with observations of children at play. Her career was marked by two "scandals," first the critical opinion that *A Young Girl's Diary* was a forgery, written by an adult, perhaps herself. Second, her brutal murder by her own nephew in 1924 may have besmirched her legacy with a "criminal" taint.[50] According to Rosemary Balsam, Hug-Hellmuth's critical fortunes have suffered by way of the "meager and denigrating" credit from Anna Freud and Melanie Klein, who were in some way her rivals.[51] Balsam has now revived Hug-Hellmuth's dignity, claiming that the men in Freud's Wednesday circle "did not notice that before their eyes Hug-Hellmuth was giving birth to analytic play therapy!"[52] In 1921 Cyril Burt, writing in the August issue of the *British Journal of Psychology,* claimed the diary was a forgery created by Hug-Hellmuth. The plot thickened when in the preface to the third German edition Hug-Hellmuth revealed that she had met the author of the diary (then a nineteen-year-old woman called Rita) who was living in a Viennese boarding house and gave her the manuscript as she was engaged to be married, before she left for the Serbian front to serve as a nurse in the First World War. Whether or not "Rita" truly existed, her character was fabricated realistically in the pages of *A Young Girl's Diary.*

Literary fiction, as well as the literary tropes that take place in the process of psychoanalysis, can and should be treated as historical material. In fact, the authorship of this document could be investigated in a psychological study unto itself. Whether the *Young Girl's Diary* was written by a person named "Rita" or Grete Lainer, or an anonymous girl somewhere between the ages of eleven and fourteen, or whether it was in fact composed by the psychoanalyst Hermine Hug-Hellmuth who presented it in Vienna in 1919, possibly from childhood recollections of her own, matters relatively little for my historical purposes. The text has a complex authorship and provenance. The fact that the diary chronicled girlhood concerns in a Viennese psychoanalytic milieu makes it "authentic" enough to be held up as literary/historical evidence

50. Balsam 2003, 328–29.
51. Balsam 2003, 337.
52. Balsam 2003, 338.

in a discussion of the age of maturity in Viennese girls in the second decade of the twentieth century.

Certainly, beyond any phenomena of despicable pederasty, young girls apparently had the agency to inspire deep romantic passion in adults: the diarist speaks of a fourteen-year-old girl causing the suicide of a grown man.[53] This brings us back to the idea of the young, innately dangerous *hetaerae*, who could injure the lives of men with their seductive powers. The fact that they were characterized as predators rather than victims made the abuse of these girls all the more palatable to male-dominated society.

The intense attention paid by grown men to such girls who were defined as *hetaerae* was clearly counter to the girls' well-being, and not only because they typically became ill and died young. The beautiful young actress Annie Kalmar (1877–1901), Karl Kraus's first love, was described by Wittels as "promiscuous, careless, and drunk," without any accounting for her condition: what was it that had ruined her at such an early age? Kalmar died of pneumonia in 1901 at the age of twenty-three. Wittels's description of Annie Kalmar as "promiscuous, careless, and drunk" stems almost directly from Cesare Lombroso's estimation of the female prostitute as a criminal. Lombroso considered many of the women on the urban streets of northern Italy to be prostitutes, especially those who were impoverished, homeless, or underemployed.[54] Such was Lombroso's somewhat morbid, misogynistic imagination about women and girls. They existed, according to him, in a degenerate state of savagery where heredity had for several generations overridden free will and produced an innate primitive state, much like that of childhood, in a certain population of women.[55] Local influences such as the nineteenth-century phenomena of tuberculosis, syphilis, morphine addiction, and alcoholism supposedly caused an increase in decadent behavior, including prostitution itself. From our twenty-first-century viewpoint, Lombroso had probably reversed cause and effect: tolerated (overt or covert) prostitution of this time weakened girls and women in such a way that they became vulnerable to tuberculosis, syphilis, morphine addiction, and alcoholism at a young age. The personification of syphilis in mid-nineteenth-century visual culture was a so-called

53. Lainer 2006, 22.

54. Lombroso 1893, 16.

55. Lombroso 1893, 10, 16, 20, 22.

grisette, like the ones invented by the French illustrator Paul Gavarni (1804–66), but with a death's head, wielding a mask, as she flirts with a healthy man.[56]

Irma Karsczewska, the so-called *Kindweib*, had venereal disease by the time she was a young teenager. Individuals like Wittels and Kraus discarded young girls when they got bored with the limited scope of their life experience and conversation. These men were misogynists, bona fide reactionary thinkers after the fashion of Otto Weininger (1880–1903) and Karl Lueger (1844–1910). Felix Salten was famous in the United States for having written *Bambi, A Life in the Woods* (1923), which became an animated Disney film in 1942. We do not know if Salten, who belonged to the literary circles of Hugo von Hofmannsthal (1874–1929) and Arthur Schnitzler (1862–1931), the so-called Jung Wien group, was actively cruel toward girls, or whether he wrote *Josefine* only for the money. (We do know that Salten made next to nothing on the proceeds from *Bambi.*)

In Schnitzler's novella *Fraülein Else*, the aging ("almost sixty-five") sexual predator Herr von Dorsday, who required Else to disrobe for his personal delectation, had caressed her face when she was about twelve or thirteen, saying, "Schon ein ganzes Fraülein," or "already a fully grown-up young lady."[57] For Else there is no escape but suicide by an overdose of the hypnotic-sedative veronal.

Wittels himself was, in any case, far from being open to a feminist point of view; he drove Karen Horney (1885–1952) out of the New York Psychoanalytic Institute in 1941 because of her differences with Freud and her pioneering attention to women's issues in psychology. Wittels objected to education for women and especially to women (like Horney) attending medical school and working as physicians. Although Kraus and Wittels were by their own lights modernists who lived far into the twentieth century, their moral customs were shaped in an earlier time when a woman's or girl's sexuality was to be reviled: exploited, laughed at, and even despised. Leo Lensing's keen critique of Edward Timms's *Freud and the Child Woman* claims that Timms, following Kraus and Wittels, was defamatory toward Irma Karsczewska and other girls (Altenberg's Albine Ruprich comes to mind) who were

56. Gilman 1985, 106–07.

57. Szalay 2000, 13–14, "reveals desires of which the patient was probably unaware."

drawn into the sexual intrigues of older men.[58] On the subject of young teenage girls, Kraus, Wittels, and perhaps even Timms tended to be reactionary thinkers, after the fashion of Otto Weininger, Karl Lueger, and the Italian criminologist Cesare Lombroso. Adolf Loos (1870–1933), by temperament and historical moment more forward-thinking than his contemporaries, commented about the aesthetic fluctuation of taste in terms of sensuality, and the recent preference for the "woman-child" in society: "The call for youth rang out. The woman-child became fashionable. People craved immaturity. The girl's psyche was dissected and exploited in literature. Peter Altenberg."[59] Loos referred to the risqué act of the Barrison sisters, who, scantily dressed as babies, smoked and held kittens to their crotches in naughty gestures.

The brothels of Austria were officially closed in 1921, but the anthropological novel *The Red House*, an exposé written by Else Jerusalem (1909), serves as a key to the social and psychological *demimonde* of Viennese prostitution. Else Jerusalem's fact-based writing illuminates the predicament of many young girls—some 50,000 at any given moment—working in brothels in turn-of-the-century Vienna. Even girls from the high bourgeoisie (comparable in social status to Ida Bauer) were procured; many of these girls were underage or even children. In *The Red House*, one of the prostitutes found lounging on a divan in the reception area is described as "a little girl of about twelve."[60] Girls were recruited from cafés, railway stations, dancing schools, and theaters, and even from the more elegant residential streets in the capital.[61] Sander Gilman tells us that from 1873 to 1883 most of the registered prostitutes in Vienna were legally minors.[62] But many of the unregistered prostitutes were still girls or prepubescent children when they were used for prostitution.

Impoverished, poorly educated girls were characterized as sexual seductresses and predators, responsible for their own condition in life as well as for the demise of grown men.[63] Whereas in Paris prostitutes were categorized as humble *grisettes*, who dedicated their lives to

58. Lensing 1996, 322–32.
59. Loos 2019, 93.
60. Jerusalem 1909, 287.
61. Jerusalem 1909, 76 and *passim*.
62. Gilman 1985, 41.
63. Gilman 1985, 43.

art and artists, or scheming *insoumise*-type *lorettes*, who aspired to bourgeois money, luxury, and fame, or even grandiose courtesans, who may have assumed a degree of actual influence, these ranks did not seem to exist in Vienna with quite the same theatrical or literary precision.[64] In the masculine fantasies of turn-of-the-century Vienna, boundaries between the seductive child and the degenerate lower class female were as blurred as they were in Lombroso's view of urban Italian women. Prostitution itself was thus configured as a form of (female) mental illness, an aspect of criminal pathology that was inherent in certain women.

I have already noted that immigrants from the provinces of the Austrian Empire were among the first to be recruited into the slavery of the brothel, with little if any means of escape. This was particularly true of Jewish girls and those from the Austro-Hungarian Crownlands of Bohemia (presently the Czech Republic) and Hungary. Budapest was a source of young female bodies for Jewish traffickers. Sarah Grossman, for example, who was known as "The Turk" for sending young women east to Constantinople, conducted business at the Café Herzl in Budapest, where honest Jewish marriage brokers were also known to hold meetings with clients.[65] The backwaters of impoverished Jewish Galicia were also exploited by procurers of young women for the prostitution trade.[66]

A popular cliché at the time was that Jewish girls from the Leopoldstadt neighborhood of Vienna were sold into prostitution by their mothers who paraded them in front of potential clients at cafés.[67] We must remember that prostitution had a wider practice than just that of individual women caught up in the tolerated sex trade. Covert prostitutes included dancers, domestic servants, waitresses, and others who were occasionally or regularly paid for sex outside the public eye. In the late imperial prostitution business, women as well as men trafficked in the young women of their own provincial regions. Jewish traffickers were particularly reviled for participating in the so-called white slave trade, and eastern European Jews (including those residing in Budapest or Vienna) were stereotyped as people who would supposedly exploit

64. Sullivan 2003, *passim*.

65. Bristow 1983, 68.

66. Wingfield 2017, 12.

67. Klein 1904, 267.

their own daughters by selling them into sexual slavery.[68] Throughout central and eastern Europe Jews were routinely slandered in the press for their supposed propensity for the vice trade. This was true in Warsaw and Lemberg (Lviv), where letters to the press by anti-Semites characterized Jews as brothel-keepers and pimps who profited by selling Christian women. One writer in Warsaw stated, "Most brothel owners are Jews with university educations. All customers are Jewish. The girls are mostly servants—Christian."[69] Adolf Hitler continued this stream of thought when describing the Austro-Hungarian capital in *Mein Kampf*: "an icy shudder ran down my spine when seeing for the first time [in Vienna] the Jew as an evil, shameless, and calculating manager of this shocking vice, the outcome of the scum of the big city."[70]

Prostitution was a complicated business, and Jewish brothel-keepers like Sarah Grossman, Madam Sachs, or the fictional madams like Elise Goldscheider were not the owners of their own houses.[71] Their expertise was in negotiating with the police and regulating the lives of the inmates living in the brothels.

It was a slippery slope for girls and young women in the city of Vienna, where vortices of misogyny, anti-Semitism, and anti-immigrant propaganda could easily swallow up unprotected young women. Life in the imperial capital placed a premium on assimilation, particularly among impoverished Jews from the eastern provinces of Galicia and Bukovina. Else Jerusalem's fictional madam, Elise Goldscheider in *The Red House*, worked as a procuress in order to keep her own daughter free from the hardship she herself had known as a Jewish girl, "free from the atmosphere of the second-hand clothes shop … free from the taint of the ghetto."[72]

Another Viennese woman of Jewish origin, Regine Riehl, was the real-life counterpart of Elise Goldscheider—a fragile-looking older woman who was indeed hardened by a life of crime, brought to trial in 1906 as a brothel madam who abused and neglected the young women in her charge. Her establishment was described by her prostitutes as

68. Wingfield 2017, 207; Vyleta 2012, 57.

69. Quoted by Bristow 1983, 61, from Korotynski private collection, City of Warsaw Archives.

70. Hitler, *Mein Kampf* 1926 quoted by Bristow 1983, 84.

71. Bristow 1983, 48–84.

72. Jerusalem 1909, 87.

the "house of hell on earth."[73] Her trial was a Viennese scandal not least because it was a "Jewish" crime: in the newspapers, Madame Riehl was a dissimulating villain, and as a Jewish person she supposedly had an innate talent for calculated lying and cheating.[74] The anti-Semitic press characterized Riehl as "a Jewish procuress," and at her trial it was stated that "Jews are almost always the entrepreneurs of vice."[75]

In *Die Fackel*, Karl Kraus wrote a series of articles about the Riehl case in 1906–7.[76] Kraus denounced the hypocrisy of the double-standard that allowed men sexual freedom while women remained the victims of class-based repression and imposed religious morality. But Kraus advocated the sexual liberation of women primarily insofar as it would free and enable men. In Kraus's cosmos, women, and especially young girls, were muses who had the ability in their very sexy naïveté to release men's creative spirit. According to this view, an abundance of female sexuality, paired with the intellectual innocence of women and girls, renewed men's intellectual vitality.[77] In Viennese society constructed along these ideals, the alluring "Weib" or "Kindweib," would live in a state of sensual passion without much "Geist," or spirit, which was still a masculine preserve. This cultural imperative required a social environment in which masculine achievement and authority could prosper as against the irrationality and even innate (or easily acquired) corruption of women.

Meanwhile, Otto Weininger's misogynistic and anti-Semitic treatise *Geschlecht und Charakter* (*Sex and Character*) of 1903 had become a kind of caricature of itself in its own time. Written in a romanticist, rather adolescent prose, it speaks of a deep malaise with modernity and a conscious reactionary hatred for women and Jews. The formulation of such thoughts took place in the modern city of Vienna, as it was a time of both women and Jews becoming more visible and active in urban spheres. Such changes had shaken the Viennese status quo as personified by Karl Lueger (1844–1910), who became mayor of Vienna in 1897 on an anti-Semitic platform. Weininger's book was an event unto itself, the introduction of a pseudoscientific text that combined

73. Wingfield 2017, 23.

74. Vyleta 2012, 140–50.

75. Vyleta 2012, 148; Wingfield 2017, 17–46.

76. Vyleta 2012, 173, n. 203.

77. Szalay 2000, 4–5 and *passim*.

racism and sexism in its frantic disparagement of all homosexuals, women, and Jews. That the work was crowned with the author's suicide the same year it was published is now a non-teleological commonplace in the history of culture. Weininger designated two kinds of women: mothers and prostitutes, romanticizing motherhood, on the one hand, and claiming that any women who had sex for any reason other than planned reproduction was in fact a prostitute, on the other. In this mode, Weininger followed Cesare Lombroso's theories of degeneracy, such that prostitution and criminality were congenital, reflecting inborn qualities determined by parentage (ancestry) and race.

Such pseudoscientific thinking blurred and clashed, of course, with the "new" sciences of sex and family relations, cultural systems, and unconscious ideation that were undertaken by Sigmund Freud in a serious, indeed groundbreaking manner. We have seen that his Wednesday evening discussion groups allowed for free-wheeling conversations about diverse topics. This group discussed the predilection of older men for young girls, which the committee (and Freud himself), strangely, did not consider as a factor of ordinary, everyday psychological life that might include bourgeois people like themselves. The discussion instead centered on a murder case: it was the case of a mature man murdering young girls—a kind of pathological fetishism turned lethal.[78] This morbid case history precluded any reference to the role of young girls as "romantic" or sexual partners for mature men of an established social caste, such as those who took part in Freud's Wednesday evening sessions. This may have been a case of unconscious group-scotomization by the members of the Psychoanalytic Society. To tighten the network of associations here, we see that Dr. Isidor Sadger (Wittels's uncle, who proposed Wittels himself for membership of the Wednesday group on March 20, 1907) was present for the discussion on that evening of January 23, 1907.[79]

Although Freud and even Sadger, to some extent, were open-minded and forward-thinking individuals, traditionalist views and even superstitions flourished in the group, which functioned as a kind of microcosm of the educated bourgeois Jewish population. Misogyny and Jewish self-stereotyping were laced through the discussions there, such as Isidor Sadger's contention that among Russian and Polish Jews,

78. Nunberg and Federn 1967, vol. 1, 88.

79. Nunberg and Federn 1967, vol. 1, 146, 81–82.

"almost every man is hysterical."[80] Or Eduard Hitschmann's statement, "It is striking, not only that neuroses, psychoses, suicides, etc., play a more important role among the Jews, but also that they have many more sexual experiences than others and,—a fact that must be particularly emphasized—take them much more seriously."[81] Such statements reiterate and even enlarge upon some of the prejudices in mainstream Austrian society. Many members of the Wednesday Psychoanalytic Society were Jewish immigrants to the capital city from various parts of the Austro-Hungarian Empire. But at times they seem to have been grasping in the dark for knowledge about their own people. The recorded discussions show that even in Freud's circle of highly educated participants, these racialist generalizations were not supported by any research into the social and economic conditions that prevailed for Jews or other ethnic groups.

Popular Austrian and German literature that was composed with a sociological premise, such as *The Red House* (1909) by Else Jerusalem and *The Diary of a Lost Girl* (1905) by Margarethe Böhme (1867–1943), can enlighten us as to the perils of an unmarried girl's future. An intelligent, compassionate young prostitute called Thymian is the first-person protagonist of Böhme's novel. In her diary, Thymian ruminates that not a single one of these girls "has plunged into this mire with full consciousness of what she was doing."[82] But there was no viable exit, and as Thymian stated, quoting from Dante's *Divine Comedy* (the public educational system in the Austro-Hungarian Empire was excellent, even for girls): "Abandon hope, all ye who enter here."

The grim historical picture is that poverty or a single "false step" in life, such as the death or disenfranchisement of one's father, or a love affair with a soldier or travelling salesman, could land a young woman into a life of shame and abjection, wherein she would soon perish. The story of "Angela" from Trieste who ended up in the Red House was a case in point. She ran away from home with a wine-merchant at age fourteen. Deserted by her man in the imperial capital, she tried to make her way as a nurse, as a model, and finally as a waitress in the night cafés, "singing indecent songs in a tiny childish voice." Madam Goldscheider's police connection, Inspector Sucher, found Angela entertaining men

80. Nunberg and Federn 1967, vol. 2, 44.
81. Nunberg and Federn 1967, vol. 2, 45.
82. Böhme [1905] 2019, 135.

in an unhealthy dive in Trieste and brought her to the Red House in Vienna for a reprieve, no matter how temporary, from the torments of public degradation.[83]

Angela's story is fiction within fiction, but she was typical of the disenfranchised girls and women who worked in Viennese brothels around the turn of the twentieth century. During the trials of Regine Riehl, a girl named Ottilie Geresch testified that she had been fourteen when recruited to the Riehl house, ostensibly as a maid. Once inside the brothel, Geresch was "styled" by the brothel keeper to look even younger, wearing a short haircut and a child's sailor suit.[84] This was an exaggerated flaunting of any regulations or customs protecting children from prostitution, and was not an isolated case.[85] Indeed, the taste for children's bodies seems to have been regularly satisfied, and in the world of prostitution, the exploitation of underage girls was systemic. Perhaps the saddest abuse of girls occurred among those "Praternymphs" and "Naturenymphs" under fifteen years of age, sick with venereal disease, who roamed the Prater looking for drunken clients, men who were themselves so desensitized that they were oblivious to infection.[86]

Painters' models and models in the photographic studios were also recruited by various houses of prostitution. Indeed, turning once more to the social history of photography, batches of photographs of "naked girls" played diverse roles in the trade, as testified by Else Jerusalem. Awareness of such large-scale photographic production and distribution can clarify the social history of numerous photographic images, including the ones published by Schultze-Naumburg in 1901. In Else Jerusalem's novel, one disgraced prostitute called Olympia, who had been from Vienna to Paris and back again, mused, "What's she got out of all of it? A few hundred photographs, two good diamonds, unset, a lot of phony jewelry and leucorrhea."[87] *Nota bene*: "*A few hundred photographs*"!

Girls of the bordellos were sent away from the houses as easily as they were taken in. This was when their beauty "faded" and they might begin to use cosmetics, dyeing their hair "flaxen blond" and applying

83. See Böhme [1905] 2019, 85.
84. Wingfield 2017, 36, n. 60.
85. Wingfield 2017, 36.
86. Wingfield 2017, 149.
87. Jerusalem 1909, 126.

conspicuous amounts of rouge, which made them look even older—or when they were sick, which was more or less inevitable under such circumstances.[88] A hand-colored postcard by the Verlag J. Deutsch titled *Wiener Frauenschönheit* decorated with the portrait-photo of an anonymous Viennese woman, heavily made-up, with light blond hair, blackened eyes, red lips, and pink cheeks, seems to illustrate the concept of such "fading beauty," artificially revived. A similar postcard of 1897 published by J. Deutsch, featuring a portrait and signature of Katharina Schratt (1853–1940), a Vienna court actress who became the long-time mistress of Emperor Franz Josef, was labeled "Gruss aus Wien" ("Greetings from Vienna"). The concept of *Wiener Frauenschönheit* had a strong scent of scandal about it at the end of the nineteenth century, and could be cited ironically with regard to certain women who, far from demure, had passed the prime of their natural beauty.

Turning back once more to *The Red House*, those girls turned out of the "better" establishments became street-walkers, public lavatory attendants, or performers of unusual sexual practices in mirror-walled rooms of a brothel.[89] So depraved were these performances, we are told, that they led before long to the premature deaths of the young women involved. After Mrs. Goldscheider retired from the Red House, under the new regime of the greedy Madame Spizzari, girls at the brothel were silently abducted or disappeared when they were considered damaged goods.[90] They were also literally for sale, as their bodies could be purchased from the madam by customers as human wares, or slaves, and taken away by these new owners, not to be seen again. This particularly cruel fate was engineered by Spizzari, who we are told had cut her teeth in the so-called white slave trade.

The Red House by Else Jerusalem was published in 1908, the same year that Freud produced *"Civilized" Sexual Morality and Modern Nervous Illness*. *The Red House* is explicit in its descriptions of the torpid, monotonous life in a Viennese brothel. The protagonist of Jerusalem's story is a young woman with an incipient social conscience, Milada Rezek, who was born and raised in the Red House under the direction of the more or less benevolent Jewish madame, Elise Goldscheider. The daughter of a prostitute, Milada becomes an efficient caretaker

88. Böhme [1905] 2019; Jerusalem 1909, 66–67.
89. Jerusalem 1909, 288.
90. Jerusalem 1909, 286.

in the Red House as a young woman. Her story and the story of the house exposes the political reality of the turn of the twentieth century. Madame Goldscheider had learned her trade in the military brothels of garrison towns in the provinces of the Austrian Empire.[91] Her most important business relationship was with a high-ranking corrupt police officer, Superintendent Sucher.[92]

In Trieste, the socialist newspaper *Il Lavoratore* stated that Regine Riehl, for instance, had profited from her police connections to "hoard underage women, falsify documents, and limit the personal freedom" of her employees.[93] Such phenomena were typical for procuresses working in Vienna. The fictional "Salon Goldscheider" was well managed and financially successful. But the lives of the young prostitutes, recruited as early as the age of twelve, were degrading and without purpose. These girls lived in a constant state of dejected apathy punctuated by episodes of physical illness. Apart from venereal infections, the prevailing illness in *The Red House* was a disease as mentally debilitating as it was physically dangerous: alcoholism—a condition that in itself fostered apathy and despair.

Else Jerusalem indicates a general low-grade mental illness in the brothel as well. There were few if any healthy egos among the more or less imprisoned residents, and suicide was not unknown, such as that of the seventeen-year-old Rosina, who in despair "threw herself from the window of the room in which she had been locked."[94] A male character in *The Red House*, a manager named Horner, was a well-educated former (disgraced) school teacher. Horner, in his constant "chat," was the purveyor of certain progressive ideas for Milada Rezek. Horner was a veritable "ego-psychologist" who made Milada conscious of her own personality and a purposeful "ego" that belonged to her alone. He introduced the idea of freedom of the "true self" that could not be tarnished by life in a brothel, namely that of the "Eternal," "Unutterable" ideal that was wrapped inside even the most enslaved bodies as an "Idea."[95] It was not until some twenty-five years later that Freud would codify the terminology "Ego" and "Id" in psychoanalysis. But these ideas

91. Jerusalem 1909, 57.

92. Jerusalem 1909, 75.

93. *Il Lavoratore* November 10, 1906, 1–2.

94. Jerusalem 1909, 286.

95. Jerusalem 1909, 116.

had evidently germinated in society on a popular stratum in advance of Freud's writings, as Else Jerusalem gathered them from the oxygen of her own experience and imagination.

Much as brothels were frequented by men, there were also Viennese women, "respectable women," who used the Red House for sexual tourism of an urban variety. Such fine ladies, who belonged to the bourgeoisie or aristocracy, would arrive in groups, dressed in black, possibly with masks to conceal their social identities, as in Eduard Manet's *Masked Ball at the Opera* of 1873 or in Paul Gavarni's illustrations of *grisettes* masked for carnival, and observe the scene, sometimes engaging in sex with a male client for their own satisfaction. These "black ladies" behaved as though they were enjoying a morbid sort of "girls' night out" at the theater, or a night of make-believe come true. They were close in character to the well-born "nymphomaniacs" who would occasionally frequent the premises for their own diversion.

Since Else Jerusalem did not define her own terms, we do not know exactly what she meant by "nymphomaniacs of good family."[96] We have already seen that there was considerable overlap among classes of women in *fin-de-siècle* Vienna, and these categories included varieties of Czech and Jewish women who were living in the capital. Elise Goldscheider was described by the philosopher Horner as a "sentimental Jewess" and he chastised her for her Jewish mentality.[97] In Horner's view it was a case of Athens versus Jerusalem: with regard to Elise Goldscheider, there was "no use trying to inject the soul of a Greek into a mind poisoned by Fichte and Spinoza." In the Austro-Hungarian worldview, Judea, or the "old-clothes shop," never really died, but rather continued to contaminate its descendants with an indelible mark.[98]

The capable Milada Rezek is characterized as a caring pragmatist at the crossroads of women's history. Her point of view and style of narration conforms to the realism and naturalism of writers like Emile Zola, where people are products of their immediate social experience. However, social idealism is also proposed, if in a roundabout manner. The books glimpsed for a moment on Milada's dressing table in *The Red House* include titles by Karl Marx (1818–83), Charles Fourier (1772–1837), and August Bebel (1830–1914), thus giving the reader

96. Jerusalem 1909, 285.
97. Jerusalem 1909, 86.
98. Jerusalem 1909, 86.

a view into Rezek's political and feminist formation, as well as that of her author, the courageous Else Jerusalem. Charles Fourier was the first writer to coin the term "feminism," and believed that all social progress took place in proportion to the emancipation of women: "The extension of the privileges of women is the fundamental cause of all social progress."[99] August Bebel's radical book *Woman and Socialism* was published in German in 1879. In Bebel's view, class struggle would contribute to women's emancipation and women would become the equal of men in all pursuits including intellect, learning, and economic power.

Let this incipient feminism, together with the photography of young girls, take us back once more to Freud's *Dora*, written in the first decade of the twentieth century. To a twenty-first-century reader in the age of "#MeToo," the facts of Dora's situation look abhorrent if not criminal. Were young women really treated with such cavalier indifference and cruelty in *fin-de-siècle* Vienna? Did Wittels and Kraus not virtually suffocate these younger women for their own pleasure? In view of the financier Jeffrey Epstein's procurement of young teenagers for his own enjoyment, ultimately taking his own life in prison in 2019, one might be tempted to universalize. But we should resist such easy equations in favor of a more specific, nuanced, cultural history. The answer has to do with the changes of societal habitus, that constant interaction of individual intellect with social systems, from the so-called seduction theory (which Freud rejected already in 1906) to the #MeToo movement of 2016. I will not presume to report on Freud's seduction theory or its critical vicissitudes. Nor will I attempt to evaluate Jeffrey Moussaieff Masson's counterargument, *The Assault on Truth* of 1984. The idea of underage children being seduced by grown men did permeate Viennese society in fantasy if not in fact. We postmoderns might abide by the time-worn Italian phrase "se non è vero è bentrovato" (if it's not true it is well conceived anyway) and let the features of mental life be considered side by side with those of biographical or biological narratives.

Can we render judgment on the fact that at the turn of the twentieth century, teenagers (beginning at the ages of thirteen or fourteen) were considered active, conscious participants in the world of adult sex? Were they children? Does childhood depend upon societal custom? Is it possible for Freud to be "discredited" or proven correct in any of his

99. Beecher 1986, 206–08, 305, 312.

theoretical writings in the twenty-first century? In a century of cultural history, social and intellectual developments can fluctuate a great deal.

In historical retrospect, Hans Zellenka and Sigmund Freud appear to have contributed to Ida Bauer's anxieties and sorrows. Freud wrote about Dora's response to Hans Zellenka's supposed erection when he embraced her as a young teenager:[100] "If I may propose that the scene of the kiss took place in this way."[101] Was Freud simply sick with countertransferential love for Ida Bauer, whom he claimed to not even like? Or was he merely typical of his age, place, and custom? Had Freud not been a typical, even quintessential, and therefore reliable reporter of his own society, he would not have been able to communicate its textures and meanings to readers like ourselves who ponder his writings, over one hundred years in his future.

In theoretical terms, psychoanalysis, visual culture, and anthropological literature cannot simply "mirror" or "eclipse" one another. Nor should they be used as methodologies to explain each other. No one single closed intellectual system can be marshaled to interpret another in a modernist plot, be it sociological, literary, psychoanalytic, or photographic.

In conclusion, I suggest that the best approach is to follow the example of the eminent historian of modern culture, Peter Joachim Fröhlich (1923–2015), known in America as Peter Gay. In honor of Peter Gay, let us allow the study of cultural history to be informed, but not overwhelmed, by psychoanalysis as well as the social history of photography.[102]

100. Freud 1901, 30.
101. Freud 1901, 31.
102. Gay 1988.

BIBLIOGRAPHY

Abraham, Karl. 1960. *Selected Papers on Psychoanalysis*. Translated by Douglas Bryan and Alix Strachey. Introduction by Ernest Jones. New York: Basic Books.

Achenbach, Michael, Thomas Ballhausen and Nicholas Wostry, eds. 2009. *Saturn: Wiener Filmerotik 1906–1910: Viennese Film Eroticism 1906–1910*. Vienna: Verlag Filmarchiv Austria.

Achenbach, Michael, and Paolo Caneppele. 1999. "Born under the Sign of Saturn: The Erotic Origins of Cinema in the Austro-Hungarian Empire." *Griffithiana: La Rivista della Cineteca del Friuli* 65: 126–39.

Achenbach, Michael, with Anton Thaller. 2009. "Saturn Produktionen 1906–1910, Filmografie." In Achenbach et al. 2009, 101–98.

Achenbach, Michael, Paolo Caneppele and Ernst Kieninger. 2000. *Projektionen der Sehnsucht: Saturn, Die erotischen Anfänge der österreischen Kinematografie*. Vienna: Filmarchiv Austria.

Ackerman, Gerald. 1986. *The Life and Work of Jean-Leon Gérôme*. New York: Sotheby Parke Bernet.

Adriaensens, Vito, and Steven Jacobs. 2015. "The Sculptor's Dream: Tableaux Vivants and Living Statues in the Films of Méliès and Saturn." *Early Popular Visual Culture* 13, no. 1: 41–65.

Aegiptische Sammlung KHM. 1896. *Auszug aus dem Jahresberichte 1896*. Transcribed photocopy provided by Elfriede Haslauer, Egyption Collections, Kunsthistorisches Museum, Vienna.

Agamben, Giorgio. 2011. *Nudities*. Translated by David Kishik and Stefan Pedatella. Stanford, CA: Stanford University Press.

Ahrem, Maximilian. 1924. *Das Weib in der Antiken Kunst*. Jena: Eugen Diedrichs.

Aksakov, Alexander. 1898. *Animismus und Spiritismus*. Leipzig: Verlag Oswald Mutze.

Amm, Marita, and Karl Holubar. 1997. "'Coca-Koller' und seine Freunde: zium, 140. Geburtstag des Jüdisch-Wienerischen Trios: Carl Koller (1857–1944), Sigmund Lustgarten (1857–1911), und Sigmund Freud (1856–1939)." *Wiener Klinische Wochenschrift* 109, no. 5: 170–75.

Andriopoulos, Stefan. 2008. *Possessed: Hypnotic Crimes, Corporate Fiction, and the Invention of Cinema*. Translated by Peter Jansen. Chicago: University of Chicago Press.

Anonymous. 1896. "A Novel Use for Röntgen Rays." *British Journal of Photography* 43 (February 28): 131.

Anonymous. 1910. "A Royal Princess." *The Sphinx* 17, no. 258 (January 1): 2.

Anzieu, Didier. 2016. *The Skin Ego*. Translated by Naomi Segal. New York and London: Routledge.

Appignanesi, Lisa, and John Forrester. 1992. *Freud's Women: Family, Patients, Followers*. New York: The Other Press.

Apter, Emily. 1991. *Feminizing the Fetish: Psychoanalysis and Narrative Expression in Turn-of-the-Century France*. Ithaca, NY, and London: Cornell University Press.

Armstrong, Richard H. 2005. *A Compulsion for Antiquity: Freud and the Ancient World*. Ithaca, NY: Cornell University Press.

Auden, W. H. 1991. "In Memory of Sigmund Freud 1939." In *W. H. Auden: Collected Poems*, edited by Edward Mendelson, 273–76. New York: Vintage.

Auer, Anna et al., eds. 1983. *Geschichte der Fotografie in Österreich* 2 vols. Bad Ischl: Verein zur Erarbeitung der "Geschichte der Fotografie in Österreich."

Baessler, Arthur. 1906. *Peruanische Mumien: Untersuchungen mit X-Strahlen*. Berlin: Georg Reimer Verlag.

Balsam, Rosemary H. 2003. "Women of the Wednesday Society: The Presentations of Drs. Hilferding, Spielrein, and Hug-Hellmuth." *American Imago* (Fall): 303–42.

Balsam, Rosemary. 2016. "Freud, The Birthing Body, and Modern Life." *Journal of the American Psychoanalytic Association* 65: 61–90.

Barker, Andrew. 1996. *Telegrams from the Soul: Peter Altenberg and the Culture of fin-de-siècle Vienna*. Columbia, SC: Camden House.

Barthes, Roland. 2006. *The Language of Fashion*. Translated by Andy Stafford and Michael Carter. New York and London: Bloomsbury Academic Press.

Baudelaire, Charles. 1964. "The Painter of Modern Life." In *The Painter of Modern Life and Other Essays*, edited and translated by Jonathan Mayne. London: Phaidon.

Bebel, August. 1904. *Woman under Socialism*. New York: Labor News Company.

Beecher, Jonathan. 1986. *Charles Fourier: The Visionary and His World*. Berkeley: University of California Press.

Benjamin, Walter. 1999. *Selected Writings*. 4 vols. Vol. 2, part 2: 1931–34. Translated by Rodney Livingstone and others. Edited by Michael W. Jennings, Howard Eilans and Gary Smith. Cambridge, MA and London: The Belknap Press of Harvard University.

Benjamin, Walter. 2015. "Small History of Photography." In *On Photography*, edited and translated by Esther Leslie, 59–95. London: Reaktion Books.

Benthien, Claudia. 2002. *Skin: On the Cultural Border between the Self and the World*. New York: Columbia University Press.

Bergstein, Mary. 1992. "Lonely Aphrodites: On the Documentary Photography of Sculpture." *Art Bulletin* 74: 475–98.

Bergstein, Mary. 2009. "Freud's Uncanny Egypt: Prolegomena." *American Imago* (Summer): 185–210.

Bergstein, Mary. 2010. *Mirrors of Memory: Freud, Photography, and the History of Art*. Ithaca, NY, and London: Cornell University Press.

Bergstein, Mary. 2014. *In Looking Back One Learns to See: Marcel Proust and Photography*. New York and Amsterdam: Rodopi [Brill].

Bergstein, Mary. 2017. "Freud, Saturn, and the Power of Hypnosis." In *Photography and the Optical Unconscious*, edited by Shawn Michelle Smith and Sharon Sliwinski, 104–33. Durham, NC, and London: Duke University Press.

Bergstein, Mary. 2020. "Radiant Matter: X-ray Photography and the Visual Imagination in Thomas Mann and Sigmund Freud." In *Photography and Imagination*, edited by Edited Margaret Olin and Amos Morris-Reich, 36–51. New York and London: Routledge.

Bergstein, Mary. 2021. "Eros in Vienna: Dreams/ Archaeology/ Photography/ Film." *American Imago* 78, no. 2: 307–39.

Bernheimer, Charles. 1997. *Figures of Ill Repute: Representing Prostitution in Nineteenth-Century France*. Durham, NC, and London: Duke University Press.

Bernheimer, Charles, and Claire Kahane, eds. 1990. *In Dora's Case: Freud—Hysteria—Feminism*. New York: Columbia University Press.

Bernstein, Susan. 2003. "It Walks: The Ambulatory Uncanny." *Modern Language Notes* 118: 1111–139.

Billing, Archibald. 1875. *The Science of Gems, Jewels, Coins, and Medals, Ancient and Modern*, with Autobiography of Pistrucci. Translated by Mrs. Billing. London: Daldy Isbister and Co.

Bing-Heidecker, Liora. 2017. "Unearthing the Spirit: The Archaeological Metaphor and the Uncanny Pathology of Romantic Ballet." *Dance Research* 35, no. 2: 165–86.

Blackshaw, Gemma. 2007. "The Pathological Body: Modernist Strategising in Egon Schiele's Self-Portraiture." *Oxford Art Journal* 30, no. 3: 377–401.

Blossveldt, Karl. 1928. *Urformen der Kunst: Photographische Pflanz Bilder*. Berlin: Verlag Ernst Wasmuth.

Blumenberg, Hans. 2010. *Paradigms for a Metaphorology*. Translated by Robert Savage. Ithaca and New York: Cornell University Press.

Bogousslavsky, Julien, Olivier Walusinski and Denis Veyrunes. 2009. "Crime, Hysteria, and Bell'Époque Hypnotism: The Path Traced by Jean-Martin Charcot and Georges Gilles de la Tourette." *European Neurology*: 193–99.

Böhme, Margarete. (1905) 2019. *Tagerbuch einer Verlorenen. Von Einer Toten*. Berlin: Friedrich Fontane. Translated by Ethel Colburn Mayne, as *The Diary of a Lost Girl* (Louise Brooks Edition). Introduction by Thomas Gladysz. Lexington, KY: Pandora's Box Press.

Bonah, Christiana, and Anja Laukötter. 2009. "Moving Pictures and Medicine in the First Half of the Twentieth Century: Some Notes on International Historical Developments and the Potential of Medical Film Research." *Gesnerus* 66: 121–46.

Bonfante, Larissa. 1989. "Nudity as a Costume in Classical Art." *American Journal of Archaeology* 93: 543–70.

Borgerson, Janet L., and Jonathan E. Schroeder. 2018. "Making Skin Visible: How Consumer Culture Imagery Commodifies Identity." *Body and Society* 24, no. 1–2: 103–36.

Boylan, Alexis L. 2020. *Visual Culture*. Cambridge, MA: MIT Press.

Bredekamp, Horst, Vera Dünkel and Birgit Schneider. 2015. *The Technical Image: A History of Styles in Scientific Imagery*. Chicago and London: University of Chicago Press.

Brinckmann, Christine M., and Rainer Herrn. 2005. "Von Ratten und Männern. Der Steinach-Film." *Montage AV. Zeitschrift für Theorie und Gesischchte audiovisueller Kommunikation Jg.* 14 no. 2: 78–100. DOI: 10.25969/mediarep/225.

Bristow, Edward J. 1983. *Prostitution and Prejudice: The Jewish Fight against White Slavery 1870–1939*. New York: Schocken Books.

Brücke, Ernst. 1891. *The Human Figure: Its Beauties and Defects. Preface by William Anderson; Illustrations by Hermann Paar*. London: H. Grevel; and Co.

Burke, Charles V. 1907. "Surgery as a Vaudeville Show." *The Medical Times* (May): 156.

Busch, Ewe. 1998. "The Progress of Radiology in 1896" and "Deutsches Röntgen Museum—Today and Future." in *The Radiology History and National Trust*: An Occasional Newsletter no. 10 (Winter): 152.

Butler, Judith. (1993) 2011. *Bodies that Matter: On the Discursive Limits of "Sex."* London and New York: Routledge.

Caneppele, Paolo, and Ernst Kieninger. 2009. "Projektion der Sehnsucht: Saturn, Die etotischen Anfänge der österreichischen Kinomategrafie (Vienna Filmarchiv Austria, 2000)." *The Moving Image* 9 (Spring): 253–56.

Cartwright, Lisa. 1995. *Screening the Body: Tracing Medicine's Visual Culture*. Minneapolis: University of Minnesota Press.

Cavallini, Eleonora. 2013. "Radiology and Art: The Invisible Revealed." https://www.bmhmagazine.com/features/radiology-and-art-the-invisible-revealed/.

Chekhov, Anton. 2004. Letters of Anton Chekhov. Translated by Constance Garnett. EBook 6408, last updated 2016.

Cep, Casey. 2021. "Why Did So Many Victorians Try to Talk with the Dead?" *The New Yorker*, May 31: 67–71.

Chiò, Adriano, Claudia Gianetto and Stella Dagna. 2016. "Professor Camillo Negro's Neuropathological Films." *Journal of the History of the Neurosciences* 25, no. 1: 39–50.

Church, Archibald, and Frederick Peterson. 1899. *Nervous and Mental Diseases*. Philadelphia: W. B. Saunders.

Coen, Deborah R. 2007. *Vienna in the Age of Uncertainty: Science, Liberalism, and Private Life*. Chicago and London: University of Chicago Press.

Cohen, Jacques H. M. 2006. "The Scandalous Dr. Doyen, or the Solitary Tragedy of a Prodigy." Translated by Karin Debbasch. *Histoire de la Santé, Bibliotheque numérique Medic*. http://www.bium.univ-paris5fr/histmed/medica/doyen_eng.htm.

Colombo, Daria. 2010. "Worthless Female Material': Nursemaids and Governesses in Freud's Cases." *Journal of the American Psychoanalytic Association* 58, no. 5: 835–59.

Crary, Jonathan. 2000. *Techniques of the Observor*. Cambridge, MA: MIT Press.

Crary, Jonathan. 2001. *Suspensions of Perception: Attention, Spectacle, and Modern Culture*. Cambridge, MA: MIT Press.

Danius, Sara. 2002. *The Senses of Modernism: Technology, Perception, and Aesthetics*. Ithaca, NY, and London: Cornell University Press.

Davies, Keith J., and Gerhard Fichtner. 2006. *Freud's Library: A Comprehensive Catalogue/Freuds Bibliothek*: Vollständiger Katalog. London: The Freud Museum and Tübingen: Edition Diskord.

Del Regato, Juan A. 1993. *Radiological Oncologists: The Unfolding of a Medical Speciality*. Ann Arbor: University of Michigan, Radiology Centennial.

Didi-Hubermann, Georges. 1982. *Invention de l'Hysterie. Charcot et l'Iconographie photographique de la Salpêtrière*. Paris: Macula.

Didi-Hubermann, Georges. 2003. *Invention of Hysteria: Charcot and the Photographic Iconography of the Salpêtrière*. Translated by Alicia Hartz. Cambridge, MA: MIT Press.

Döblin, Alfred. 1991. *Journey to Poland*. Translated by Joachim Neugroschel. Edited by Heinz Graber. New York: Paragon House Publishers.

Douglas, Mary. 1966. *Purity and Danger: The Analysis of Concepts of Totem and Taboo*. London: Routledge and Kegan Paul.

Dowden, Stephen D., ed. 1999. *A Companion Guide to Thomas Mann's The Magic Mountain*. Columbia, SC: Camden House.

Doyen, Eugéne. 1899. "Dr. E. Doyen Gave a Cinematic Demonstration of Gynaecological Operations." *London Medical Press and Circular* 3 January 1900, 8–9.

Doyen, Eugène-Louis. 1899. "Le Cinematographie et l'Enseigement de la Chirurgie." *Revue Critique de médecine et de chirurgie* 15 (August): 1–4.

Doyen, Eugène. 1917. *With Louis Spencer Brown Surgical Therapeutics and Operative Technique*. New York: William Wood and Company.

Du Maurier, George. 1998. *Trilby. Introduction by Elaine Showalter, notes by Dennis Denisoff*. Oxford: Oxford University Press.

Dünkel, Vera. 2016. *Röntgenblick und Schattenbild: Genese und Ästhetik einer neuen Art von Bildern*. Berlin: Edition Imorde.

Eder, Josef Maria. 1886. *Die Moment-photographie in ihrer Anwendung auf Kunst und Wissenschaft*, 2nd edition. Halle an der Saale: W. Knapp.

Eder, Josef Maria. 1889. "Aufnahmen von Geisteskranken zu Zwecken der Psychiatrie." *Photographische Korrespondenz* no. 349: 466–67.

Eder, Josef Maria. 1891. *Die Photographie bei Künstlichem Licht*. Halle: Wilhelm Knapp.

Eder, Josef Maria. 1932. *Geschichte der Photographie*, vol. 1 & vol. 2, 4th edition Halle (Saale): Wilhelm Knapp.

Eder, Josef Maria. 1945. *History of Photography*. Translated by Edward Epstean. New York: Dover.

Eder, Josef Maria. 2013. *Photographie als Wissenschaft: Positionen um 1900*. Edited by Maren Gröning and Ulrike Matzer. Series Photogramme, edited by Bernd Stiegler. Munich: Wilhelm Fink Verlag.

Eder, Josef Maria and Eduard Valenta. 1896. *Versuche über Photographie mittelst der Röntgen'schen Strahlung. Hrsg.Mit Genehmigung des K. K. Ministerums für Cultus und Unterricht von der K. K. Lehr- und Versuchs Anstalt für Photographie und Reproductionsverfahren in Wien*. Vienna: R. Luchner [W. Müller].

Eichler, Fritz, and Ernst Kris. 1927. *Die Kameen in Kunsthistorischen Museum: Beschreibender Katalog*. Vienna: Anton Schroll.

Eladany, Abeer Helmy. 2011. "A Study of a Selected Group of Third Intermediate Period Mummies in the British Museum." PhD diss., University of Manchester.

Elcott, Noam M. 2016a. *Artificial Darkness: An Obscure History of Modern Art and Media*. Chicago and London: University of Chicago Press.

Elcott, Noam M. 2016b. "The Phantasmagoric Dispositif: An Assembly of Bodies and Images in Real Time and Space." *Grey Room* 62: 42–71. https://doi.org/10.1162/GREY_a_00187.

Elkins, James. 1999. *Pictures of the Body: Pain and Metamorphosis*. Stanford, CA: Stanford University Press.

Ellis, Andrew W., Oliver Raitmayr and Christian Herbst. 2015. "The Ks: The Other Couple in the Case of Freud's Dora." *Journal of Austrian Studies* 48, no. 4 (Winter): 1–26.

English, Charlie. 2021. *The Gallery of Miracles and Madness: Insanity, Art, and Hitler's First Mass-Murder Programme*. London and Dublin: William Collins.

Eugeni, Ruggero. 2019. "Imaginary Screens: The Hypnotic Gesture and Early Film." In *Screen Geneologies: From Optical Device to Environmental Medium*, edited by Craig Buckley, Rüdiger Campe and Francesco Casetti, 269–91. Amsterdam: Amsterdam University Press.

Faber, Monika. 2003. "Josef Maria Eder and Scientific Photography 1855–1918." In *The Eye and the Camera: The Albertina Collection of Photographs*, edited by Monika Faber and Klaus Albrecht Schroeder, 142–69. Vienna and Paris: Éditions de Seuil.

Faber, Monika. 2006. "Photography." In *Vienna 1900: Art, Life, and Culture*, edited by Christian Brandstätter, 226–37. New York: Vendome Press.

Fend, Mechthild. 2005. "Bodily and Pictorial Surfaces: Skin in French Art and Medicine, 1790–1860." *Art History* 28, no. 3 (June): 311–39.

Fend, Mechthild. 2017. *Fleshing out Surfaces: Skin in French Art and Medicine 1650–1850*. Manchester: Manchester University Press.

Finzi, Daniela. 2018. "Narrative Strategies and Hermeneutic Desire: Constructions of a Case History." In *Dora, Hysteria, and Gender*, edited by Daniela Finzi and Herman Westerlink, 17–31. Louvain: Leuven University Press.

Foster, Ian. 1993. "Adventures in the Human Zoo: Peter Altenberg's Ashantee in Context." In *Theatre and Performance in Austria: From Mozart to Jelinek*

(*Austrian Studies IV*), edited Robertson Ritchie and Edward Timms, 36–60. Edinburgh: Edinburgh University Press.

Franklin, James. 2004. "Mozart, Mesmer, and Medicine." *Hektsoen International: A Journal of Medical Humanities*. Paper given at Chicago Literary Club, February 16.

Freud, Ernst L., ed. 1992. *Letters of Sigmund Freud*. Translated by Tania and James Stern. New York: Dover.

Freud, Sigmund. 1889. "Review of August Forel's Hypnotism." *SE* 1: 91–102.

Freud, Sigmund. 1891. "Hypnosis." *SE* 1: 105–14.

Freud, Sigmund. 1893. "A Case of Successful Treatment by Hypnotism." *SE* 1: 117–32.

Freud, Sigmund. 1895. "Studies on Hysteria." *SE* 2: 1–47.

Freud, Sigmund. 1899. "Screen Memories." *SE* 3: 301–22.

Freud, Sigmund. 1900. "The Interpretation of Dreams" [1899]. *SE* 4–5: 4: 1–338 and 5: 339–723.

Freud, Sigmund. 1901. "The Psychopathology of Everyday Life." *SE* 6: 43–52.

Freud, Sigmund. 1905a. "Three Essays on the Theory of Sexuality" [1901]. *SE* 7: 123–243.

Freud, Sigmund. 1905b. "Fragment of an Analysis of a Case of Hysteria." *SE* 7: 7–112.

Freud, Sigmund. 1907. "Delusions and Dreams in Jensen's Gradiva" [1906]. *SE* 9: 7–95.

Freud, Sigmund. 1915a. "Mourning and Melancholia." *SE* 14: 239–58.

Freud, Sigmund. 1915b. "Instincts and Their Vicissitudes." *SE* 14: 117–40.

Freud, Sigmund. 1917. "Mourning and Melancholia." *SE* 14: 243–58.

Freud, Sigmund. 1919. "The Uncanny." *SE* 17: 219–52.

Freud, Sigmund. 1923. "The Ego and the Id." *SE* 19: 19–27.

Freud, Sigmund. 1924. "The Economic Problem of Masochism." *SE* 19: 157–70.

Freud, Sigmund. 1927. "Fetishism." *SE* 21: 152–57.

Freud, Sigmund. 1933. "Femininity." *SE* 22: 112–35.

Freud, Sigmund. 1937. "Analysis Terminable and Interminable." *SE* 23: 216–53.

Freud, Sigmund. 1953–74. *The Standard Edition of the Complete Psychological Works of Sigmund Freud*. Edited and Translated by James Strachey in collaboration with Anna Freud, assisted by Alix Strachey and Alan Tyson. London: Hogarth Press.

Freud, Sigmund, and Josef Breur. 1893–95. *Studies in Hysteria*. *SE* 2.

Frizot, Michel. 1998. *A New History of Photography*. Cologne: Konemann.

Gaertner. 1898. "Stricker's Unterrichtsmethode." In *30 Jahre Experimentelle Pathologie Herrn Prof. S. Stricker zur Feier seines 25 Jährigen Jubiläums als ordentlicher Professor der Institutes Allgemeinen und Experimentelle Pathologie und zur Erinnerung an den 30Jährigen Bestand des Institutes für experimentelle Pathologie in Wien: gewidmet von Freunden und Schülern*, edited by anonymous, 54–62. Leipzig, Wien: Deuticke. Max Planck-

Institute for the History of Science, Berlin, ISSN 1866–4784-http://vlp.mpiwg-berlin.mpg.de/.

Gamwell, Lynn, and Richard Wells. 1989. *Sigmund Freud and Art: His Personal Collection of Antquities*. Exhibition catalogue. Binghamton: State University of New York Press.

Gautier, Théophile. 1976. "The Tourist." In *My Fantoms*, 113–49. Translated by Richard Holmes. New York: New York Review of Books.

Gautier, Théophile. 2021. *Charles Baudelaire, His Life*. Middletown, DE: Streetlib Press.

Gay, Peter. 1985. *Freud for Historians*. Oxford and New York: Oxford University Press.

Gay, Peter. 1988. *Freud, A Life for Our Time*. New York: W. W. Norton.

Geertz, Clifford. 1976. "Art as a Cultural System." *MLN* 91, no. 6, Comparative Literature (December): 1473–499.

Geimer, Peter, ed. 2002. *Ordnungen und Sicherheit: Photographie in Wissenschaft, Kunst, und Technologie*. Frankfurt: Suhrkamp.

George, Alys X. 2020. *The Naked Truth: Viennese Modernism and the Body*. Chicago and London: University of Chicago Press.

Gerlach, Martin. 1902–1904. *Formenwelt aus dem Naturreiche: Photographische Naturaufnahmen von Martin Gerlach. Mikroskopische Vergrösserungen von Universitäts-Lehrer Hugo Hinterberger*. Vienna and Leipzig: Verlag Martin Gerlach & Co.

Gerson, Jeannie Suk. 2021. "What if Trigger Warnings Don't Work?" *The New Yorker*, September 28.

Gilman, Sander L. 1985. *Difference and Pathology: Stereotypes of Sexuality, Race, and Madness*. Ithaca, NY, and London: Cornell University Press.

Glasser, Otto. 1931. *Wilhelm Conrad Röntgen und die Gesichte von Röntgenstrahlen. Mit einem Beitrag Persönliches über W. C. Röntgen von Margret Boveri, Berlin*. Berlin: Verlag Julius Springer.

Goldberg, Vicki. 1998. "Art and Science Sing the Body Transparent." *The New York Times*, December 20, 2–17.

Goldstein, Leigh. 2009. "Review of M. Achenbach, P. Caneppele, and E. Kieninger, *Projektion der Sehnsucht: Saturn, Die erotischen Anfänge de österreichischen Kinematografie*. Vienna: Filmarchiv Austria." *Moving Image* no. 9 (Spring): 253–56.

Grasset, Joseph. 1896. "Un 'homme mumie,'" *Nouvelle Iconographie* 9: 257–64.

Grasset, Joseph. 1910. *The Marvels Beyond Science: Being a Record of Progress Made in the Reduction of Occult Phenomena to a Scientific Basis. Preface by Emile Faguet*. Translated by René Jacques Tubeuf. London and New York: Funk & Wagnalls.

Green, Aaron. 2019. "English Translation of 'Sempre Libera' from Verdi's 'La Traviata.'" https://www.liveabout.com/sepre-libera-lyrics-and-text.

Greenberg, Harvey R. n.d. "Freud at the Bijou." http:www.doctorgreenberg.net/Freud.htm (retrieved May 9, 2011).

Gröning, Maren. 2008. "Almost a Game of Chance: Josef Maria Eder and Scientific Photography." Translated from German by Russell Stockman, in Keller 2008, 65–72.

Guida, James. 2013. "A Flâneur for All Seasons." *The New Yorker*, March 7.

Gunning, Tom. 2008a. "Invisible Worlds, Visible Media." In Keller 2008, 51–63.

Gunning, Tom. 2008b. "Uncanny Reflections, Modern Illusions: Sighting the Modern Optical Uncanny." In *Uncanny Modernity: Cultural Theories, Modern Anxieties*, edited by Jo Collins and John Jervis, 68–90. London and New York: Palgrave Macmillan.

Haeckel, Ernst. 1998. *Kunstformen der Natur. Die einhundert Farbtafeln. Foreword by Richard P. Hartmann. Contributions by Olaf Breidbach and Irenäus Eibl-Eibesfeldt*. Munich: Prestel Verlag.

Hall, G. Stanley. 1897. "A Study of Fears." *The American Journal of Psychology* 8, no. 2 (January): 147–249.

Hambourg, Maria Morris, Pierre Apraxine et al., eds. 1993. *The Waking Dream: Photography's First Century*. Exhibition Catalog. New York: Metropolitan Museum of Art.

Hammond, Charles H., Jr. 2019. "Review of Wingfield 2017." *Journal of Austrian Studies* 52, nos. 1–2 (Spring-Summer): 161–63.

Hansson, Nils, with Matthis Kirschel, Per Södersten, Friedrich H. Moll, and Heiner Fangerau. 2020."'He Gave Us the Cornerstone of Sexual Medicine': A Nobel Plan but No Nobel Prize for Eugen Steinach." *Urologia Internationalis* 104: 501–09.

Harriet, Wilhelm. 1904. *Gesichte de Prostitution aller Völker*. Berlin: R. Jacobsthal.

Haslauer, Elfriede. 2007. "Egypt in Nineteenth-Century Vienna, a Phantasm?" Translated by Jon Winbigler. *Visual Resources* 23 (special issue: *Visual Documentation in Freud's Vienna*, edited by Mary Bergstein): 85–103.

Hau, Michael. 2003. *The Cult of Health and Beauty in Germany: A Social History, 1890–1930*. London and Chicago: University of Chicago Press.

Havelock-Ellis, Henry. 2018. *Studies in the Psychology of Sex*, 6 vols, 1897–1928. New York: Alpha Editions.

Henderson, Linda Dalrymple. 1988. "X-rays and the Quest for Invisible Reality in the Art of Kupka, Duchamp, and the Cubists." *Art Journal* 47 (Winter): 323–40.

Henderson, Linda Dalrymple. 1989. "Francis Picabia, Radiometers, and X-Rays in 1913." *Art Bulletin* 71, no. 1 (March): 114–23.

Hinterberger, Hugo. 1897. "Über Röntgenstrahlen." *Jahrbuch für Photographie und Reprodutionstechnik* 11: 65–68, figs. 16–17.

Holzknecht, Guido. 1931. Obituaries. "Professor Guido Holzknecht: Ein Opfer seines Berufes." *Neue Freie Presse Abendblatt* (evening edition): 1–2.

Howe, Kathleen Stewart. 1994. *Excursions along the Nile: The Photographic Discovery of Ancient Egypt*. Exhibition Catalogue. Santa Barbara, CA: Santa Barbara Museum of Art.

Huerta Floriano, Miguel Angel. 2008. "The Cinema as Therapy: Psychoanalysis in the Work of Woody Allen." *J Med JMM* 4 (November): 17–26.

Hug-Hellmuth, Hermine. 1923. *Preface to the third German edition of A Young Girl's Diary*. Translated by Eden Paul and Cedar Paul, vii–xiii. New York: Thomas Seltzer.

Hustvedt, Asti. 2011. *Medical Muses: Hysteria in Nineteenth-Century Paris*. New York and London: W. W. Norton.

L'Illustration. 1896. "X-Ray of a Hand." January 25 and February 1.

Iverson, Margaret. 1998. "In the Blind Field: Hopper and the Uncanny." *Art History* 21, no. 3: 409–29.

Jablonski, Nina G. 2013. *Skin: A Natural History*. London, Berkeley, and Los Angeles: University of California Press.

James, Henry. (1890) 1995. *The Tragic Muse*. London: Penguin.

Jarvis, Brooke. 2020. "Your Body is a Wonderland." *The New Yorker*, August 3 and 10: 66–70.

Jaspers, Kristina, and Wolf Unterberger, eds. 2006. *Kino im Kopf: Psychologie und Film seit Sigmund Freud*. Berlin: Betz & Fischer.

Jensen, Wilhelm. 1903. *Gradiva: ein pompejanisches phantasiestück*. Dresden: C. Reissner.

Jensen, Wilhelm. 1917. *Delusion and Dream: An Interpretation in the Light of Psychoanalysis of Gradiva*. Translated by H. M. Downey. New York: Moffat Yard.

Jentsch, Ernst. (1906) 2008. "On the Psychology of the Uncanny." In *Uncanny Modernity: Cultural Theories, Modern Anxieties*, edited by Jo Collins and John Jervis, 216–28. New York: Palgrave Macmillan.

Jerusalem, Else. 1909. *Der heilige Skarabeus*. Berlin: Samuel Fischer Verlag.

Jerusalem, Else. 1932. *The Red House*. Translated by R. I. Marchant. New York: McCauley Co.

Jerusalem, Else. 2016. *Liberazione e altreprose inedite*. Translated and edited by Claudia Ciardi. Pistoia: Via del Vento.

Jung, C. G. 1961. *Memories, Dreams, Reflections*. Translated by Richard and Clara Winston. New York: Vintage.

Kandel, Eric. 2012. *The Age of Insight: The Quest to Understand the Unconscious in Art, Mind and Brain from Vienna 1900 to the Present*. New York: Random House.

Karamanou, M., C. Antoniou, A. J. A. Stratigos, Z. Z. Saradaki and G. Androutzos. 2013. "The Eminent Dermatologist Moriz Kaposi (1837–1902) and the First Description of Idiopathic Multiple Pigmented Sarcoma of the Skin." *Journal of the Balkan Union of Oncology* 18, no. 4: 1101–105.

Keller, Corey, ed. 2008. *Brought to Light: Photography and the Invisible 1840–1900*. Exhibition Catalog, San Francisco Museum of Modern Art. New Haven, CT, and London: Yale University Press.

Kelles, Jamie Lauren. 2019. "How ASMR Became a Sensation." *The New York Times Magazine*, April 4.

Kelley, Susanne. 2012. "Perceptions of Jewish Female Bodies through Gustav Klimt and Peter Altenberg." *Imaginations*, May 12: 109–22.

Kenaan, Hagi. 2020. *Photography and Its Shadow*. Stanford, CA: Stanford University Press.

Kevles, Bettyann Holtzman. 1997. *Naked to the Bone: Medical Imaging in the Twentieth Century*. New Brunswick, NJ: Rutgers University Press.

Kieninger, Ernst. 2000. "'Herrenabende' Erotik im Wanderkino." In Achenbach, Caneppele, and Kieninger 2000, 43–73.

Kiesewetter, Karl. 1909. *Gesichte des neuen Occultismus*, 2nd edition. Edited by Robert Blum. Leipzig: Max Altmann.

Klein, Berthold. 1904. *Geschichte der Prostituten aller Völker*. Berlin: Jacobsthal.

König, Walter. 1896. *14 (Vierzehn) Photographien mit Röntgen-Strahlen: Aufgenommen im physikalischen Verein zu Frankfurt A. M.* Leipzig: J. A. Barth. See fol. "Kniegelenke einer Ägyptischer Kindermumie aus dem Senckenbergischen Museum zu Frankfurt a M." Re: Inventory # ÄS 18. Photo by Stephanie Zesch.

Krauss, Friedrich Salomon. 1904. *Streifzüge im Reich der Frauenschönheit*. Leipzig: A. Schumanns Verlag.

Kristeva, Julia. 1989. *Black Sun: Depression and Melancholia*. Translated by Leon Roudiez. New York: Columbia University Press.

Krukenberg, Hermann. 1920. *Der Gesichtsausdruck des Menschen*. Stuttgart: Ferdinand Enke.

Kury, Astrid. 2000. "Heiligenscheine eines elektrischen Jahrhunderts sehen anders aus …": *Okkultismus und die Kunst der Wiener Moderne*. Vienna: Passagen Verlag.

Lainer, Grete (attributed to). 2006. *A Young Girl's Diary. Preface with a letter from Sigmund Freud*. Translated by Eden and Cedar Paul. Introduction by Julia Swindells. New York: Dover.

Lalvani, Suren. 1996. *Photography, Vision, and the Production of Modern Bodies*. Albany: State University of New York Press.

Laplanche, J., and J. B. Pontalis 1973. *The Language of Psychoanalysis*. Translated by Donald Nicholson-Smith. Introduction by Daniel La Gache. New York and London: W. W. Norton. First French edition 1967.

Laskow, Sarah. 2017. "A Machine That Made Stockings Helped Kick Off the Industrial Revolution." *Pants Week*, September 19.

Lawrence, Joseph P. 1999. "Transfiguration in Silence: Hans Castorp's Uncanny Awakening." In Dowden 1999, 1–13.

Lechner, Astrid. 2005. *Martin Gerlachs Formenwelt aus dem Naturreiche: Fotografien als Vorlager für Kunstler um 1900*. Vienna: Christian Brandstätter Verlag.

Lefebvre, Thierry. 2004. *La Chair et le Celluloïd: Le Cinéma Chirurgical du Docteur Doyen. Prefaces by Dr. Alain Ségal, Jean Doyen, and Marie-Véronique Clin*. Paris: Jean Doyen.

Lensing, Leo. 1996. "Review article of Fritz Wittels: 'Freud and the Child Woman': The Memoirs of Fritz Eittels or 'The Kraus Affair': A Textual 'Reconstruction' of Fritz Wittels's Psychoanalytic Autobiography." *The German Quarterly* 69, no. 3 (Summer): 322–32.

Lensing, Leo. 2001. "Der Mädchensammler: Peter Altenbergs Ansichtskartenalben." *Figurationen* 2, no. 2: 71–91.

Levy, Max. 1900. "Die Entwicklung der Röntgentechnik in den Jahren 1898/1900." *Jahrbuch für Reproductionstechnik*, 321–37.

Levi, Neil. 2014. *Modernist Form and the Myth of Jewification*. New York: Fordham University Press.

Lev Kenaan, Vered. 2021. "Digging with Freud: From Hysteria to the Birth of a New Philology." *American Imago* 78, no. 2: 341–66.

Levingston, Steven. 2014. *Little Demon in the City of Light*. New York and London: Doubleday.

Lippit, Akira Mizuta. 2013. "Modes of Visuality: Psychoanalysis, X-ray, Cinema." In *The Spectralities Reader: Ghosts and Haunting in Contemporary Cultural Theory*, edited by Maria del Pilar Blanco and Esther Peeren, 257–78. London: Bloomsbury.

Loentz, Elizabeth. 2003. "The Problem and Challenge of Jewishness in the City of Schnitzler and Anna O." In *A Companion Guide to the Works of Arthur Schnitzler*, edited by Dagmar C. G. Lorentz, 79–102. Rochester, NY: Camden House.

Loentz, Elizabeth. 2007. *Let Me Continue to Speak the Truth: Berthe Pappenheim as Author and Activist*. Cincinnati: Hebrew Union College Press.

Lombroso, Cesare, with Guglielmo Ferrero. 2004. *Criminal Women, the Prostitute, and the Normal Woman*. Translated by Mary Gibson and Nicole Hahn Rafter. Durham, NC: Duke University Press.

Loos, Adolf. 2019. *Ornament and Crime: Thoughts on Design and Materials*. Translated by Shaun Whiteside. New York and London: Penguin and Random House.

Lukiesh, Matthew. 1916. *Light and Shade and Their Applications*. New York: D. Van Nostrand.

Luxenberg, Alisa. 2001. "'The Art of Correctly Painting the Expressive Lines of the Human Face': Duchenne de Boulogne's Photographs of Human Expression and the École des Beaux-Arts." *History of Photography* 25, no. 2 (Summer): 101–12.

MacIntire, John. 1897. "X-ray Records for the Cinematograph." *Archives of Sciagraphy* 1, no. 37.

Mahony, Patrick. 1996. *Freud's Dora: A Psychoanalytic, Historical, and Textual Study*. New Haven, CT, and London: Yale University Press.

Makela, Maria. 2015. "Rejuvenation and Regen(d)eration: Der Steinachfilm, Sex Glands, and Weimar-Era Visual and Literary Culture." *German Studies Review* 38, no. 1: 35–62.

Malcolm, Janet. 1984. *In the Freud Archives*. New York: Alfred A. Knopf.

Malcolm, Janet. 1987. "Reflections: J'appelle un chat un chat." *The New Yorker*, April 20: 84–102, reprinted in Bernheimer and Kahane 1990, 305–25.

Malcolm, Janet. 1997. "The Real Thing." In *Diana and Nikon: Essays on Photography (expanded edition)*, 190–207. New York: Aperture.

Malerba, Luigi. 2002. *La Composizione del Sogno*. Turin: Einaudi.

Malinowski, Bronislaw. 1989. *A Diary in the Strict Sense of the Term*. Translated by Norbert Guterman. Introduction by Raymond Firth. Preface by Valetta Malinowska. Stanford, CA: Stanford University Press.

Manon, Hugh S. 2007–08. "X-ray Visions: Radiography, Chiaroscuro and the Fantasy of Unsuspicion in Film Noir." *Film Criticism* 3232, no. 2 (Winter): 2–27.

Mann, Thomas. (1928) 1999. *The Magic Mountain*. Translated by H. T. Lowe-Porter. New York and London: Vintage, Random House.

Marcus, Steven. 1990. "Freud and Dora: Story, History, Case History." In Bernheimer and Kahane, 1990, 56–91.

Marinelli, Lydia, ed. 1998. *"Meine … alter und dreckigen Götter": Aus Sigmund Freuds Sammmlungen*. Vienna: Stroemfeld.

Masschelein, Annaleen. 2011. *The Unconcept: The Freudian Uncanny in Late-Twentieth-Century Theory*. Albany: State University of New York.

Masson, Jeffrey Moussaieff. 1984. *The Assault on Truth: Freud's Suppression of the Seduction Theory*. New York: Farrar, Strauss, & Giroux.

Mayer, Andreas. 2013. *Sites of the Unconscious: Hypnosis and the Emergence of the Psychoanalytic Setting*. Chicago: University of Chicago Press.

Mayreder, Rosa. 2009. *Gender and Culture*. Translated by Pamela S. Saur. Afterword by Susanne Hochreiter. Riverside, CA: Ariadne Press.

McCarthy, Mary. 1959. "A City of Stone." *The New Yorker*, August 22: 38–48.

McKernon, Luke. 2014. "Dr. Gheorghe Marinescu (1863–1938)." In *Who's Who of Victorian Cinema*. www.victorian-cinema.net/.

McKibben, Bill. 2022. "A Deer in the Headlights." *New York Times Sunday*, February 6: 18.

Meredith, Stephen C.. 1999. "Mortal Illness on the Magic Mountain." In Dowden 1999, 109–40.

Molnar, Michael, ed. and trans. 1992. *The Diary of Sigmund Freud 1929–1939*. New York: Scribners.

Moonan, Wendy. 2005. "A Look at the Past Recounted in Miniature." *New York Times*, August 19.

Morris-Reich, Amos. 2016. *Race and Photography: Racial Photography as Scientific Evidence, 1876–1980*. Chicago and London: University of Chicago Press.

Mulvey, Laura. 1975. "Visual Pleasure and Narrative Cinema." *Screen* 16, no. 3: 6–18.

Musatti, Cesare. 1961. *Gradiva: Un Racconto di Wilhelm Jensen e un studio analitico di Sigmund Freud con un commento di Ceare L. Musatti*. Turin: Editore Boringhieri.

Nead, Lynda. 2007. *The Haunted Gallery: Painting, Photography, Film ca. 1900*. New Haven, CT, and London: Yale University Press.

Newhall, Beaumont. 1946. "Review of 'History of Photography' by Josef Maria Eder and Edward Epstean." *The Art Bulletin* 28(2): 135–36.

Niewenglowski, G. H. 1890. *Applications scientifiques de la Photographie*. Paris: Masson Gautier-Villars.

Niewenglowski, G. H. 1898. *Technique et Applications des Rayons X*. Paris: Radiguet.

Niewenglowski, G. H. 1924. *Les Rayons X et le Radium*. Paris: Hachette.

Nochlin, Linda. 2007. *Courbet*. New York: Thames and Hudson.

Nunberg, Hermann, and Federn, Ernst, eds. 1962–81. *Minutes of the Vienna Psychoanalytic Society*. New York: International Universities Press.

O'Donoghue, Diane. 2004. "Negotiations of Surface: Archaeology in the in the Early Strata of Psychoanalysis." *Journal of the American Psychoanalytic Association* 52, no. 53: 653–71.

O'Donoghue, Diane. 2019. *On Dangerous Ground: Freud's Visual Culture of the Unconscious*. London and New York: Bloomsbury Academic Press.

Ortner, Sherry. 1974. "Is Female to Male as Nature is to Culture?" In *Women, Culture, and Society*, edited by M. Z. Rosaldo and L. Lamphere, 67–87. Stanford, CA: Stanford University Press.

Ovid. 1955. *Metamorphoses*. Translated by Mary Inness. London and New York: Penguin.

Packer, Sharon. 2007. *Movies and the Modern Psyche*. Westport, CT, and London: Praeger.

Panek, Richard. 2004. *The Invisible Century: Einstein, Freud, and the Search for Hidden Universes*. New York: Penguin Books.

Papadaki, Evangelia. 2021. "Feminist Perspectives on Objectification." In *Stanford Encyclopedia of Philosophy*. Stanford, CA: The Metaphysics Research Lab, Department of Philosophy, Stanford University.

Paulsen, Kris. 2017. "Review of Noam Elcott, *Artificial Darkness: An Obscure History of Modern Art and Media*. Chicago: University of Chicago Press." *CAA reviews*, October 26: 143. DOI: 10.3202/caa.reviews.

Pemmer, Hans, and Ninni Lackner. 1974. *Der Prater: Von den Anfangen bis zur Gegenwart (Wiener Heimatkunde)*. Vienna: Jugend und Volk.

Le Petit Parisien. 1890. *Supplément littéraire illustré*, June 15: 1.

Philoctetesctr. 2009. "Freud, Psychoanalysis, and the Philippson Bible." YouTube. https://www.youtube.com/watch?v=GBy2mOMM1hE.

Pinney, Christopher. 2011. *Photography and Anthropology*. London: Reaktion Books.

Pistrucci, Bendetto. 1875. "Autobiography of Pistrucci." Translated by Mrs. Billing. Appendix to Billing 1875, 135–226.

Prendergast, Mark. 2003. *Mirror/Mirror: A History of the Human Love Affair with Reflection*. New York: Basic Books.

Pringle, Heather. 2001. *The Mummy Congress: Science, Obsession, and the Everlasting Dead*. New York: Theia.

Quinn, Susan. 1995. *Marie Curie: A Life*. Cambridge, MA: Da Capo Press.

Quintieri, Rosalinda. 2021. *Dolls, Photography, and the Late Lacan: Doubles Beyond the Uncanny*. Oxford and New York: Routledge.

Rahimi, Sadeq. 2013. "The Ego, the Ocular, and the Uncanny: Why Are Metaphors of Vision Central in Accounts of The Uncanny?" *The International Journal of Psychoanalysis*, 94, no. 3: 453–76.

Rahimi, Sadeq. 2021. *The Hauntology of Everyday Life*. Los Angeles: Palgrave Macmillan.

Rampley, Matthew. 2013. *The Vienna School of Art History: Empire and the Politics of Scholarship, 1847–1918*. University Park: Penn State University Press.

Rank, Otto. 1971. *Double: A Psychoanalytic Study*. Translated and edited by Harry Tucker Jr. Chapel Hill: University of North Carolina Press.

Redniss, Lauren. 2010. *Radioactive*. New York: Harper Collins.

Reichert, Ramonn. 2007. "Das Kino in der Klinik: Medientechniken des Unbewusstem um 1900." In *Kino im Kopf: Psychologie und Film seit Sigmund Freud*, edited by Christina Jaspers and Wolf Unterberger, 23–29. Vienna: Bertz und Fischer.

Reiner, M. 1890. *Arbeiten auf dem Institut für allgemeine und experimentelle Pathologie des Prof. Dr. S. Stricker*. Vienna: Alfred Hölder.

Reinhardt, Jennifer, Chicago School of Media Theory.

Riedel, Samantha. 2022. "Remembering Dora Richter, One of the First Women to Receive Gender-Affirming Surgery." *Them*. March 15.

Riviere, Joan. 1929. "Womanliness as a Masquerade." *International Journal of Psychoanalysis* 10: 303–13.

Röntgen, W. C. 1945. "On a New Kind of Rays (Preliminary Communication)." Translated by G. F. Barker. In *Dr. W. C. Röntgen*, edited by Otto Glasser, 41–52. Springfield, IL: Charles E. Thomas.

Roeske, Thomas. 2001. "Traces of Psychology: The Art Historical Writings of Ernst Kris." *American Imago* 58, no. 1: 463–77.

Rose, Jacqueline. 2005. "Dora—Fragment of an Analysis" In *Sexuality in the Field of Vision*, 28–47. London and New York: Verso Books.

Rose, Louis. 1988. "Freud and Fetishism: Previously Unpublished Minutes of the Vienna Psychoanalytic Society." Translated and edited by Louis Rose. *Psychoanalytic Quarterly* 57: 156.

Rosen, Jeff. 1987. "The Printed Photograph and the Logic of Progress in Nineteenth-Century France." *Art Journal* (Winter): 305–11.

Rosenbaum, Max. 1984. "Anna O. (Berthe Pappenheim): Her History." In *Anna O.: Fourteen Contemporary Reinterpretations*, edited by Max Rosenbaum and Melvin Muroff, 1–25. New York: The Free Press.

Rousseau, Louis, and Achille Devéria. 1853–55. *Photographie Zoologique ou représentation des animaux rares des Collections du Muséum d'Histoire Naturelle*. París: S.n.

Royle, Nicholas. 2003. *The Uncanny*. Manchester: Manchester University Press.

Russel, Lawrence K. 1896. "Lines to an X-ray Portrait of a Lady." *Life*, 27 (689).

Russo, Mary. 1994. *The Female Grotesque: Risk, Excess, and Modernity*. New York and London: Routledge.

Said, Edward. 1978. *Orientalism*. New York: Pantheon.

Said, Edward. 2003. *Freud and the Non-European*. New York: Verso.

Salten, Felix. 2018. *Josefine Mutzenbacher oder Die Geschichte einer Wienerischen Dirne von ihr selbst erzählt by Anon. in Vienna, Austria, 1906*. Translated by Ilona J. Hämäläinen. Helsinki: Books on Demand.

Satzinger, Helmut. 1994. *Das Kunsthistorische Museum in Wien: Die Ägyptisch-Orientalische Sammlungen*. Vienna: Turtleback.

Sauerteig, Lutz D. H. 2012. "Loss of Innocence: Albert Moll, Sigmund Freud and the Invention of Childhood Sexuality around 1900." *Medical History* 56, no. 2: 156–83.

Savill, Thomas Dixon. 1904. "Hysterical Skin Symptoms and Eruptions." *The Lancet*, January 30.

Savill, Thomas Dixon. 1910. "Obituary: Thomas Dixon Savill, MD, MRCP Lond, Physician West End Hospital for Diseases of the Nervous System and St. John's Hospital for Skin Diseases." *British Medical Journal*, January 22: 238.

Scherer, Frank F.. 2011. "Ufa Orientalism: The "Orient" in Early German Film: Lubitsch and May." *Cinema Journal*, Special Issue, 1: 90–98.

Schettini, Laura. "Negro, Camillo." In *Dizionario Biografico degli Italiani*, 78.

Schmidgen, Henning. 2011. "1900—The Spectatorium: On Biology's Audiovisual Archive." *Grey Room* 43 (Spring): 42–65.

Schmidt, Gunnar. 1998. "1895 Freud/Röntgen." *Fotogeschichte* 68, no. 69: 167–76.

Schnitzler, Arthur. 1925. *Fräulein Else*. Translated by F. H. Lyon. London: Pushkin Press.

Schnitzler, Arthur. 1970. *My Youth in Vienna*. Foreword Frederic Morton. Translated by Catherine Hutter. New York: Holt, Rinehart, and Winston.

Schultz, Karla. 1999. "Technology as Desire: X-ray Vision in *The Magic Mountain*." In Dowden 1999, 158–76.

Schultze-Naumburg, Paul. 1901. *Die Kultur des Weiblichen Körpers als Grundlage der Frauenkleidung*. Leipzig: Eugen Diederichs.

Schultze-Naumburg, Paul. 1928. *Kunst und Rasse*. Munich: J. F. Lehmanns Verlag.

Schur, Max. 1972. *Freud: Living and Dying*. New York: International Universities Press.

Sengoopta, Chandak. 2000. "Tales from the Vienna Labs: The Eugen Steinach–Harry Benjamin Correspondence." *Favourite Edition*: Newsletter of the Friends of the Rare Book Room, New York academy of Medicine, no. 2 (Spring): 1–7.

Simmel, Georg. 1984. *On Women, Sexuality, and Love*. Translated by Guy Oakes. New Haven, CT: Yale University Press.

Smith, Shawn Michelle, and Sharon Sliwinski, eds. 2017. *Photography and the Optical Unconscious*. Durham, NC: Duke University Press.

Södersten, Per David Crews, Cheryl Logan and Rudolf Werner Soukup. 2013. "Eugen Steinach – the First Neuroenocrinologist." *Endocrinology* 155, no. 3 (March): 688–95. DOI: 10.1210/en.3013-1816.

Sontag, Susan. 1978. *Illness as a Metaphor*. New York: Farrar, Strauss & Giroux.

Sontag, Susan. 1989. *Aids and Its Metaphors*. New York: Farrar, Strauss & Giroux.

Steindorff, Georg. 1900. *Die Blütezeit des Pharaonenreichs*. Bielefeld: Valhagen and Klasing.

Stratz, Carl Heinrich. (1898) 1925. *Die Schönheit des Weiblichen Körpers* (den Haag, 1898). Stuttgart: Verlag Ferdinand Enke.

Stratz, Carl Heinrich. 1903. *Was sind Juden? Eine ethnographisch-anthropologische Studie*. Vienna: F. Temsky and Leipzig: G. Freytag.

Stratz, Carl Heinrich. (1901) 1911. *Die Rassenschönheit des Weibes*, 7th edition. Stuttgart: Verlag Ferdinand Enke.

Stricker, Salomon. 1879. *Studien über das Bewusstsein*. Vienna: Braumüller.

Strümpell, Ludfwig Adolf. 1877. *Die Nature und Entstehung der Träume*. Leipzig: Verlag von Veit & Co.

Strümpell, Ludwig Adolf. 1883–84. *Lehrbuch der speciellen Pathologie und Therapie der inneren Krankheiten*. 2 vols. Leipzig: F. C. W. Vogel.

Strümpell, Ludwig Adolf. 1886. A *Textbook of Medicine: For Students and Practitioners*, American edition. New York: Appleton.

Sullivan, Courtney Ann. 2003. "Classification, Containment, Contamination, and the Courtesan: The Grisette, Lorette, and Demi-mondaine in Nineteenth-Century French Fiction." PhD diss., University of Texas at Austin.

Szalay, Eva Ludwiga. 2000. "From Bourgeois Daughter to Prostitute: Representations of the 'Wiener Fräulein' in Kraus's 'Prozess Veith' and Schnitzler's 'Fräulein Else.'" *Modern Austrian Literature* 33, no. 3/4: 1–28.

Timms, Edward, and Ritchie Robertson, eds. 1990. *Vienna 1900: From Altenberg to Wittgenstein*. Austrian Studies 1. Edinburgh: Edinburgh University Press.

Tögel, Christfried, ed. 2002. *Unser Herz zeigt nach dem Süden: Reisebriefe von Sigmund Freud 1895–1923*. Berlin: Aufbau Verlag.

Torkel, Kurt. 1907. "Kinetescope show." *The Medical Times*, March.

Trilling, Lionel. 1947. "Freud and Literature." *Horizon* (September): 182–200.

Van Dijck, José. 2005. *The Transparent Body: A Cultural Analysis of Medical Imaging*. Seattle and London: University of Washington Press.

Vogel, Carol. 2007. "Mummy's Log: Visited Scan God in Land of the Dead." *New York Times*, August 6: B1, B5.

Von Doderer Heimito. 2021. *The Strudlhof Steps: Or Melzer and the Depth of the Years*. Translated by Vincent Kling. Afterword Daniel Kehlman. New York: The New York Review of Books.

Von Schelling, Friedrich Wilhelm Joseph. 2008. *Historical-Critical Introduction to the Philosophy of Mythology*. Translated by Mason Richey. Edited by Markus Zisselsberger. Albany: State University of New York Press.

Von Tischendorf, K. 1896. *Mittheilungen uber Aufnahmen mit Röntgen-Strahlen. Separatabdruck aus der Photographische Korrespondenze*. Vienna: Photographische Korrespondenz.

Vyleta, Daniel Mark. 2012. *Crime, Jews and News: Vienna 1895–1914*. Oxford and New York: Berghahn.

Wallace, David Foster. 2009. *This Is Water: Some Thoughts, Delivered on a Significant Occasion, about Living a Compassionate Life*. New York, Boston, and London: Little, Brown & Co.

Walters, Caroline Jessica. 2012. "Discourses of Heterosexual Female Masochism and Submission from the 1880s to the Present Day." PhD diss., University of Exeter.

Warner, Marina. 2006. *Phantasmagoria: Spirit Visions, Metaphors, and Media into the Twenty-first Century*. Oxford: Oxford University Press.

Weininger, Otto. 1903. *Geschlecht und Charakter*. Vienna and Leipzig: Wilhelm Braumüller. Translated by Ladislaus Löb. Edited by Daniel Steuer and Laura Marcus. Introduction by Daniel Steuer. New York: Putnam's Sons.

Weininger, Otto. 1907. *Sex and Character*. Translated by Ladislaus Löb. Edited by Daniel Steuer and Laura Marcus. Introduction by Daniel Steuer. New York: Putnam's Sons.

Weissman, Gerald. 1990. *The Doctor with Two Heads*. New York: Vintage.

Werbart, Andrzej. 2019. "'The Skin Is the Cradle of the Soul': Didier Anzieu on the Skin-Ego, Boundaries, and Boundlessness." *Journal of the American Psychoanalytic Association*, March 18. DOI: 10.1177/003065119829701.

Werfel, Franz. 1937. *Twilight of a World*. New York: Viking.

Weygandt, Wilhelm. 1902. *Atlas und Grundriss der Psychiatrie*. Munich: J. F. Lehmann.

Wheeling, Kate. 2017. "How Electroconvulsive Therapy Became a Nazi Weapon." *Pacific Standard*, August 25.

Wilder, Kelley. 2009. *Photography and Science*. London: Reaktion Books.

Wingfield, Nancy M. 2017. *The World of Prostitution in Late Imperial Austria*. Oxford and New York: Oxford University Press.

Wittels, Fritz. 1995. *Freud and the Child Woman: The Memoirs of Fritz Wittels*. Edited, with a preface and commentary, by Edward Timms. New Haven, CT, and London: Yale University Press.

Wittkowsky, Vera. 2021. "The Phantasmagoric Dispositif: An Approach to Uncanniness." MA thesis, Universität für künstlerische und industrielle Gestaltung Linz, Institut für Medien Interface Cultures.

Yourcenar, Marguerite. 1990. "That Mighty Sculptor, Time." Translated by Walter Kaiser. *The New Criterion* (June): 85–87.

Zilcosky, John. 2008. "Uncanny Encounters: Adventure Literature, Psychoanalysis, and Ethnographic Exhibitions." In *Literature and Science / Literatur und Wissenschaft*, edited by Monika Schmitz-Emans, 139–57. Würzburg: Könighausen & Neumann.

Zilcosky, John. 2016. *Uncanny Encounters: Literature, Psychoanalysis, and the End of Alterity*. Evanston, IL: Northwestern University Press.

Zilcosky, John. 2018. "'The Times in Which We Live': Freud's The Uncanny, World War I, and the Trauma of Contagion." *Psychoanalyis and History* 20, no. 2: 165–90.

Zohn, Harry. 1997. "Karl Kraus and the Critics." *Literary Criticism in Perspective*, no. 43: 140–57.

Zweig, Stefan. 1964. *The World of Yesterday*. Introduction by Harry Zohn. Lincoln: University of Nebraska Press.

Filmography

Fellini, Federico. 1957. *Le Notti di Cabiria*.

Marinescu, Gheorghe. 1898. *Walking Difficulties in Organic Hemiplegia*.

Marinescu, Gheorghe. 1899. *A Case of Hysterical Hemiplegia Cured through Hypnotic Suggestion*.

Marinescu, Gheorghe. 1990. *Walking Difficulties due to Progressive Locomotory Ataxia*.

INDEX

www.ingramcontent.com/pod-product-compliance
Lightning Source LLC
LaVergne TN
LVHW020325220926
848484LV00001BB/6